ברכון שלום רב

The Shalom Rav Birkon

KOREN JERUSALEM

Rabbi Shalom Rosner

ברכון שלום רב
SHALOM RAV BIRKON

COMPILED AND EDITED BY
Marc Lesnick

KOREN PUBLISHERS JERUSALEM

The Shalom Rav Birkon
First Edition, 2025

Koren Publishers Jerusalem
POB 4044, Jerusalem 9104001, ISRAEL
POB 8531, New Milford, CT 06776-8531, USA

www.korenpub.com

The publication of this book was made possible
through the generous support of *The Jewish Book Trust.*

ISBN 978-965-7845-36-3, hardcover

Printed and bound in Israel

לעילוי נשמת חיים מאיר בן יהושע ז״ל

This birkon is dedicated to the memory of my dear father z"l,
Dr. Fred Rosner, who returned his soul to his Creator
during the preparation of this work.

My father, my first rebbi, was a giant in Torah, a giant in medicine, and a giant in middot. He, along with my dear mother a"h, instilled and imbued in all of his progeny a thirst for mitzvot, a love for Hashem, and the desire to use every minute to the fullest. At the Shabbos table, he went in order, singing each and every zemer in the birkon. He relished the opportunity to connect with Hashem and his family through song, being mindful of the meaning of the words being chanted. The birkon is a most appropriate way to memorialize his dedication, commitment, and love, both for Hashem as well as for all those around him.

May his memory be a blessing
and serve to guide us for years to come.

This birkon is dedicated in honor of our dear parents

Rabbi David & Eileen z"l Lesnick

Shaya z"l & Rhona Bar Chama

Who have served as role models
for us and our children as individuals dedicated
to Torah, avoda, and gemilut hasadim.

And to our dear children

Ariel & Rinat, Ori, Noam, and Shahar

Adena & Netanel

Sarit & Yonatan, Zohar, and Nili

Rami & Achinoam, Aviv, and Lavi

Amichai & Dalia

Each of whom continually brings us tremendous nahat.

Tamar & Marc Lesnick

זָכוֹר אֶת יוֹם הַשַּׁבָּת לְקַדְּשׁוֹ,
קַרְנוֹ כִּי גָבְהָה נֵזֶר עַל רֹאשׁוֹ.
עַל כֵּן יִתֵּן הָאָדָם לְנַפְשׁוֹ,
עֹנֶג וְגַם שִׂמְחָה בָּהֶם לוֹ לְמָשְׁחָה.
הַשּׁוֹמֵר שַׁבָּת, הַבֵּן עִם הַבַּת,
לָאֵל יֵרָצוּ כְּמִנְחָה עַל מַחֲבַת.

לזכר נשמת

אהרן אשר זעליג בן יעקב יצחק ז״ל

אבינו וסבנו, שקולו ורוחו מילאו את ביתנו ביופיים של שירי שבת. הוא לימד אותנו לא רק את המנגינות, אלא גם את המשמעות העמוקה יותר מאחורי המילים – הקדושה והשמחה שהשבת מביאה. באמצעות הדוגמה שהוא נתן לנו, למדנו איך כוחן של זמירות שבת מחבר אותנו למסורת, לאמונה ואחד לשני. אנו מקווים כי הערך של ספר זה ישמש הוקרה הולמת לזכרו, ימשיך את מורשת השיר, האהבה והמסירות שהוא חלק איתנו בנדיבות כה רבה.

In loving memory of our father and grandfather, **George Saks** *z"l, whose voice and spirit filled our home with the beauty of zemirot on Shabbat. He taught us not only the melodies, but the deeper meaning behind the words of the zemirot – the sanctity and joy that Shabbat brings. Through his example, we learned the power of song in connecting us to tradition, to faith, and to each other. It is our hope that the merit of this book serves as a fitting tribute to his memory, continuing the legacy of song, love, and devotion he shared with us.*

משפחות סאקס

In honor of our parents

Rochelle and Leo Goldberg

on their 60th wedding anniversary

and in memory of

Elliot Goldberg

יצחק אייזיק בן הרב אליעזר

Zack Meller

יחזקאל פסח יהודה בן שלמה

Josh, Evelyn and Phillip Goldberg
Adrianne and Shaun Meller
Rebecca and Guy Mizrachi
Aliza and Zoe Meller

In loving memory of our parents

חיים מאיר וחנה שרה רוזנר ז״ל

who made every Shabbat and Chag special and memorable for their children, grandchildren, and great-grandchildren. They exemplified the significance of Torah and showed us the tremendous importance of family. We were very blessed to have them as our parents and role models, full of warmth, support and unconditional love, always giving and doing everything for us and always making each of us feel special.

They are greatly missed.

Mitchel and Lydia Rosner, Miriam Goldberg,
Aviva and Michael Taragin, Shalom and Tamar Rosner
and their families

In honor of our dear brother

Rabbi Shalom Rosner

who continues to be an outstanding source of Torah for Klal Yisrael. May you continue to spread Torah, with such knowledge, passion, and enthusiasm, all over the world.

And in honor of Tamar, who provides unlimited support and assistance to him and the entire community.

Mitchel, Lydia, Miriam, Aviva, and Michael

In honor and appreciation of

Rabbi Shalom and Dr. Tamar Rosner

In honor of our parents

Evie and Alden Leifer

Suzanne and Avi Stokar

For making zemirot a staple of our Shabbat tables.

And to our siblings
for the cherished memories and joy of singing together.

ונרחיב פה ונמלאנה לשוננו לך רינה

Mira and Daniel Stokar

In memory of

Drs. Stanley and Frances Minkowitz

Sheindy and Jerry Minkowitz

לעילוי נשמת
שמואל בן ישראל צבי
זיסל בת יצחק
ישראל בן שמעון

from the Braun Family

With deep appreciation to Rabbi Rosner's harbatzos Torah and his continuous dedication to helping us learn all aspects of Torah.
May Hashem reward you and your family for helping us all grow.
Caroline and Morris Massel

In loving memory of our dear son, Eli Moshe Zimbalist, HY"D

לזכר נשמת אליהו משה שלמה בן שמעון איתן ושרה צימבליסט, הי״ד
שמסר את נפשו על קדושת ה׳ בט׳ בסיוון ה׳תשפ״ד
נזכור את אהבתו לארץ ישראל, לתורת ישראל ולעם ישראל.
היה ענו ואהוב על כולם, בעל לב זהב וידי זהב.

Sara and Simmy Zimbalist & Family

In memory of
יחזקאל צבי בן משה הלוי
He was honored to be called a talmid of Rav Rosner.

Dovid & Faygie Meisels
Yitzchok & Tamar Meisels, Avigayil, Meira & Shmuel
Eitan & Devorah Rozenberg, Chava, Tehilla & Chezi
Yehuda, Yoni & Yaakov

LZ"N Avrohom Menachem ben Eliyahu Meir
A Holocaust survivor who loved to sing Shabbos zmiros with his family.

תודה רבי, שתלך מחיל אל חיל! קלמן אוסובל

In honor of our dear friends and neighbors, Rabbi Shalom and Dr. Tamar Rosner, with whom we and our children continue to share many Shabbat meals in each other's homes.
מזמור שיר ליום השבת – טוב להודות לה׳ ולזמר לשמך עליון
Wishing us all many years of continued ברכה, הצלחה, *and friendship.*
Chani and Jason Schwartz and family

Friends

Aharon Goldwasser

Marcelle A. Agus

Meir and Shandee Fuchs

Daniel Blender

Bracha and Dovid Schreiber

Becca and Yosef Madowicz

Cindy & Jonathan Sherman and Family

Davida & Gary Stadtmauer

Steven and Michelle Farbman

לע"נ הרב אברהם אריה בן ר' יעקב הכהן
והרב יצחק זלמן בן הרב אברהם שלמה

Susan, Michael, Simcha Nachman,
Elchanan Yosef & Tuvia Leib Geller

Eliezer Rosenblatt

Phyllis and Jack Rubel

Joel and Debbie Spier

Rozen family

CONTENTS

Preface

In a Jewish library, there are *sefarim* that we "learn" and *sefarim* that we "read." *Humashim, mishnayot,* and Talmud are studied and learned, while *siddurim, Tehillim,* and *birkonim* are read and recited at various appropriate times. This is not the ideal reality, however. All *sefarim* contain material that needs to be studied, analyzed, and appreciated. The latter group's recitation would be much more meaningful if we first put in the time for preparation and study. Imagine what our *tefilla* would look like if we had an *"iyun" seder* in *siddur,* preparing for our meeting with Hashem.

Birkon Shalom Rav is a humble contribution toward this end. The *birkon,* found on every Shabbat table, is a potentially inspirational treasure for each and every Shabbat meal. From the mitzvot of *Kiddush, Havdala,* and *Birkat HaMazon,* to the lifecycle events of *sheva berakhot* and *brit mila,* and of course the *Rishonim*-authored *zemirot,* our *birkon* is an overflowing reservoir of material to uplift our Shabbat experience and to edify our spiritual yearnings. In this *birkon,* commentary has been presented to peruse during the singing, or better yet, to prepare beforehand to share with all the attendees, to make the mitzva or *zemer* that much more meaningful.

I had planned to publish a *birkon* at some point in the future, but upon my father's passing this past summer, I knew that this had to become my priority. My father's Shabbat was filled with *ruhniyut.* He learned the *parasha* on Friday night and had a 7 a.m. *havruta* each Shabbat morning before *Shaharit.* He also sang, in order, every single *zemer* in the *birkon.* Whether he was teaching us the European tunes he learned in his youth, or joining our more modern rhythms, my father relished the singing time with the family, imparting to us *simha* and emotion at each meal. He and my mother *a"h* together led our family's Shabbat table for sixty-three wonderful years. May this *birkon* be an eternal testament to their commitment and devotion to Shabbat, to Hashem, and to their family.

Rabbi Shalom Rosner
Beit Shemesh, 2025

Introduction

Rav Shalom Rosner has a unique ability to transmit Torah from a variety of sources in a simple and concise manner. I cannot comprehend how Rav Rosner is able to give so many *shiurim* on a weekly basis on various topics, including *parasha, Nakh, daf yomi, Hilkhot Shabbat* (*Tzurba D'Rabbanan*), *Semikhat Haver*, and others, all while serving as Rav of a shul and as the Rosh Bet Midrash at Machon Lev.

About a year ago, Rav Rosner approached me at a *simha* we were attending and said, "You know, we really should print a *Shalom Rav birkon*." Shortly thereafter, Rav Rosner initiated a weekly *shiur* that served as the basis for this *birkon*.

In *Parashat Vayeshev* (37:2), Rashi states:

> בקש יעקב לישב בשלוה, קפץ עליו רגזו של יוסף. צדיקים מבקשים לישב בשלוה, אמר הקדוש ברוך הוא לא דיין לצדיקים מה שמתוקן להם לעולם הבא, אלא שמבקשים לישב בשלוה בעולם הזה.
>
> Yaakov wished to live in tranquility, but the troubles with Yosef suddenly came upon him. When the righteous wish to live in tranquility, the Holy One, blessed be He, says: "Is it not enough for the righteous what has been prepared for them in the World to Come, that they also wish to live in tranquility in this world?"

Yaakov lived quite a difficult life, running from Esav and dealing with the devious Lavan. Once he returns to Israel with a family, he just wants to keep a low profile and take it easy. Yet, as many commentators state

◂ see *Shalom Rav*

(see *Shalom Rav Al HaTorah, Parashat Vayeshev*), man's duty to serve the community and spread Torah never ends.

Rav Rosner has the attitude that there is constantly more to achieve. There is always so much more to learn and to teach; his job is never completed. May *HaKadosh Barukh Hu* grant Rav Rosner a long, healthy, happy, and fruitful life so that he can continue to spread Torah!

Our Shabbat meals have been enhanced by Rav Rosner's *divrei Torah* on the *parasha*, and I am excited that we will now be able to further enrich our Shabbat with *divrei Torah* on *zemirot* and *Birkat HaMazon*. I apologize in advance to Rav Rosner and to the readers if there are any errors. They are likely my fault. I tried my best to enable the reader to hear Rav Rosner's voice while transmitting the "oral" word in a reader-friendly "written" manner.

I would like to take this opportunity to sincerely thank Rav Rosner, who has had such a profound impact on my life and on the lives of each of my family members. We are all guided by his inspiring thoughts and ideas. I would also like to take this opportunity to thank Rav Asher Weiss, who has inspired me personally in so many ways.

I owe a debt of gratitude to my father, who is my guiding light. We share *divrei Torah* on a daily basis. Practically everything that I share with others that I did not hear from Rav Rosner and Rav Weiss comes from my father. I look up to my father, who is a businessman and yet spends hours each day learning Torah and preparing for *shiurim* that he gives in his community. May Hashem bless my dear Aba with health so that he can continue to spread Torah for many more years.

My mother passed away a little over two years ago. Each week, she would share with me her thoughts on the weekly entries in *Shalom Rav Al HaTorah*. I know she would have appreciated reading and discussing the content of this *birkon*. May she look down from above and be rewarded for having inspired me to continue to make Torah accessible to readers.

I would also like to thank Matthew Miller, Rabbi Reuven Ziegler, Aryeh Grossman, Ita Olesker, Caryn Meltz, David Silverstein, Meira Mintz, Tani Bayer and Tali Simon for their support and uncompromising efforts in ensuring that this *birkon* be presented in the most professional manner.

Aharon, aharon haviv – I would like to express my deepest appreciation to my *eshet hayil*, Tamar. Without her encouragement, support, and

◂ partnership

partnership, I would not have been able to achieve this feat or any other. She is a true *ezer kenegdo*, and I cherish our relationship. In addition, I want to thank each of our children, their spouses, and my grandchildren: Ariel and Rinat and their children, Ori, Noam, and Shahar; Adena and Netanel Weil; Sarit and Yonatan Kurtzman and their children, Zohar and Nili; Rami and Achinoam and their children, Aviv and Lavi; and Amichai and Dalia, with whom I discuss Rav Rosner's *divrei Torah* during our Shabbat meals together. It brings me great *nahat* when I hear them share these thoughts with others. May Hashem continue to watch over each of you and enable you to continue to positively influence others through your tremendous acts of *hesed* and through Torah.

I would also like to thank all my friends and shul buddies, as well as Rav Rosner "junkies" with whom we share Torah and who have encouraged me to continue to print Rav Rosner's *shiurim*. I hope that all who use this *birkon* enjoy the content, internalize it, and share it with others. May the singing of *zemirot* be more meaningful, and may its words reach the heavens!

Marc Lesnick
Beit Shemesh, 2025

ברכון שלום רב

BIRKON SHALOM RAV

ליל שבת

SHABBAT EVENING

Candle Lighting

On Erev Shabbat that is not a Yom Tov, cover the eyes with the hands after lighting the candles, and say:

בָּרוּךְ Blessed are You, LORD our God, King of the Universe, who has made us holy through His commandments, and has commanded us to light the Sabbath light.

Essentially, whose home court is the location? When we enter the *Mikdash,* we are guests in God's home and act accordingly. We are more respectful of the location. We take off our shoes, and we do not use it as a shortcut. In contrast, when we are in shul, it is our home court and God is the guest, so standards are a bit lower. We can wear shoes, yet we respect the *kedusha* of the location and do not allow people to use our property as a shortcut.

The Rav explains that the relationship between the *Beit HaMikdash* and a *Beit HaKenesset* in *space* is parallel to the relationship between Yom Tov and Shabbat in *time*. On Yom Tov we are obligated to perform *aliya leregel*. We leave our homes and journey to the *Beit HaMikdash,* which is considered God's domain. Therefore, we dress in fancier garments and are in a greater state of happiness, excited to be a guest in God's palace. We do not have a *Kabbalat Yom Tov* prayer, welcoming the Yom Tov, since conceptually, we are going to Him. On Shabbat, in contrast, God comes to us, to our home, and the standards are therefore lowered. Appropriate, but not the most expensive clothing, suffices. We have *Kabbalat Shabbat,* since we are welcoming in the Shabbat Queen. It is our responsibility to create the proper atmosphere in our homes on Shabbat and Yom Tov to merit to be in the intense presence of the *Shekhina.*

HADLAKAT NEIROT SHABBAT

WHY TWO SHABBAT CANDLES?

The Rambam in *Hilkhot Shabbat* (5:1) discusses the importance of lighting candles on Friday night:

> ולוקח שמן ומדליק את הנר שזה בכלל עונג שבת, אפילו אין לו מה יאכל שואל על הפתחים.
>
> One takes oil and lights a candle, as this is part of *oneg Shabbat*; even if one does not have anything to eat, he should borrow money for wicks.

Yet, later in *Hilkhot Shabbat* (30:5), the Rambam writes:

הדלקת נרות

On ערב שבת *that is not a* יום טוב*, cover the eyes with the hands after lighting the candles, and say:*

בָּרוּךְ אַתָּה יהוה אֱלֹהֵינוּ מֶלֶךְ הָעוֹלָם
אֲשֶׁר קִדְּשָׁנוּ בְּמִצְוֹתָיו וְצִוָּנוּ לְהַדְלִיק נֵר שֶׁל שַׁבָּת.

SHABBAT: HASHEM VISITS WITH US

In a yahrzeit *shiur,*[1] Rav Yosef Dov Soloveitchik asked the following three questions with respect to the comparison of Shabbat and Yom Tov:

1. Why is it that on Erev Yom Tov there is no *Kabbalat Yom Tov* prayer, similar to what we recite as *Kabbalat Shabba*t on Erev Shabbat? Why do we not recite *Lekhu Neranena* or *Lekha Dodi* on Erev Yom Tov?
2. In Massekhet Moed Katan 23b, Tosafot asks why it is that a *mo'ed* breaks the customs of *aveilut* (mourning), while Shabbat does not. Tosafot explains that only on Yom Tov is there *simha,* while on Shabbat there is *oneg. Aveilut* can coexist with *oneg,* but not with *simha.* But that just begs the question: Why is there no *simha* on Shabbat?
3. The Hagahot Maimoniyot (*Hilkhot Yom Tov,* ch. 6) states that on Yom Tov one should wear special clothes that are even nicer than what one adorns on Shabbat. Why is that so?

To answer these questions, the Rav draws upon an analogy from another area of Halakha. In Massekhet Megilla (28), the Gemara declares that a desolate shul retains its *kedusha* (sanctity), comparable to the *Beit HaMikdash.* After all, shul is referred to as a *mikdash me'at* (a small temple). There are numerous halakhic parallels between a shul and the *Mikdash.* Thus, for example, one cannot use a shul or the *Mikdash* as a shortcut or treat either of them in a disgraceful way. Yet, there are also distinctions between them. One cannot wear shoes or a money belt in the *Mikdash,* but in a shul one is permitted to wear shoes and carry a wallet. Why the distinction?

The Gemara in Berakhot (62b) tells us in the name of Rava: *Ki beito* – A shul is like one's home. That is why a shortcut is not allowed (as you would not allow neighbors to use your living room as a shortcut), while shoes may be worn (as they would be worn in one's home). The Rav expands this idea, explaining that both a shul and the *Mikdash* are places where we meet God intensely; the only distinction is who is the host and who is the guest.

1 Rav Yosef Dov Soloveitchik, *Shiurim LeZekher Avi Mori.*

On Erev Yom Tov, say the following blessing and then light the candles from an existing flame. If also Shabbat, cover the eyes with the hands after lighting the candles and say the following blessing, adding the words in parentheses.

בָּרוּךְ Blessed are You, Lord our God, King of the Universe,
who has made us holy through His commandments,
and has commanded us to light (the Sabbath light and)
the festival light.

The blessing "Sheheḥeyanu" ("Who has given life") is said on Yom Tov evenings, except on the last two evenings of Pesaḥ. (In Israel, it is not said on the last evening of Pesaḥ.)

בָּרוּךְ Blessed are You, Lord our God, King of the Universe,
who has given us life, sustained us, and brought us to this time.

---

and Yom Kippur candles.[2] The *berakha* is always "*lehadlik ner*" in the singular, as the *ikkar* (primary) mitzva is to light a single candle, although the custom is to light more than one candle.

The *Shulhan Arukh* (263:1) writes in *Hilkhot Shabbat* that there is a custom to light two candles, symbolizing *shamor* and *zakhor*, the two terms used in connection with Shabbat in the first and second *luhot*. *Shamor* represents the prohibitions, and zakhor reflects the positive commandments with respect to Shabbat. This is based on a *gemara* (Shabbat 33b), which recounts the story of R. Shimon Bar Yohai and his son: After spending an extensive period in a cave, they leave the cave and see a man walking with two bundles of myrtle branches (*hadasim*) on Erev Shabbat. They ask why he needs the two bundles, and he responds, "This is for Shabbat - one is for *shamor* and the other for *zakhor*." Although Rav Shimon Bar Yohai and his son had been in a cave for several years in an intense way with unadulterated pure *kedusha*, they learned a lesson from this anonymous man - that one can infuse *kedusha* into every aspect on one's life, especially at the Shabbat table.

שהחיינו – SHEHEHEYANU

The *Shulhan Arukh* does not mention that women should recite *birkat Sheheheyanu* when lighting Yom Tov candles. Rav Yaakov Emden (*She'eilot Yaavetz* 103, quoted in *Mishna Berurah* 263:23) prefers to have the *berakha* of

2 The *berakha* recited on Yom Kippur candles is one of seven *berakhot* recited once a year in *Eretz Yisrael*: *(1) Lehadlik ner shel Yom HaKippurim; (2) Al biur hametz; (3) Nahem; (4) Birkat ha'ilanot; (5) Al akhilat matza; (6) Al akhilat maror; and (7) Asher ge'alanu.*

Sheheheyanu

On ערב יום טוב, say the following blessing and then light the candles from an existing flame. If also שבת, cover the eyes with the hands after lighting the candles and say the following blessing, adding the words in parentheses.

בָּרוּךְ אַתָּה יהוה אֱלֹהֵינוּ מֶלֶךְ הָעוֹלָם
אֲשֶׁר קִדְּשָׁנוּ בְּמִצְוֹתָיו
וְצִוָּנוּ לְהַדְלִיק נֵר שֶׁל (שַׁבָּת וְשֶׁל) יוֹם טוֹב.

The blessing שֶׁהֶחֱיָנוּ is said on יום טוב evenings, except on the last two evenings of פסח. (In ארץ ישראל, it is not said on the last evening of פסח.)

בָּרוּךְ אַתָּה יהוה אֱלֹהֵינוּ מֶלֶךְ הָעוֹלָם
שֶׁהֶחֱיָנוּ וְקִיְּמָנוּ, וְהִגִּיעָנוּ לַזְּמַן הַזֶּה.

צריך לתקן ביתו מבעוד יום מפני כבוד השבת. ויהיה נר דלוק ושולחן ערוך לאכול ומטה מוצעת שכל אלו לכבוד שבת הן.

> *One should prepare his home for Shabbat. A candle should be lit, the table set, and bed made, as all of these preparations are for kavod Shabbat.*

In chapter 5, the Rambam relates candle lighting to *oneg Shabbat*, while in chapter 30 he links candle lighting to *kavod Shabbat*. Which is it?

The Brisker Rav (*Grah al HaShas* 11) explains, based on an idea expressed by the Vilna Gaon (*Orah Hayim* 529:1), that *kavod* relates to actions that we perform *prior* to the commencement of Shabbat, such as taking a shower, cooking, setting the table, etc., and that is the context of the Rambam's statement in chapter 30. Actions that we perform or engage in *during* Shabbat, such as singing, eating, or resting, are forms of *oneg Shabbat*.

Lighting candles has a duality and is considered both *kavod* and *oneg*. When one celebrates a special occasion and desires to create a certain mood, one lights candles on the table out of respect for the event. This is a form of *kavod Shabbat*. At the same time, entering a room and seeing the candles and enjoying the ambiance is a form of *oneg Shabbat*. Candle lighting is a unique mitzva that encompasses both *kavod and oneg Shabbat*. The candles help set the mood and provide one with enjoyment from their light. May we always be able to "enlighten" the manner in which we prepare (*kavod*) and experience (*oneg*) each Shabbat.

THE NUMBER OF CANDLES

There is a mitzva to light not only Shabbat candles but also Yom Tov candles

On Erev Yom Kippur, cover the eyes with the hands after lighting the candles, and say (on Shabbat add the words in parentheses):

בָּרוּךְ Blessed are You, Lord our God, King of the Universe,
who has made us holy through His commandments,
and has commanded us to light (the Sabbath light and)
the light of the Day of Atonement.

בָּרוּךְ Blessed are You, Lord our God, King of the Universe,
who has given us life, sustained us, and brought us to this time.

Some add:

יְהִי May it be Your will, Lord our God and God of our ancestors, that the Temple be speedily rebuilt in our days, and grant us our share in Your Torah. And may we serve You there in reverence, as in the days of old and as in former years. *Mal. 3*

Prayer after candle lighting (add the words in parentheses as appropriate):

יְהִי May it be Your will, Lord my God and God of my forebears, that You give me grace – me (and my husband/and my father/and my mother/and my sons and my daughters) and all those close to me, and give us and all Israel good and long lives. And remember us with a memory that brings goodness and blessing; come to us with compassion and bless us with great blessings. Build our homes until they are complete, and allow Your Presence to live among us. And may I merit to raise children and grandchildren, each one wise and understanding, loving the Lord and in awe of God, people of truth, holy children, who will cling on to the Lord and light up the world with Torah and with good actions, and with all the kinds of work that serve the Creator. Please, hear my pleading at this time, by the merit of Sarah and Rebecca, Rachel and Leah our mothers, and light our candle that it should never go out, and light up Your face, so that we shall be saved, Amen.

Sheheheyanu when lighting candles for centuries. There is an emotional attachment to this mitzva, so we should encourage women to continue to recite *Sheheheyanu* when lighting candles for Yom Tov.

On ערב יום כיפור, cover the eyes with the hands after lighting the candles, and say (on שבת add the words in parentheses):

בָּרוּךְ אַתָּה יהוה אֱלֹהֵינוּ מֶלֶךְ הָעוֹלָם
אֲשֶׁר קִדְּשָׁנוּ בְּמִצְוֹתָיו
וְצִוָּנוּ לְהַדְלִיק נֵר שֶׁל (שַׁבָּת וְשֶׁל) יוֹם הַכִּפּוּרִים.

בָּרוּךְ אַתָּה יהוה אֱלֹהֵינוּ מֶלֶךְ הָעוֹלָם
שֶׁהֶחֱיָנוּ וְקִיְּמָנוּ, וְהִגִּיעָנוּ לַזְּמַן הַזֶּה.

Some add:

יְהִי רָצוֹן מִלְּפָנֶיךָ יהוה אֱלֹהֵינוּ וֵאלֹהֵי אֲבוֹתֵינוּ, שֶׁיִּבָּנֶה בֵּית הַמִּקְדָּשׁ
בִּמְהֵרָה בְיָמֵינוּ, וְתֵן חֶלְקֵנוּ בְּתוֹרָתֶךָ, וְשָׁם נַעֲבָדְךָ בְּיִרְאָה כִּימֵי
עוֹלָם וּכְשָׁנִים קַדְמֹנִיּוֹת. וְעָרְבָה לַיהוה מִנְחַת יְהוּדָה וִירוּשָׁלָםִ כִּימֵי מלאכי ג
עוֹלָם וּכְשָׁנִים קַדְמֹנִיּוֹת:

Prayer after candle lighting (add the words in parentheses as appropriate):

יְהִי רָצוֹן מִלְּפָנֶיךָ יהוה אֱלֹהַי וֵאלֹהֵי אֲבוֹתַי, שֶׁתְּחוֹנֵן אוֹתִי (וְאֶת אִישִׁי/ וְאֶת אָבִי/ וְאֶת אִמִּי/ וְאֶת בָּנַי וְאֶת בְּנוֹתַי) וְאֶת כָּל קְרוֹבַי, וְתִתֶּן לָנוּ וּלְכָל יִשְׂרָאֵל חַיִּים טוֹבִים וַאֲרֻכִּים, וְתִזְכְּרֵנוּ בְּזִכְרוֹן טוֹבָה וּבְרָכָה, וְתִפְקְדֵנוּ בִּפְקֻדַּת יְשׁוּעָה וְרַחֲמִים, וּתְבָרְכֵנוּ בְּרָכוֹת גְּדוֹלוֹת, וְתַשְׁלִים בָּתֵּינוּ וְתַשְׁכֵּן שְׁכִינָתְךָ בֵּינֵינוּ. וְזַכֵּנִי לְגַדֵּל בָּנִים וּבְנֵי בָנִים חֲכָמִים וּנְבוֹנִים, אוֹהֲבֵי יהוה יִרְאֵי אֱלֹהִים, אַנְשֵׁי אֱמֶת זֶרַע קֹדֶשׁ, בַּיהוה דְּבֵקִים וּמְאִירִים אֶת הָעוֹלָם בַּתּוֹרָה וּבְמַעֲשִׂים טוֹבִים וּבְכָל מְלֶאכֶת עֲבוֹדַת הַבּוֹרֵא. אָנָּא שְׁמַע אֶת תְּחִנָּתִי בָּעֵת הַזֹּאת בִּזְכוּת שָׂרָה וְרִבְקָה וְרָחֵל וְלֵאָה אִמּוֹתֵינוּ, וְהָאֵר נֵרֵנוּ שֶׁלֹּא יִכְבֶּה לְעוֹלָם וָעֶד, וְהָאֵר פָּנֶיךָ וְנִוָּשֵׁעָה. אָמֵן.

Sheheheyanu recited later in the night, because when one lights candles it is not yet Yom Tov. The *Tzitz Eliezer* (14:53) defends the practice and declares that women have been following this custom of including the blessing of

Blessing the Children

On the evenings of Shabbat and Yom Tov, many have the custom to bless their children.

To sons, say:

יְשִׂמְךָ May God make you
like Ephraim and Manasseh. *Gen. 48*

To daughters, say:

יְשִׂימֵךְ May God make you
like Sarah, Rebecca, Rachel and Leah.

יְבָרֶכְךָ May the LORD bless you and protect you. *Num. 6*
May the LORD make His face shine on you
and be gracious to you.
May the LORD turn His face toward you
and grant you peace.

---

any adverse repercussions by switching his hands and providing the younger of the brothers with the greater blessing. We bless our children that they should be able to establish the relationship that existed between Efraim and Menashe, so they can avoid sibling rivalry and live in peace and harmony together. Witnessing one's children respect each other brings the greatest *nahat* and joy to a parent.

Rabbi Zalman Sorotzkin: First to Live as Jews in Exile

Another approach as to why we bless our children to emulate Efraim and Menashe is suggested by Rabbi Zalman Sorotzkin, the author of *Oznayim LaTorah.*

Just moments before the *berakha*, Yaakov asks, "Who are these children?" What did Yaakov mean? He saw in the future that their descendants wouldn't be perfect, so he asked, "Do they deserve *berakhot*?" Yosef answered, "Hashem gave them to me." Then Yaakov agreed to bless them.

Why did Yaakov's attitude change? *Hazal* tell us that at that moment, Yaakov wanted to reveal when the redemption would come. He saw clearly

before

ברכת הבנים

On ליל שבת *and* ליל יום טוב*, many have the custom to bless their children.*

To sons, say:

יְשִׂמְךָ אֱלֹהִים כְּאֶפְרַיִם וְכִמְנַשֶּׁה: בראשית מח

To daughters, say:

יְשִׂימֵךְ אֱלֹהִים כְּשָׂרָה רִבְקָה רָחֵל וְלֵאָה.

יְבָרֶכְךָ יהוה וְיִשְׁמְרֶךָ: במדבר ו
יָאֵר יהוה פָּנָיו אֵלֶיךָ וִיחֻנֶּךָּ:
יִשָּׂא יהוה פָּנָיו אֵלֶיךָ וְיָשֵׂם לְךָ שָׁלוֹם:

BLESSING OUR CHILDREN

It is customary to bless one's children each Friday night with *Birkat Kohanim* (the blessing the *kohanim* are charged to convey to *Am Yisrael*), with an introductory phrase of "*Yesimkha E-lohim keEfraim ukeMenashe* – Hashem should make you like Efraim and Menashe." Why do we bless our children to be like Efraim and Menashe? Aren't there greater *tzaddikim*, such as Avraham, Yitzhak, and Yaakov, or Moshe Rabbeinu, whom we would prefer our children emulate? What is so unique about Efraim and Menashe that we want our children to be modeled after their character traits?

We will offer three explanations.

Bnei Yissakhar: No Sibling Rivalry

In *Igra DeKalla*, the Bnei Yissakhar's commentary on the Torah, he suggests that Efraim and Menashe were the first siblings in history that we know of who do not exhibit sibling rivalry. Until then, we witness many sets of brothers who engaged in disputes, including Kayin and Hevel, Yizhak and Yishmael, Yaakov and Esav, and Yosef and his brothers. We bless our children to be like Efraim and Menashe with respect to the aspect of brotherly love. Yaakov was aware of their special relationship, and he therefore did not fear

Yam Simha: No Generation Gap

The *Yam Simha*[3] suggests yet another explanation as to why we bless our children to emulate Efraim and Menashe. He infers an answer from a previous *pasuk*, where Yaakov says:

אפרים ומנשה כראובן ושמעון יהיו לי.

> Efraim and Menashe shall be mine like Reuven and Shimon. (*Bereshit* 48:5)

We know the reality that every generation experiences a spiritual decline from the previous generation, what we call *yeridat hadorot*. Every generation that is further from the source, further from *maamad Har Sinai*, drops a spiritual notch. Yet, Yaakov saw that Menashe and Efraim didn't fall spiritually. Instead they jumped in their spiritual level – they were just like his own sons.

The Gemara (Sanhedrin 105b) states:

בכל אדם מתקנא חוץ מבנו ותלמידו.

> A person is jealous of everyone in the world other than his son and his *talmid*.

A father thinks, *If only my son would outdo what I do!* Therefore, every Friday night, when a father gives this *berakha* to his child, his hope is: "Outshine me. Don't contribute to *yeridat hadorot*. Be greater than me!" That is why we bless our sons to be like Menashe and Efraim specifically. They were two people who didn't experience *yeridat hadorot* and were on par with their father.[4]

A similar idea is expressed by Rav Yosef Dov Soloveitchik.[5] He cites a *gemara* (Kiddushin 30a) that states:

אמר רבי יהושע בן לוי כל המלמד בן בנו תורה מעלה עליו הכתוב כאילו קיבלה מהר סיני.

---

3 Rabbi Yisrael Moshe Fried, *Yam Simha* (1997), 143.

4 In a similar vein, Yaakov learned with Yosef's children, and in a way, Yaakov was stating that when one learns Torah, it transcends any generational gap. Imagine entering a time machine and landing in a different era. If a Jew were to meet Rashi or the Rambam, a most interesting discussion about Torah would ensue. When one shares Torah, there is no generation gap. To Yaakov, this is what Efraim and Menashe symbolized, and that is the blessing we wish to convey to our children.

5 *Harerei Kedem*, vol. 2 (Israel: 2004), sec. 122, p. 356.

before him the whole future of *Klal Yisrael*, the tragedies, the physical and the spiritual destruction. He saw every detail: pogroms, crusades, assimilation, and the freedom that has led to spiritual depravation.

When Yaakov saw all that, he said, "Who are these people I see in the future who will sometimes willingly throw off the yoke of Torah?" But then Yosef said, "These are the children that Hashem gave me," and Yaakov saw children who were able to withstand the pressures of Egypt. He saw grandchildren who learned Torah. Even though Yaakov foresaw the corruption of the future, he gave *berakhot* – specifically blessing his descendants to be like these children, who managed to withstand the corruption and depravity of the society around them.

Efraim and Menashe were enslaved along with the rest of *Klal Yisrael*. They didn't exclude themselves by claiming to be Egyptian. They accepted upon themselves the yoke of exile, as part of all their Jewish brethren. Yaakov saw where they were coming from and that they had managed to succeed spiritually despite that. Therefore, he blessed his descendants to be like them, to be able to survive in an unfriendly environment, in an environment that went against everything they believed in.

We choose to bless our children to emulate Menashe and Efraim, people who were able to remain strong and committed to Judaism irrespective of the adverse culture and environment in which they were surrounded. This is the *berakha* that every parent wants to convey – that their children should not be influenced by the negative values of the society around them, no matter which country they live in.

Rabbi Sorotzkin points out that the secret of Menashe and Efraim's success boils down to the education their father provided for them. The *pasuk* says:

ויברכם ביום ההוא לאמור בך יברך ישראל לאמר ישמך א־להים כאפרים וכמנשה.

> So he blessed them on that day, saying, "Through you, Israel will bless, saying, 'May God make you like Efraim and like Menashe.'" (*Bereshit* 48:20)

When Yaakov said "*bekha*" ("through you"), he was talking to Yosef. Says Rabbi Sorotzkin, the greatest measure of a person is what type of *hinukh* he provides to his children. Whether his education succeeds or not is beyond his control. We can only do our best, and the rest is *siyata dishmaya*. Yet, we have to do our utmost to ensure that our children are being given the best education possible.

Many people sing each of the four verses of the following song three times:

שָׁלוֹם עֲלֵיכֶם Welcome, ministering angels, angels of the Most High,
from the Supreme King of kings,
the Holy One, blessed be He.

Enter in peace, angels of peace, angels of the Most High,
from the Supreme King of kings,
the Holy One, blessed be He.

---

they should carry the torch into the next generation, passing on the fire of Har Sinai. It's really a *tefilla* when we give this *berakha*, a *tefilla* of the father that he should be *zokhe* to pass on the torch of tradition.[6]

שלום עליכם – SHALOM ALEIKHEM

The Gemara tells us in Shabbat (119b):

> תניא ר׳ יוסי בר יהודה אומר שני מלאכי השרת מלוין לו לאדם בע״ש מבית הכנסת לביתו אחד טוב ואחד רע, וכשבא לביתו ומצא נר דלוק ושלחן ערוך ומטתו מוצעת, מלאך טוב אומר יהי רצון שתהא לשבת אחרת כך ומלאך רע עונה אמן בעל כרחו, ואם לאו, מלאך רע אומר יהי רצון שתהא לשבת אחרת כך ומלאך טוב עונה אמן בעל כרחו.

> R. Yosei bar Yehuda says: Two ministering angels accompany a person on Shabbat evening from the shul to his home, one good angel and one evil angel. And when he reaches his home and finds a candle lit and a table set and his bed made, the good angel says: "May it be Your will that it shall be like this for another Shabbat." And the evil angel answers against his will: "Amen." And if the person's home is not prepared for Shabbat in that manner, the evil angel says: "May it be Your will that it shall be so for another Shabbat," and the good angel answers against his will: "Amen."

Two angels accompany a person home on Shabbat evening to evaluate whether or not the household has prepared for Shabbat. This reflects that we each need to make sure that we prepare for the special meeting with Hashem on

6 See *Reflections of the Rav*, vol. 2 (Hoboken, NJ: Ktav, 1989), 17, where Rav Soloveitchik provides an emotional description of his experience of feeling the *baalei mesora* entering the room while he is studying Torah.

Many people sing each of the four verses of the following song three times:

שָׁלוֹם עֲלֵיכֶם מַלְאֲכֵי הַשָּׁרֵת, מַלְאֲכֵי עֶלְיוֹן
מִמֶּלֶךְ מַלְכֵי הַמְּלָכִים, הַקָּדוֹשׁ בָּרוּךְ הוּא.

בּוֹאֲכֶם לְשָׁלוֹם מַלְאֲכֵי הַשָּׁלוֹם, מַלְאֲכֵי עֶלְיוֹן
מִמֶּלֶךְ מַלְכֵי הַמְּלָכִים, הַקָּדוֹשׁ בָּרוּךְ הוּא.

> R. Yehoshua ben Levi says: "Anyone who teaches Torah to his grandson is treated by the Torah as having received it from Mount Sinai.

The Rambam (*Hilkhot Talmud Torah* 1:2) adds that there is a special merit of learning Torah with a grandchild, and it is greater in some ways than learning with a child.

The problem, notes Rav Soloveitchik, is that the Rambam also says that if you have a choice between your son and grandson for *talmud Torah*, your son comes first. If you only have enough money to pay for a *melamed* for either your son or your grandson, your son's education is your primary obligation, which seems to mean the opposite of the previous words of the Rambam.

Which is it, then? We can find our answer based on a Ramban, says Rav Soloveitchik. The Ramban in *Sefer HaMitzvot* (addition to negative commandment 2), counts a separate negative mitzva that the Rambam doesn't count: the mitzva to never forget the experience of Mount Sinai.

There are two elements of Torah that we have to transmit to the next generation. The first is *talmud Torah*, which is actual information in the form of Halakha, Mishna, Gemara – the whole breadth of Torah. The second is the Har Sinai element, which is *emunat haTorah*, the development of our tradition, our Jewish identity, and our passion for Torah.

When it comes to the first type, says Rav Soloveitchik, a son takes precedence over a grandson, whereas when it comes to passing on the torch to the next generation, the continuity of the Jewish People, it is considered a greater accomplishment to pass it on to someone two generations down.

Maybe this is why we bless our children to be like Efraim and Menashe. Yaakov was the first person to have such a relationship with his grandchildren, in which a grandfather learned Torah with his grandsons. We're giving the *berakha* to our children that not only should they learn Torah from us, but

Bless me with peace, angels of peace, angels of the Most High,
from the Supreme King of kings,
the Holy One, blessed be He.

Go in peace, angels of peace, angels of the Most High,
from the Supreme King of kings,
the Holy One, blessed be He.

---

maximize this special time and exclusive opportunity to enhance our connection to our Creator each Shabbat.

It is told that the late Lubavitcher Rebbe never slept on Shabbat. He expressed that on Shabbat he felt as if he was on a shopping spree. If one were to be granted a certain amount of time in a store to gather as many items as possible for free, he would not take a break. He would utilize every second to be able to maximize the opportunity. Shabbat was like a spiritual shopping spree for the Rebbe. He would appreciate and cherish each moment and did not desire to waste it on sleep.

מלאכי השרת, מלאכי השלום – MALAKHEI HASHARET, MALAKHEI HASHALOM

In the opening paragraph of *Shalom Aleikhem*, we refer to the angels as *malakhei hasharet* (servicing angels), while in the following stanzas we refer to the angels as *malakhei hashalom* (angels of peace). Why does the term used to refer to the angels change from *malakhei hasharet* to *malakhei hashalom*?

The Sar Shalom of Belz (cited in Rav Biderman's *birkon*) offers an explanation based on Avraham's encounter with the angels. The *pesukim* at the beginning of *Parashat Vayera* depicting the angels' visit to Avraham read as follows: First the angels are percieved as being above Avraham *(nitzavim alav)*. Avraham then moves toward them *(vayaratz likratam)* to greet them. He is then equal to them. Avraham has food prepared for them and provides it to them, and he is then referred to as *omed aleihem* – he is above them. When the *malakhim* enter our home, they are *malakhei hasharet*; they are the servants of God and are above us. Once the angels witness how we prepare and honor the Shabbat, we are raised to their level and are perceived as servants of God as well. Now the angels are referred to as *malakhei hashalom*, since their being subservient to Hashem is no longer exclusive to them, after they see how we honor Shabbat. They are at peace (*shalom*) with us because each of us is a servant of *HaKadosh Barukh Hu*.

בָּרְכוּנִי לְשָׁלוֹם מַלְאֲכֵי הַשָּׁלוֹם, מַלְאֲכֵי עֶלְיוֹן
מִמֶּלֶךְ מַלְכֵי הַמְּלָכִים, הַקָּדוֹשׁ בָּרוּךְ הוּא.

צֵאתְכֶם לְשָׁלוֹם מַלְאֲכֵי הַשָּׁלוֹם, מַלְאֲכֵי עֶלְיוֹן
מִמֶּלֶךְ מַלְכֵי הַמְּלָכִים, הַקָּדוֹשׁ בָּרוּךְ הוּא.

Shabbat. The Gemara (Kiddushin 41) discusses that it is better for an individual to perform a mitzva by himself rather than via a messenger: *Mitzva bo yoter mibeshluho*. The Gemara applies this principle to two mitzvot: marriage and Shabbat preparations. The *Shulhan Arukh (Orah Hayim* 272) also discusses that a person should engage in preparations for Shabbat himself. Let us not think that personal, physical exertion in Shabbat preparations are beneath us. The more we are physically involved, the more honor we are demonstrating.

צאתכם לשלום – TZETKHEM LESHALOM

Bidding Farewell to the Angels

In *Shalom Aleikhem*, we welcome the angels into our home. The last paragraph seems somewhat puzzling, however. We recite "*tzetkhem leshalom*"; we bid them farewell. Wouldn't we want the angels to remain with us? Why are we so quick to usher them out of our homes on Friday night?

The Beit Yaakov (Rav Yaakov Emden) writes in his siddur that we do not know how our meal will turn out – we may be embarrassed to have the angels remain with us. This explanation is not too confidence-building.

The Shaarei Teshuva (*Shulhan Arukh* 272) cites the Hida, who suggests that we do not know exactly when the angels will leave. It is not that we are asking them to leave now. The angels are welcome to remain with us; we just want to be sure to respectfully bid them farewell, so we do so formally now.

Rav Avraham Schorr (*HaLeket VeHalibuv*), citing the Shem MiShmuel (*Vayigash*), offers an insightful explanation. Shabbat is considered a special time of unification (*yihud*) of *Am Yisrael* and Hashem. Just like a *hatan and kalla* (bride and groom) need to be alone to consummate their marriage, so too *Am Yisrael* and Hashem need to enter the "*yihud* room" – the twenty-five hours of Shabbat. It is a special time that we have with Hashem, and even the angels cannot be present, so we politely bid them farewell. We should

כִּי מַלְאָכָיו He will command His angels about you, *Ps. 91*
to guard you in all your ways.
May the LORD guard your going out and your return, *Ps. 121*
from now and for all time.

Some say:

רִבּוֹן כָּל הָעוֹלָמִים Master of all worlds, LORD of all souls, LORD of peace, mighty, blessed and great King, King who speaks peace, King who is glorious, enduring and pure, King who gives life to worlds, King who is good and does good, King alone and unique, great King who robes Himself in compassion, King who reigns over all kings, who is exalted and supports those who fall, King who is Author of creation, who redeems and rescues, who is radiant and ruddy, King who is holy, high and exalted, King who hears prayer, King whose way is just: I thank You, LORD my God and God of my ancestors, for all the loving-kindness You have done and will do for me, and all the members of my household and all my fellow creatures. Blessed are Your angels, holy and pure, who do Your will. LORD of peace, King to whom peace belongs, bless me with peace, and grant me and the members of my household, and all Your people the house of Israel, a good and peaceful life. King exalted over all the heavenly array, who formed me and who formed creation, I entreat Your radiant presence, that You find me and all the members of my household worthy of grace and good favor in Your eyes and the eyes of all people and all who see us, that we may serve You. May we be worthy to receive Sabbaths amidst great joy, wealth and honor, and few sins. May You remove from me and all the members of my household and all Your people the house of Israel all sickness and disease, all poverty, hardship and destitution. Grant us a virtuous desire to serve You in truth, awe and love. May we find honor in Your eyes and the eyes of all who see us, for You are the King of honor: to You it belongs, to You it accords. Please, King who reigns over all kings, command Your angels, ministering angels who minister to the Most High, to act compassionately toward me when they enter my house on our holy day, for I have lit my lights, spread my couch and changed my clothes in honor of the Sabbath; I have come to Your House to lay my pleas before You that You remove my sighs; I have testified that in six days You created all things, and said it a second time, and will testify to it a third time over my cup, in joy, as You commanded me to remember it, delighting in the extra soul You have given me. On it [the Sabbath] I shall rest as You have commanded me, thereby to serve You. So too I will declare Your greatness in joyful song, for I have set the LORD before me, that You may have compassion upon me in my exile, redeeming me and awakening my heart to Your love. Then I will keep Your commands and statutes without sadness, praying correctly as is right and fitting. Angels of peace, come in peace and bless me with peace; declare blessed the table I have prepared, and go in peace, now and forever. Amen, Selah.

כִּי מַלְאָכָיו יְצַוֶּה־לָּךְ, לִשְׁמָרְךָ בְּכָל־דְּרָכֶיךָ: תהלים צא

יהוה יִשְׁמָר־צֵאתְךָ וּבוֹאֶךָ, מֵעַתָּה וְעַד־עוֹלָם: תהלים קכא

Some say:

רִבּוֹן כָּל הָעוֹלָמִים, אֲדוֹן כָּל הַנְּשָׁמוֹת, אֲדוֹן הַשָּׁלוֹם. מֶלֶךְ אַבִּיר, מֶלֶךְ בָּרוּךְ, מֶלֶךְ גָּדוֹל, מֶלֶךְ דּוֹבֵר שָׁלוֹם, מֶלֶךְ הָדוּר, מֶלֶךְ וָתִיק, מֶלֶךְ זַךְ, מֶלֶךְ חֵי הָעוֹלָמִים, מֶלֶךְ טוֹב וּמֵטִיב, מֶלֶךְ יָחִיד וּמְיֻחָד, מֶלֶךְ כַּבִּיר, מֶלֶךְ לוֹבֵשׁ רַחֲמִים, מֶלֶךְ מַלְכֵי הַמְּלָכִים, מֶלֶךְ נִשְׂגָּב, מֶלֶךְ סוֹמֵךְ נוֹפְלִים, מֶלֶךְ עֹשֶׂה מַעֲשֵׂה בְרֵאשִׁית, מֶלֶךְ פּוֹדֶה וּמַצִּיל, מֶלֶךְ צַח וְאָדֹם, מֶלֶךְ קָדוֹשׁ, מֶלֶךְ רָם וְנִשָּׂא, מֶלֶךְ שׁוֹמֵעַ תְּפִלָּה, מֶלֶךְ תָּמִים דַּרְכּוֹ. מוֹדֶה אֲנִי לְפָנֶיךָ, יהוה אֱלֹהַי וֵאלֹהֵי אֲבוֹתַי, עַל כָּל הַחֶסֶד אֲשֶׁר עָשִׂיתָ עִמָּדִי וַאֲשֶׁר אַתָּה עָתִיד לַעֲשׂוֹת עִמִּי וְעִם כָּל בְּנֵי בֵיתִי וְעִם כָּל בְּרִיּוֹתֶיךָ, בְּנֵי בְרִיתִי. וּבְרוּכִים הֵם מַלְאָכֶיךָ הַקְּדוֹשִׁים וְהַטְּהוֹרִים שֶׁעוֹשִׂים רְצוֹנֶךָ. אֲדוֹן הַשָּׁלוֹם, מֶלֶךְ שֶׁהַשָּׁלוֹם שֶׁלּוֹ, בָּרְכֵנִי בַשָּׁלוֹם, וְתִפְקֹד אוֹתִי וְאֶת כָּל בְּנֵי בֵיתִי וְכָל עַמְּךָ בֵּית יִשְׂרָאֵל לְחַיִּים טוֹבִים וּלְשָׁלוֹם. מֶלֶךְ עֶלְיוֹן עַל כָּל צְבָא מָרוֹם, יוֹצְרֵנוּ, יוֹצֵר בְּרֵאשִׁית, אֲחַלֶּה פָנֶיךָ הַמְּאִירִים, שֶׁתְּזַכֶּה אוֹתִי וְאֶת כָּל בְּנֵי בֵיתִי לִמְצֹא חֵן וְשֵׂכֶל טוֹב בְּעֵינֶיךָ וּבְעֵינֵי כָּל בְּנֵי אָדָם וּבְעֵינֵי כָּל רוֹאֵינוּ לַעֲבוֹדָתֶךָ. וְזַכֵּנוּ לְקַבֵּל שַׁבָּתוֹת מִתּוֹךְ רֹב שִׂמְחָה וּמִתּוֹךְ עֹשֶׁר וְכָבוֹד וּמִתּוֹךְ מִעוּט עֲוֹנוֹת. וְהָסֵר מִמֶּנִּי וּמִכָּל בְּנֵי בֵיתִי וּמִכָּל עַמְּךָ בֵּית יִשְׂרָאֵל כָּל מִינֵי חֹלִי וְכָל מִינֵי מַדְוֶה וְכָל מִינֵי דַלּוּת וַעֲנִיּוּת וְאֶבְיוֹנוּת. וְתֵן בָּנוּ יֵצֶר טוֹב לְעָבְדְּךָ בֶּאֱמֶת וּבְיִרְאָה וּבְאַהֲבָה. וְנִהְיֶה מְכֻבָּדִים בְּעֵינֶיךָ וּבְעֵינֵי כָל רוֹאֵינוּ, כִּי אַתָּה הוּא מֶלֶךְ הַכָּבוֹד, כִּי לְךָ נָאֶה, כִּי לְךָ יָאֶה. אָנָּא, מֶלֶךְ מַלְכֵי הַמְּלָכִים, צַוֵּה לְמַלְאָכֶיךָ, מַלְאֲכֵי הַשָּׁרֵת, מְשָׁרְתֵי עֶלְיוֹן, שֶׁיִּפְקְדוּנִי בְּרַחֲמִים וִיבָרְכוּנִי בְּבוֹאָם לְבֵיתִי בְּיוֹם קָדְשֵׁנוּ, כִּי הִדְלַקְתִּי נֵרוֹתַי וְהִצַּעְתִּי מִטָּתִי וְהֶחֱלַפְתִּי שִׂמְלוֹתַי לִכְבוֹד יוֹם הַשַּׁבָּת וּבָאתִי לְבֵיתְךָ לְהַפִּיל תְּחִנָּתִי לְפָנֶיךָ, שֶׁתַּעֲבִיר אַנְחָתִי, וָאָעִיד אֲשֶׁר בָּרָאתָ בְשִׁשָּׁה יָמִים כָּל הַיְצוּר, וָאֶשְׁנֶה וַאֲשַׁלֵּשׁ עוֹד לְהָעִיד עַל כּוֹסִי בְּתוֹךְ שִׂמְחָתִי, כַּאֲשֶׁר צִוִּיתַנִי לְזָכְרוֹ וּלְהִתְעַנֵּג בְּיֶתֶר נִשְׁמָתִי אֲשֶׁר נָתַתָּ בִּי. בּוֹ אֶשְׁבֹּת כַּאֲשֶׁר צִוִּיתַנִי לְשָׁרְתֶךָ, וְכֵן אַגִּיד גְּדֻלָּתְךָ בְּרִנָּה, וְשִׁוִּיתִי יהוה לִקְרָאתִי שֶׁתְּרַחֲמֵנִי עוֹד בְּגָלוּתִי לְגָאֳלֵנִי לְעוֹרֵר לִבִּי לְאַהֲבָתֶךָ. וְאָז אֶשְׁמֹר פִּקּוּדֶיךָ וְחֻקֶּיךָ בְּלִי עֶצֶב, וְאֶתְפַּלֵּל כַּדָּת כָּרָאוּי וְכַנָּכוֹן. מַלְאֲכֵי הַשָּׁלוֹם, בּוֹאֲכֶם לְשָׁלוֹם, בָּרְכוּנִי לְשָׁלוֹם, וְאִמְרוּ בָּרוּךְ לְשֻׁלְחָנִי הֶעָרוּךְ, וְצֵאתְכֶם לְשָׁלוֹם מֵעַתָּה וְעַד עוֹלָם, אָמֵן סֶלָה.

אֵשֶׁת־חַיִל A woman of strength, who can find? Prov. 31
Her worth is far beyond pearls.
Her husband's heart trusts in her,
and he has no lack of gain.
She brings him good, not harm,
all the days of her life.
She seeks wool and linen,
and works with willing hands.
She is like a ship laden with merchandise,
bringing her food from afar.
She rises while it is still night,
providing food for her household, portions for her maids.
She considers a field and buys it;
from her earnings she plants a vineyard.
She girds herself with strength,
and braces her arms for her tasks.
She sees that her business goes well;
her lamp does not go out at night.

The Rambam in *Hilkhot Ishut* (15:19) describes the way in which a man is obligated to respect his wife:

וכן צוו חכמים שיהיה אדם מכבד את אשתו יותר מגופו ואוהבה כגופו. ואם יש לו ממון מרבה בטובתה כפי ממונו. ולא יטיל עליה אימה יתרה. ויהיה דבורו עמה בנחת. ולא יהיה עצב ולא רגזן:

Similarly, our Sages commanded that a man honor his wife more than his own person and love her as he loves his own person. If he has financial resources, he should offer her benefits in accordance with his resources. He should not cast a superfluous measure of fear over her. He should talk with her gently, being neither sad nor angry.

A husband should honor his wife with gifts and love her as he loves himself. In *Mikhtav MiEliyahu* (vol. 1), Rav Dessler explains that the root of all love

begins

אֵֽשֶׁת־חַיִל מִי יִמְצָא משלי לא
וְרָחֹק מִפְּנִינִים מִכְרָהּ:
בָּטַח בָּהּ לֵב בַּעְלָהּ
וְשָׁלָל לֹא יֶחְסָר:
גְּמָלַתְהוּ טוֹב וְלֹא־רָע
כֹּל יְמֵי חַיֶּיהָ:
דָּרְשָׁה צֶמֶר וּפִשְׁתִּים
וַתַּעַשׂ בְּחֵפֶץ כַּפֶּיהָ:
הָיְתָה כָּאֳנִיּוֹת סוֹחֵר
מִמֶּרְחָק תָּבִיא לַחְמָהּ:
וַתָּקָם בְּעוֹד לַיְלָה
וַתִּתֵּן טֶרֶף לְבֵיתָהּ, וְחֹק לְנַעֲרֹתֶיהָ:
זָמְמָה שָׂדֶה וַתִּקָּחֵהוּ
מִפְּרִי כַפֶּיהָ נָטְעָ כָּרֶם:
חָגְרָה בְעוֹז מָתְנֶיהָ
וַתְּאַמֵּץ זְרוֹעֹתֶיהָ:
טָעֲמָה כִּי־טוֹב סַחְרָהּ
לֹא־יִכְבֶּה בַלַּיְלָ נֵרָהּ:

אשת חיל – ESHET HAYIL

Appreciating Our Wives

Shlomo HaMelekh authored the famous *Eshet Hayil* prayer, which appears in the last chapter of *Mishlei* (31). Each line starts with another letter of the *alef-bet*, in alphabetical order, and is sung as an expression of gratitude to the mother of the home for taking care of the household all week and especially for undertaking all the preparations for Shabbat.

She holds the distaff in her hand,
and grasps the spindle with her palms.
She reaches out her palm to the poor,
and extends her hand to the needy.
She has no fear for her family when it snows,
for all her household is clothed in crimson wool.
She makes elegant coverings;
her clothing is fine linen and purple wool.
Her husband is well known in the gates,
where he sits with the elders of the land.
She makes linen garments and sells them,
and supplies merchants with sashes.
She is clothed with strength and dignity;
she can laugh at the days to come.
She opens her mouth with wisdom,
and the law of kindness is on her tongue.
She watches over the ways of her household,
and never eats the bread of idleness.
Her children rise and call her happy;
her husband also praises her:
"Many women have excelled,
but you surpass them all."
Charm is deceptive and beauty vain:
it is the God-fearing woman who deserves praise.
Give her the reward she has earned;
let her deeds bring her praise in the gates.

---

begins with giving. The more one gives, the more one loves. The more one invests in a relationship, the stronger it becomes. As we usher in the Shabbat, we immediately express our gratitude to our spouse, to set the tone of love, affection, and *shalom bayit* that should permeate the home throughout Shabbat.

KIDDUSH

יָדֶיהָ שִׁלְּחָה בַכִּישׁוֹר
וְכַפֶּיהָ תָּמְכוּ פָלֶךְ:
כַּפָּהּ פָּרְשָׂה לֶעָנִי
וְיָדֶיהָ שִׁלְּחָה לָאֶבְיוֹן:
לֹא־תִירָא לְבֵיתָהּ מִשָּׁלֶג
כִּי כָל־בֵּיתָהּ לָבֻשׁ שָׁנִים:
מַרְבַדִּים עָשְׂתָה־לָּהּ
שֵׁשׁ וְאַרְגָּמָן לְבוּשָׁהּ:
נוֹדָע בַּשְּׁעָרִים בַּעְלָהּ
בְּשִׁבְתּוֹ עִם־זִקְנֵי־אָרֶץ:
סָדִין עָשְׂתָה וַתִּמְכֹּר
וַחֲגוֹר נָתְנָה לַכְּנַעֲנִי:
עוֹז־וְהָדָר לְבוּשָׁהּ
וַתִּשְׂחַק לְיוֹם אַחֲרוֹן:
פִּיהָ פָּתְחָה בְחָכְמָה
וְתוֹרַת־חֶסֶד עַל־לְשׁוֹנָהּ:
צוֹפִיָּה הֲלִיכוֹת בֵּיתָהּ
וְלֶחֶם עַצְלוּת לֹא תֹאכֵל:
קָמוּ בָנֶיהָ וַיְאַשְּׁרוּהָ
בַּעְלָהּ וַיְהַלְלָהּ:
רַבּוֹת בָּנוֹת עָשׂוּ חָיִל
וְאַתְּ עָלִית עַל־כֻּלָּנָה:
שֶׁקֶר הַחֵן וְהֶבֶל הַיֹּפִי
אִשָּׁה יִרְאַת־יהוה הִיא תִתְהַלָּל:
תְּנוּ־לָהּ מִפְּרִי יָדֶיהָ
וִיהַלְלוּהָ בַשְּׁעָרִים מַעֲשֶׂיהָ:

Kiddush for Shabbat Evening

For Kiddush on Yom Tov see page 28,
and on Rosh HaShana, see page 32.

Quietly: And it was evening, and it was morning – *Gen. 1*
יוֹם הַשִּׁשִּׁי the sixth day.

Then the heavens and the earth were completed, and all their array. *Gen. 2*
With the seventh day, God completed the work He had done.
He ceased on the seventh day from all the work He had done.
God blessed the seventh day and declared it holy,
because on it He ceased from all His work
He had created to do.

אשר ברא אלוקים לעשות – ASHER BARA ELOKIM LAASOT

It Is Our Turn

We conclude the first paragraph of *Kiddush* on Friday night with the words "*asher bara Elokim laasot,*" "that God had created to do." The last word, *laasot,* "to do," seems superfluous. This *pasuk,* which is quoted from the first chapter of *Bereshit,* could have ended with the statement "*asher bara Elokim,*" "that God created." What does the word "*laasot*" add to the phrase?

Hashem created the entire world. As the description of the six days of creation is concluded, God tells man: I have created this world; now it is your turn to do your share, *laasot.* Now you take over. You be creative. Work hard to maximize your potential and achieve great accomplishments.

A similar idea is expressed in the *Sefer HaHinukh* (mitzva 2) in connection with the mitzva of *brit mila.* If God wanted us to be circumcised, why didn't He create us circumcised? Just finish the job! He created us with lungs, kidneys, and a heart. Couldn't He have just taken off that extra piece of skin? The *Sefer HaHinukh* explains that *HaKadosh Barukh Hu* created us up to a certain point and then wanted us to take over. We have to act in order to perfect ourselves and our world. This is also why our custom is to mention Pinhas at the beginning of every *brit.* As Rashi mentions in *Parashat Pinhas* (*Bemidbar* 25:11), God stepped aside so Pinhas could act in a way that would sanctify God's name. This is precisely congruous to a *brit mila.* Man perfects

his physical

קידוש לליל שבת

For קידוש *on* יום טוב *see page 29,*
and on ראש השנה*, see page 33.*

Quietly וַיְהִי־עֶרֶב וַיְהִי־בֹקֶר בראשית א
יוֹם הַשִּׁשִּׁי:
וַיְכֻלּוּ הַשָּׁמַיִם וְהָאָרֶץ וְכָל־צְבָאָם: בראשית ב
וַיְכַל אֱלֹהִים בַּיּוֹם הַשְּׁבִיעִי מְלַאכְתּוֹ אֲשֶׁר עָשָׂה
וַיִּשְׁבֹּת בַּיּוֹם הַשְּׁבִיעִי מִכָּל־מְלַאכְתּוֹ אֲשֶׁר עָשָׂה:
וַיְבָרֶךְ אֱלֹהִים אֶת־יוֹם הַשְּׁבִיעִי, וַיְקַדֵּשׁ אֹתוֹ
כִּי בוֹ שָׁבַת מִכָּל־מְלַאכְתּוֹ, אֲשֶׁר־בָּרָא אֱלֹהִים, לַעֲשׂוֹת:

KIDDUSH

Human Sanctification

There is a mitzva to recite *Kiddush*, which is a fulfillment of the biblical imperative of *zakhor et yom haShabbat lekadsho*. It is one of the six *zekhirot* referenced in the Torah. Why do we need to perform an act of *Kiddush* if Shabbat is set? With respect to Yom Tov, *beit din* determines (based on the new month) the actual date upon which a particular Yom Tov falls. However, with respect to Shabbat, the weekly cycle is set and we take no part in its determination (see Beitza 21a). Why, then, do we recite *Kiddush* to sanctify the day, when it is sanctified by itself without our declaration?

Rav Yosef Dov Soloveitchik explains, based on a *gemara* in Nedarim (13a), that a *bekhor behema tehora*, the firstborn of a kosher animal, is automatically deemed a *korban*. This is the only automatic *korban*; all other sacrifices need to be designated. Nevertheless, there is a specific mitzva to designate it. The Torah wants there to be a personal element, irrespective of the fact that the animal is holy and considered a *korban* even absent any human act. Similarly, although Shabbat is sanctified without any human interaction, the Torah wants us to participate in infusing holiness into the day. Each individual should have a personal element in the sanctification of Shabbat.

When saying Kiddush for others, add:
Please pay attention, my masters.

Blessed are You, LORD our God, King of the Universe,
who creates the fruit of the vine.

Blessed are You, LORD our God, King of the Universe,
who has made us holy through His commandments,
who has favored us,
and in love and favor
gave us His holy Sabbath as a heritage,
a remembrance of the work of creation.
It is the first among the holy days of assembly,
a remembrance of the exodus from Egypt.
For You chose us and sanctified us from all the peoples,
and in love and favor
gave us Your holy Sabbath as a heritage.
Blessed are You, LORD, who sanctifies the Sabbath.

You have the wrong bag!" The porter, certain that the luggage he was carrying fit the description given by the guest, continued with his journey. When he arrived at the entrance to the hotel, the guest again told the porter that he had made a mistake. The porter asked with amazement, "How do you know? It accurately fits the description you gave me!" The guest responded, "My suitcase is nearly empty. It is not heavy. But the bag you were carrying seemed quite hefty. Therefore, it must be the wrong suitcase."

We are the chosen people. If we feel that mitzva observance is a burden, then we are carrying the wrong package. We ought to appreciate Torah and mitzvot and recognize that what we have been granted is not cumbersome, but truly a gift. As the *mishna* says at the end of Massekhet Makkot:

רצה הקדוש ברוך הוא לזכות את ישראל, לפיכך הרבה להם תורה ומצות.

> Hashem wanted to provide merit to Yisrael; therefore He granted them Torah and mitzvot.

God has blessed us with many ways to connect to Him through the various mitzvot.

God Sanctified

When saying קידוש *for others, add:*

סַבְרִי מָרָנָן

בָּרוּךְ אַתָּה יהוה אֱלֹהֵינוּ מֶלֶךְ הָעוֹלָם
בּוֹרֵא פְּרִי הַגָּפֶן.

בָּרוּךְ אַתָּה יהוה אֱלֹהֵינוּ מֶלֶךְ הָעוֹלָם
אֲשֶׁר קִדְּשָׁנוּ בְּמִצְוֹתָיו, וְרָצָה בָנוּ
וְשַׁבַּת קָדְשׁוֹ בְּאַהֲבָה וּבְרָצוֹן הִנְחִילָנוּ
זִכָּרוֹן לְמַעֲשֵׂה בְרֵאשִׁית
כִּי הוּא יוֹם תְּחִלָּה לְמִקְרָאֵי קֹדֶשׁ, זֵכֶר לִיצִיאַת מִצְרָיִם
כִּי בָנוּ בָחַרְתָּ וְאוֹתָנוּ קִדַּשְׁתָּ מִכָּל הָעַמִּים
וְשַׁבַּת קָדְשְׁךָ בְּאַהֲבָה וּבְרָצוֹן הִנְחַלְתָּנוּ.
בָּרוּךְ אַתָּה יהוה, מְקַדֵּשׁ הַשַּׁבָּת.

---

his physical body and is charged with perfecting his spiritual essence as well. (See more related to this idea in the section on *brit mila* later in the book.)

Similarly, commenting at the end of *Parashat Shelah*, the Meshekh Hokhma states that the *tzitzit* contain strings that appear like an unfinished garment. The *tzitzit* remind us of the 613 mitzvot, and we are to "finish the job" by properly adhering to those *taryag* mitzvot, weaving the world around us.

That is what we say in *Kiddush* every Friday night. *HaKadosh Barukh Hu* did everything for us, all the miracles of *yetzi'at Mitzrayim*. Now begins man's task – *laasot* – to perfect himself and the world around him, to conduct himself in a way that will sanctify Hashem's name throughout the world.

The Chosen People

The Dubno Maggid offers an allegory to highlight how we need to feel as the chosen people. A tourist arrived in a foreign city, and the porter went to the guest's wagon to collect his luggage. The guest watched from afar as the porter shlepped his suitcase. The porter was huffing and puffing as he carried the heavy load. The guest yelled out to the porter, "That is not my suitcase!

On Shabbat Ḥol HaMo'ed Sukkot, if Kiddush is made in the sukka, add:

Blessed are You, Lord our God, King of the Universe,
who has made us holy through his commandments
and has commanded us to dwell in the sukka.

It is customary for all present to drink of the wine.

---

presumptuous to think I can span this gap and connect to Hashem. That is the purpose of a *birkat hamitzva*. If I recognize that God commanded me to perform this act, then I can perform the mitzva and it can sanctify me to connect to Hashem. A mitzva is not just a physical act; it connects us to Hashem. The *birkat hamitzva* serves as a *matir* as well, enabling me to become close to Hashem via the performance of this specific mitzva.

זכר ליציאת מצרים – ZEKHER LEYETZI'AT MITZRAYIM

Continuous Active Involvement in the World

It is understandable that we refer to Shabbat as a reminder of creation, *zekher lemaaseh bereshit*, as it is the day that God rested after completing the creation of the world. But what is intended when we refer to Shabbat as *zekher leyetzi'at Mitzrayim*, a reminder of *yetzi'at Mitzrayim*?

The Tur (271) offers two explanations. In *Parashat Emor*, when the Torah lists the *mo'adim*, Shabbat is listed first – which perhaps explains why we include in *Kiddush* the statement "*Ki hu yom tehila lemikra'ei kodesh*": It is the initial day listed when the Torah enumerates the *mo'adim*. Shabbat is the first of the *mikra'ei kodesh*, the holy days, and those days (the *shalosh regalim*) were established in remembrance of *yetzi'at Mitzrayim*.

The Ramban believes that Shabbat itself is in remembrance of *yetzi'at Mitzrayim*. How so? *Yetzi'at Mitzrayim* exhibited the fact that God not only created the world, but is still actively involved and can perform supernatural miracles. Shabbat and *yetzi'at Mitzrayim* go hand in hand illustrating God as the *creator* who continues to *actively manage* the world (*hashgaha*).

On שבת חול המועד סוכות*, if* קידוש *is made in the* סוכה*, add:*

בָּרוּךְ אַתָּה יהוה אֱלֹהֵינוּ מֶלֶךְ הָעוֹלָם
אֲשֶׁר קִדְּשָׁנוּ בְּמִצְוֹתָיו וְצִוָּנוּ לֵישֵׁב בַּסֻּכָּה.

It is customary for all present to drink of the wine.

God Sanctified Us with Mitzvot

In the second half of *Kiddush*, we include the statement "*asher kidshanu bemitzvotav*," "God sanctified us with His mitzvot." Rav Yosef Dov Soloveitchik[7] cites the Rambam (*Hilkhot Berakhot* 1:3-4), who enumerates three categories of *berakhot*: (1) *hanaa*, recited before obtaining pleasure (e.g., eating, smelling); (2) *shevah*, praising God; and (3) mitzva, recited for the performance of a mitzva. Then the Rambam seems to equate two of these categories, stating:

וכשם שמברכין על ההנייה כך מברכין על כל מצוה.

> And just as one recites a blessing on pleasure, so too one recites a blessing prior to performing a mitzva.

The Rambam seems to connect two categories of *berakhot*, as he uses the term "*keshem*" – just like we recite a *berakha* before we obtain pleasure, so too, we recite a *berakha* prior to the performance of a mitzva. What does one have to do with the other? A *berakha* said on pleasure is a type of *matir*: Before I obtain enjoyment in this world, I have to request permission. The Gemara (Berakhot 35a) states: "*Vekhol haneheneh min ha'olam hazeh belo berakha – maal*," "Anyone who derives enjoyment in this world without blessing God is stealing." How is this relevant to a *berakha* on a mitzva?

Rav Soloveitchik explains that just as pleasure derived from this world requires a *matir*, a mitzva similarly requires a *matir*. After all, how can I as a human being think that a physical act that I perform, such as shaking a *lulav* or putting on *tefillin*, will sanctify me and connect me to God? It is

---

7 Rav Soloveitchik, *Shiurei HaRav, Tefilla* 7.

Kiddush for Festival Evening

On Shabbat add:

quietly: And it was evening, and it was morning – *Gen. 1*

יוֹם הַשִּׁשִּׁי the sixth day.

Then the heavens and the earth were completed, and all their array. *Gen. 2*
With the seventh day, God completed the work He had done.
He ceased on the seventh day from all the work He had done.
God blessed the seventh day and declared it holy,
because on it He ceased from all His work He had created to do.

On other evenings Kiddush starts here:

When saying Kiddush for others, add:
Please pay attention, my masters.

Blessed are You, LORD our God, King of the Universe,
who creates the fruit of the vine.

On Shabbat, add the words in parentheses.

בָּרוּךְ Blessed are You, LORD our God, King of the Universe,
who has chosen us from among all peoples,
raised us above all tongues,
and made us holy through His commandments.
You have given us, LORD our God, in love
(Sabbaths for rest), festivals for rejoicing,
holy days and seasons for joy,
(this Sabbath day and) this day of:

On Pesaḥ: the festival of Matzot,
the time of our freedom

On Shavuot: the festival of Shavuot,
the time of the giving of our Torah

On Sukkot: the festival of Sukkot,
our time of rejoicing

On Shemini Atzeret & Simḥat Torah: the festival of the eighth day, Shemini Atzeret,
our time of rejoicing

קידוש לליל שלוש רגלים

On שבת *add:*

בראשית א	*quietly* וַיְהִי־עֶרֶב וַיְהִי־בֹקֶר

יוֹם הַשִּׁשִּׁי:

בראשית ב	וַיְכֻלּוּ הַשָּׁמַיִם וְהָאָרֶץ וְכָל־צְבָאָם:

וַיְכַל אֱלֹהִים בַּיּוֹם הַשְּׁבִיעִי מְלַאכְתּוֹ אֲשֶׁר עָשָׂה

וַיִּשְׁבֹּת בַּיּוֹם הַשְּׁבִיעִי מִכָּל־מְלַאכְתּוֹ אֲשֶׁר עָשָׂה:

וַיְבָרֶךְ אֱלֹהִים אֶת־יוֹם הַשְּׁבִיעִי, וַיְקַדֵּשׁ אֹתוֹ

כִּי בוֹ שָׁבַת מִכָּל־מְלַאכְתּוֹ, אֲשֶׁר־בָּרָא אֱלֹהִים, לַעֲשׂוֹת:

On other evenings the קידוש *starts here:*

When saying קידוש *for others, add:*

סַבְרִי מָרָנָן

בָּרוּךְ אַתָּה יהוה אֱלֹהֵינוּ מֶלֶךְ הָעוֹלָם, בּוֹרֵא פְּרִי הַגָּפֶן.

On שבת*, add the words in parentheses.*

בָּרוּךְ אַתָּה יהוה אֱלֹהֵינוּ מֶלֶךְ הָעוֹלָם

אֲשֶׁר בָּחַר בָּנוּ מִכָּל עָם, וְרוֹמְמָנוּ מִכָּל לָשׁוֹן

וְקִדְּשָׁנוּ בְּמִצְוֹתָיו

וַתִּתֶּן לָנוּ יהוה אֱלֹהֵינוּ בְּאַהֲבָה

(שַׁבָּתוֹת לִמְנוּחָה וּ) מוֹעֲדִים לְשִׂמְחָה

חַגִּים וּזְמַנִּים לְשָׂשׂוֹן

אֶת יוֹם (הַשַּׁבָּת הַזֶּה וְאֶת יוֹם)

בפסח: חַג הַמַּצּוֹת הַזֶּה, זְמַן חֵרוּתֵנוּ

בשבועות: חַג הַשָּׁבוּעוֹת הַזֶּה, זְמַן מַתַּן תּוֹרָתֵנוּ

בסוכות: חַג הַסֻּכּוֹת הַזֶּה, זְמַן שִׂמְחָתֵנוּ

בשמע״צ ובש״ת: הַשְּׁמִינִי חַג הָעֲצֶרֶת הַזֶּה, זְמַן שִׂמְחָתֵנוּ

(with love), a holy assembly in memory of the exodus from Egypt.
For You have chosen us and sanctified us above all peoples,
and given us as our heritage (Your holy Sabbath in love and favor and)
Your holy festivals for joy and gladness.
Blessed are you, LORD,
who sanctifies (the Sabbath,) Israel and the festivals.

On Motza'ei Shabbat, the following Havdala is added:

בָּרוּךְ Blessed are You, LORD our God, King of the Universe,
who creates the lights of fire.

Blessed are You, LORD our God, King of the Universe,
who distinguishes between sacred and secular,
between light and darkness,
between Israel and the nations,
between the seventh day and the six days of work.
You have made a distinction between the holiness of the Sabbath
and the holiness of festivals,
and have sanctified the seventh day above the six days of work.
You have distinguished and sanctified Your people Israel
with Your holiness.
Blessed are You, LORD,
who distinguishes between sacred and sacred.

On Sukkot, say the following blessing. On the first night it is said before the blessing "who has given us life"; on the second night, after it (some say it before on both nights).

בָּרוּךְ Blessed are You, LORD our God, King of the Universe,
who has made us holy though His commandments,
and has commanded us to dwell in the sukka.

The following blessing is omitted on the last two nights of Pesaḥ (in Israel, the last night).

בָּרוּךְ Blessed are You, LORD our God, King of the Universe,
who has given us life, sustained us, and brought us to this time.

It is customary for all present to drink of the wine.

(בְּאַהֲבָה) מִקְרָא קֹֽדֶשׁ, זֵֽכֶר לִיצִיאַת מִצְרָֽיִם
כִּי בָֽנוּ בָחַֽרְתָּ וְאוֹתָֽנוּ קִדַּֽשְׁתָּ מִכָּל הָעַמִּים
(וְשַׁבָּת) וּמוֹעֲדֵי קָדְשֶֽׁךָ (בְּאַהֲבָה וּבְרָצוֹן)
בְּשִׂמְחָה וּבְשָׂשׂוֹן הִנְחַלְתָּֽנוּ.
בָּרוּךְ אַתָּה יהוה
מְקַדֵּשׁ (הַשַּׁבָּת וְ) יִשְׂרָאֵל וְהַזְּמַנִּים.

On מוצאי שבת*, the following* הבדלה *is added:*

בָּרוּךְ אַתָּה יהוה אֱלֹהֵֽינוּ מֶֽלֶךְ הָעוֹלָם
בּוֹרֵא מְאוֹרֵי הָאֵשׁ.

בָּרוּךְ אַתָּה יהוה אֱלֹהֵֽינוּ מֶֽלֶךְ הָעוֹלָם
הַמַּבְדִּיל בֵּין קֹֽדֶשׁ לְחֹל
בֵּין אוֹר לְחֹֽשֶׁךְ
בֵּין יִשְׂרָאֵל לָעַמִּים
בֵּין יוֹם הַשְּׁבִיעִי לְשֵֽׁשֶׁת יְמֵי הַמַּעֲשֶׂה.
בֵּין קְדֻשַּׁת שַׁבָּת לִקְדֻשַּׁת יוֹם טוֹב הִבְדַּֽלְתָּ,
וְאֶת יוֹם הַשְּׁבִיעִי מִשֵּֽׁשֶׁת יְמֵי הַמַּעֲשֶׂה קִדַּֽשְׁתָּ,
הִבְדַּֽלְתָּ וְקִדַּֽשְׁתָּ אֶת עַמְּךָ יִשְׂרָאֵל בִּקְדֻשָּׁתֶֽךָ.
בָּרוּךְ אַתָּה יהוה, הַמַּבְדִּיל בֵּין קֹֽדֶשׁ לְקֹֽדֶשׁ.

On סוכות*, say the following blessing. On the first night it is said before the blessing* שֶׁהֶחֱיָֽנוּ*; on the second night, after it (some say it before on both nights).*

בָּרוּךְ אַתָּה יהוה אֱלֹהֵֽינוּ מֶֽלֶךְ הָעוֹלָם
אֲשֶׁר קִדְּשָֽׁנוּ בְּמִצְוֹתָיו וְצִוָּֽנוּ לֵישֵׁב בַּסֻּכָּה.

The following blessing is omitted on the last two nights of פסח *(in* ארץ ישראל*, the last night).*

בָּרוּךְ אַתָּה יהוה אֱלֹהֵֽינוּ מֶֽלֶךְ הָעוֹלָם
שֶׁהֶחֱיָֽנוּ וְקִיְּמָֽנוּ וְהִגִּיעָֽנוּ לַזְּמַן הַזֶּה.

It is customary for all present to drink of the wine.

Kiddush for Rosh HaShana Evening

On Shabbat add:

quietly: And it was evening, and it was morning – *Gen. 1*

יוֹם הַשִּׁשִּׁי the sixth day.

Then the heavens and the earth were completed, and all their array. *Gen. 2*
With the seventh day, God completed the work He had done.
He ceased on the seventh day from all the work He had done.
God blessed the seventh day and declared it holy,
because on it He ceased from all His work He had created to do.

On other evenings start Kiddush here:

When saying Kiddush for others: Please pay attention, my masters.

Blessed are You, LORD our God, King of the Universe,
who creates the fruit of the vine.

On Shabbat, add the words in parentheses.

בָּרוּךְ Blessed are You, LORD our God,
King of the Universe,
who has chosen us from among all peoples,
raised us above all tongues,
and made us holy through His commandments.
You have given us, LORD our God, in love,
this (Sabbath and this) Day of Remembrance,
a day of (remembering) blowing the shofar (in love),
a holy assembly in memory of the exodus from Egypt,
for You have chosen us and sanctified us above all peoples,
and Your word is true and endures for ever.
Blessed are You, LORD,
King over all the earth,
who sanctifies (the Sabbath,) Israel
and the Day of Remembrance.

קידוש לליל ראש השנה

On שבת *add:*

quietly וַיְהִי־עֶרֶב וַיְהִי־בֹקֶר בראשית א

יוֹם הַשִּׁשִּׁי:

וַיְכֻלּוּ הַשָּׁמַיִם וְהָאָרֶץ וְכָל־צְבָאָם: בראשית ב

וַיְכַל אֱלֹהִים בַּיּוֹם הַשְּׁבִיעִי מְלַאכְתּוֹ אֲשֶׁר עָשָׂה

וַיִּשְׁבֹּת בַּיּוֹם הַשְּׁבִיעִי מִכָּל־מְלַאכְתּוֹ אֲשֶׁר עָשָׂה:

וַיְבָרֶךְ אֱלֹהִים אֶת־יוֹם הַשְּׁבִיעִי, וַיְקַדֵּשׁ אֹתוֹ

כִּי בוֹ שָׁבַת מִכָּל־מְלַאכְתּוֹ, אֲשֶׁר־בָּרָא אֱלֹהִים, לַעֲשׂוֹת:

On other evenings start קידוש *here:*

When saying קידוש *for others* סַבְרִי מָרָנָן

בָּרוּךְ אַתָּה יהוה אֱלֹהֵינוּ מֶלֶךְ הָעוֹלָם, בּוֹרֵא פְּרִי הַגָּפֶן.

On שבת*, add the words in parentheses.*

בָּרוּךְ אַתָּה יהוה אֱלֹהֵינוּ מֶלֶךְ הָעוֹלָם

אֲשֶׁר בָּחַר בָּנוּ מִכָּל עָם

וְרוֹמְמָנוּ מִכָּל לָשׁוֹן

וְקִדְּשָׁנוּ בְּמִצְוֹתָיו

וַתִּתֶּן לָנוּ יהוה אֱלֹהֵינוּ בְּאַהֲבָה

אֶת יוֹם (הַשַּׁבָּת הַזֶּה וְאֶת יוֹם) הַזִּכָּרוֹן הַזֶּה, יוֹם (זִכְרוֹן) תְּרוּעָה

(בְּאַהֲבָה) מִקְרָא קֹדֶשׁ, זֵכֶר לִיצִיאַת מִצְרָיִם

כִּי בָנוּ בָחַרְתָּ וְאוֹתָנוּ קִדַּשְׁתָּ מִכָּל הָעַמִּים

וּדְבָרְךָ אֱמֶת וְקַיָּם לָעַד.

בָּרוּךְ אַתָּה יהוה, מֶלֶךְ עַל כָּל הָאָרֶץ

מְקַדֵּשׁ (הַשַּׁבָּת וְ) יִשְׂרָאֵל וְיוֹם הַזִּכָּרוֹן.

On Motza'ei Shabbat, the following Havdala is added:

בָּרוּךְ Blessed are You, LORD our God, King of the Universe,
who creates the lights of fire.

Blessed are You, LORD our God, King of the Universe,
who distinguishes between sacred and secular,
between light and darkness, between Israel and the nations,
between the seventh day and the six days of work.
You have made a distinction between the holiness of the Sabbath
and the holiness of festivals,
and have sanctified the seventh day above the six days of work.
You have distinguished and sanctified Your people Israel
with Your holiness.
Blessed are You, LORD, who distinguishes between sacred
and sacred.

The following blessing is said on both nights of Rosh HaShana.
On the second night, new fruit is placed on the table, and one should have in mind that the blessing is also on the new fruit.

בָּרוּךְ Blessed are You, LORD our God, King of the Universe,
who has given us life, sustained us, and brought us to this time.

It is customary for all present to drink of the wine.

On מוצאי שבת, the following הבדלה is added:

בָּרוּךְ אַתָּה יהוה אֱלֹהֵינוּ מֶלֶךְ הָעוֹלָם
בּוֹרֵא מְאוֹרֵי הָאֵשׁ.

בָּרוּךְ אַתָּה יהוה אֱלֹהֵינוּ מֶלֶךְ הָעוֹלָם
הַמַּבְדִּיל בֵּין קֹדֶשׁ לְחֹל,
בֵּין אוֹר לְחֹשֶׁךְ
בֵּין יִשְׂרָאֵל לָעַמִּים
בֵּין יוֹם הַשְּׁבִיעִי לְשֵׁשֶׁת יְמֵי הַמַּעֲשֶׂה.
בֵּין קְדֻשַּׁת שַׁבָּת לִקְדֻשַּׁת יוֹם טוֹב הִבְדַּלְתָּ
וְאֶת יוֹם הַשְּׁבִיעִי מִשֵּׁשֶׁת יְמֵי הַמַּעֲשֶׂה קִדַּשְׁתָּ
הִבְדַּלְתָּ וְקִדַּשְׁתָּ אֶת עַמְּךָ יִשְׂרָאֵל בִּקְדֻשָּׁתֶךָ.
בָּרוּךְ אַתָּה יהוה, הַמַּבְדִּיל בֵּין קֹדֶשׁ לְקֹדֶשׁ.

The following blessing is said on both nights of ראש השנה.
On the second night, new fruit is placed on the table, and one should have in mind that the blessing is also on the new fruit.

בָּרוּךְ אַתָּה יהוה אֱלֹהֵינוּ מֶלֶךְ הָעוֹלָם
שֶׁהֶחֱיָנוּ וְקִיְּמָנוּ וְהִגִּיעָנוּ לַזְּמַן הַזֶּה.

It is customary for all present to drink of the wine.

Zemirot for Shabbat Evening

כָּל מְקַדֵּשׁ All who fittingly sanctify the seventh day,
All who protect the Sabbath properly from desecration,
Will have great reward in accord with their deed.
"Each in his own camp, each under his own banner." *Num. 1*

Lovers of the LORD, who await the building of the Temple,
Be glad and joyful on the Sabbath as if receiving the gift
of God's inheritance,
Raise your hands in holiness and say to God:
"Blessed is the LORD who has given rest to His people Israel." *1 Kings 8*

---

different nations, each with its own religion, customs, and observances. How is it possible to ensure that each tribe would excel in its area and achieve its goals without creating a rift in the nation?

Rav Kamenetsky suggests in *Emet LeYaakov* that the key is in the timing. If flags are so important, why then were they not assigned immediately after the exodus from Egypt? Why wait a year?

The safety net protecting a society against dissolution is to have some type of common denominator, a spiritual glue, that would unify all of the tribes. Immediately after leaving Egypt, there was no unifying element. That is why the flag positioning did not start then. Only after experiencing the Splitting of the Sea, receiving the Torah, and building the *Mishkan* did the generation that left Egypt become a unified people. Now, with the *Aron HaBrit* in the center of the encampment, they could each have their own flag, with unique colors representing their different aspirations, without risking schism. This was possible because they were all connected by the Torah.

Just like a person has various organs that cooperate because they share a common body and soul, so too do the twelve tribes each serve a different function and carry a different banner, while sharing a common belief in the Torah.

People can differ yet be united if they share a common focal point. The

center

זמירות לליל שבת

כָּל מְקַדֵּשׁ שְׁבִיעִי כָּרָאוּי לוֹ
כָּל שׁוֹמֵר שַׁבָּת כַּדָּת, מֵחַלְּלוֹ
שְׂכָרוֹ הַרְבֵּה מְאֹד עַל פִּי פָעֳלוֹ
אִישׁ עַל־מַחֲנֵהוּ וְאִישׁ עַל־דִּגְלוֹ: במדבר א

אוֹהֲבֵי יהוה הַמְחַכִּים לְבִנְיַן אֲרִיאֵל
בְּיוֹם הַשַּׁבָּת שִׂישׂוּ וְשִׂמְחוּ כִּמְקַבְּלֵי מַתַּן נַחֲלִיאֵל
גַּם שְׂאוּ יְדֵיכֶם קֹדֶשׁ וְאִמְרוּ לָאֵל
בָּרוּךְ יהוה אֲשֶׁר נָתַן מְנוּחָה לְעַמּוֹ יִשְׂרָאֵל: מלכים א, ח

ZEMIROT

כל מקדש שביעי – KOL MEKADESH SHEVI'I

Celebrating Shabbat in Our Own Way

כל מקדש שביעי כראוי לו... איש על מחנהו ואיש על דגלו.

> All who fittingly sanctify the seventh day.... Each in his own camp, each under his own banner.

What is the mention of the flag meant to convey? This is clearly a reference to the flags related to each tribe as depicted in *Parashat Bemidbar*, but what do these flags have to do with the sanctification of Shabbat? Rav Mordechai Willig (*Am Mordechai* on Massekhet Shabbat, p. 11) explains the connection based on the words of Rav Yaakov Kamenetsky.

What is the significance of each tribe being designated with its own unique flag? Wouldn't it have been more befitting to have one common flag for the entire nation? It seems like color war between the tribes.

Indeed, there is a danger in designating separate flags for each tribe. Each flag was a different color and had a different symbol. Each tribe had different talents and specific goals. It can be very dangerous to have twelve groups that are each striving for something different. They could end up becoming twelve

Seekers of the LORD, offspring of His beloved Abraham,
Who are slow to leave the Sabbath but hasten to enter it,
Who rejoice to keep it and make its *eiruv* –
"This is the day the LORD has made; let us rejoice and be glad in it." *Ps. 118*

Remember Moses' Torah, from which the laws of Sabbath are learned,
Engraved is the seventh day like a bedecked bride between her companions,
The pure inherit it and sanctify it with the words:
"All that He had made...
With the seventh day God completed the work He had done." *Gen. 2*

It is a sacred day from beginning to end,
All Jacob's offspring will honor it as the King's word and decree,
Resting on it and rejoicing with delights of food and drink.
"All the congregation of Israel will observe it." *Ex. 12*

המאחרים לצאת מהשבת וממהרים לבוא – HAME'AHARIM LATZET MEHASHABBAT U'MEMAHARIM LAVO

Finishing Shabbat Late and Starting It Early

There is a statement in the *zemer* praising those who delay the termination of Shabbat and who hasten its entrance. Many commentaries question the order of this statement. Shouldn't it be reversed to reflect the proper chronological order? First one would usher in the Shabbat, and then delay its termination. Why is it presented in the opposite order, first praising one who delays the termination of Shabbat and then one who ushers it in early?

Perhaps this is because first one has to experience the awesomeness of Shabbat, and then he will surely extend it. After one appreciates Shabbat, he will usher in the next Shabbat early.

Rav Mirski (*Hegyonei Halakha*) discusses the reason for extending Shabbat. As human beings, we do not know the exact time that Shabbat begins and ends, so we have to add to it. We begin a little early and end a little late.

דּוֹרְשֵׁי יהוה זֶרַע אַבְרָהָם אוֹהֲבוֹ
הַמְאַחֲרִים לָצֵאת מִן הַשַּׁבָּת וּמְמַהֲרִים לָבוֹא
וּשְׂמֵחִים לְשָׁמְרוֹ וּלְעָרֵב עֵרוּבוֹ
זֶה־הַיּוֹם עָשָׂה יהוה, נָגִילָה וְנִשְׂמְחָה בוֹ: תהלים קיח

זִכְרוּ תּוֹרַת מֹשֶׁה בְּמִצְוַת שַׁבָּת גְּרוּסָה
חֲרוּתָה לַיּוֹם הַשְּׁבִיעִי,
כְּכַלָּה בֵּין רֵעוֹתֶיהָ מְשֻׁבָּצָה
טְהוֹרִים יִירָשׁוּהָ, וִיקַדְּשׁוּהָ בְּמַאֲמַר כָּל אֲשֶׁר עָשָׂה
וַיְכַל אֱלֹהִים בַּיּוֹם הַשְּׁבִיעִי מְלַאכְתּוֹ אֲשֶׁר עָשָׂה: בראשית ב

יוֹם קָדוֹשׁ הוּא, מִבּוֹאוֹ וְעַד צֵאתוֹ
כָּל זֶרַע יַעֲקֹב יְכַבְּדוּהוּ, כִּדְבַר הַמֶּלֶךְ וְדָתוֹ
לָנוּחַ בּוֹ וְלִשְׂמֹחַ בְּתַעֲנוּג אָכוֹל וְשָׁתֹה
כָּל־עֲדַת יִשְׂרָאֵל יַעֲשׂוּ אֹתוֹ: שמות יב

---

center of the nation in the desert was the *Mishkan*. As long as each group's practices are in accordance with Halakha, it is acceptable and perhaps even preferable to wave a distinct flag – to have a different ideology – while respecting differing halakhic opinions. With the Torah at the center, we can maintain our unity while expressing divergent opinions.

Rabbi Willig explains that the reference to flags in this *zemer* relates to an individual who observes Shabbat "as befits him." Shabbat is a different experience for each person. As long as one is careful not to desecrate it, one can experience it in a personal way. One person may appreciate the singing, another the *shiurim*, and a third the *cholent* – all "as befits him"! We are bound together by our Shabbat observance, even though there may be different nuances in each individual's observance. Each person can wave his Shabbat flag as the tribes did in the desert, as long as there is the unifying factor of avoiding any desecration of Shabbat.

Extend Your loving-kindness to those who know You, zealous
and retributive God,
Those who keep the seventh day, fulfilling "Remember" and
"Observe,"
Grant them the joy of Jerusalem rebuilt, make them shine with
the light of Your face.
"Fill them with the rich plenty of Your House, give them drink
from Your river of delights." *Ps. 36*

Help those who, on the seventh day,
rest from plow and harvest,
Who walk slowly, and eat three meals to bless You.
May their righteousness shine like the light
of the seven days,
LORD God of Israel, grant completion. *1 Sam. 14*

Some add:

LORD, God of Israel, Savior for all times.

The following verse is often omitted:

(Make them holy in Your commands,
and pure as the very sky is pure.
Bring them to rest with Your spirit,
as cattle descend from mountain to valley,
May their Sabbaths bring them to dwell in the moon [shaped]
inheritance [the Sanhedrin],
"Like streams stretched out,
like gardens on the river side.") *Num. 24*

---

that *Hazal* initiated the recitation of the *tefilla* of *Tzidkatekha Tzedek* during Minha on Shabbat. Once Moshe died, we no longer had the *amud ha'anan* or the *amud ha'esh*. Therefore, that very Shabbat, we had to add to Shabbat, delaying its termination. The *zemer* lists the addition to the end of Shabbat prior to the addition to its beginning because, since Moshe died on Shabbat, the first act of adding to Shabbat that we performed was delaying the termination of Shabbat.

מְשֹׁךְ חַסְדְּךָ לְיוֹדְעֶיךָ, אֵל קַנּוֹא וְנוֹקֵם
נוֹטְרֵי יוֹם הַשְּׁבִיעִי זָכוֹר וְשָׁמוֹר לְהָקֵם
שַׂמְּחֵם בְּבִנְיַן שָׁלֵם, בְּאוֹר פָּנֶיךָ תַּבְהִיקֵם
יִרְוְיֻן מִדֶּשֶׁן בֵּיתֶךָ, וְנַחַל עֲדָנֶיךָ תַשְׁקֵם: תהלים לו

עֲזֹר לַשּׁוֹבְתִים בַּשְּׁבִיעִי
בֶּחָרִישׁ וּבַקָּצִיר עוֹלָמִים
פּוֹסְעִים בּוֹ פְּסִיעָה קְטַנָּה
סוֹעֲדִים בּוֹ, לְבָרֵךְ שָׁלֹשׁ פְּעָמִים
צִדְקָתָם תַּצְהִיר כְּאוֹר שִׁבְעַת הַיָּמִים
יהוה אֱלֹהֵי יִשְׂרָאֵל, הָבָה תָמִים: שמואל א, יד

Some add:

יהוה אֱלֹהֵי יִשְׂרָאֵל, תְּשׁוּעַת עוֹלָמִים.

The following verse is often omitted:

(קַדְּשֵׁם בְּמִצְוֹתֶיךָ, וְטַהֲרֵם כְּעֶצֶם הַשָּׁמַיִם לָטֹהַר
רוּחֲךָ תְּנִחֶמוֹ, כַּבְּהֵמָה תֵּרֵד בַּבִּקְעָה מִן הָהָר
שַׁבְּתֵיהֶם תְּשַׁכְּנֵם בְּנַחֲלַת הַסַּהַר
כִּנְחָלִים נִטָּיוּ, כְּגַנֹּת עֲלֵי נָהָר:) במדבר כד

Hashem, though, knows the exact time and does not need to add to it at all. Additionally, in the *midbar* there was no need for *tosefet Shabbat* (adding to Shabbat), as we had symbols that highlighted the exact moment when day became night and vice versa: The *amud ha'anan* (cloud) and *amud ha'esh* (fire) informed us of when it was day and night and led us through the desert. Moshe Rabbeinu died on a Shabbat afternoon. That is one of the reasons

מְנוּחָה וְשִׂמְחָה Rest and joy, light for all Jews,
Is the Sabbath day, day of delights;
Those who keep and recall it bear witness
That in six days all creation was made.

The highest heavens, land and seas,
The hosts of heaven, high and sublime;
Sea monsters, humans and all wild beasts,
Were created by God, the Lord,
who formed all worlds.

It was He who spoke to His treasured people:
"Keep it to make it holy from beginning to end."
The holy Sabbath is His day of delight,
For on it God rested from all His work.

Why the emphasis on food on Shabbat? Bereshit Rabba (11:4) tells the story of Rabbi Yehuda HaNasi inviting Antoninus to his home for a Shabbat meal. The guest enjoyed the food so much that he returned for another meal on Tuesday. This time, he was surprised to find that food did not taste the same. He asked Rabbi Yehuda HaNasi what was different. Which spice had he left out? Antoninus boasted that with his great wealth, he could easily obtain whatever ingredient was lacking. But Rabbi Yehuda answered, "What is missing is the spice of Shabbat. On the other days of the week, the food does not taste the same. There is a special spiritual and physical element of Shabbat that elevates the flavor of the food."

צור עולמים – TZUR OLAMIM

The Greatest Artist

We refer to Hashem in this *zemer* as "*tzur olamim*" – the one who formed all worlds. The Gemara in Berakhot (10a) makes the *drasha*: there is no *tzayar* (artist) like God (the word צור can be read צייר). The Rambam says (*Hilkhot Yesodei HaTorah* 2:1–2) that the way to reach high levels of *ahavat* and *yirat Hashem* is to open our eyes and see the way in which God created the world

and its

מְנוּחָה וְשִׂמְחָה אוֹר לַיְּהוּדִים
יוֹם שַׁבָּתוֹן, יוֹם מַחֲמַדִּים
שׁוֹמְרָיו וְזוֹכְרָיו הֵמָּה מְעִידִים
כִּי לְשִׁשָּׁה כֹּל בְּרוּאִים וְעוֹמְדִים.

שְׁמֵי שָׁמַיִם, אֶרֶץ וְיַמִּים
כָּל צְבָא מָרוֹם גְּבוֹהִים וְרָמִים
תַּנִּין וְאָדָם וְחַיַּת רְאֵמִים
כִּי בְּיָהּ יהוה צוּר עוֹלָמִים.

הוּא אֲשֶׁר דִּבֶּר לְעַם סְגֻלָּתוֹ
שָׁמוֹר לְקַדְּשׁוֹ מִבּוֹאוֹ עַד צֵאתוֹ
שַׁבַּת קֹדֶשׁ יוֹם חֶמְדָּתוֹ
כִּי בוֹ שָׁבַת אֵל מִכָּל מְלַאכְתּוֹ.

מנוחה ושמחה – MENUHA VESIMHA

ברוב מטעמים – BEROV MATAMIM

The Spice of Shabbat

Every Shabbat, we have a *neshama yeteira* (Beitza 17a) that infuses us with a *ruhniyut* lift. The Shita Mekubetzet (ad loc.) claims that we have an ability to better comprehend and achieve a deeper understanding of Torah on Shabbat. But throughout the *zemirot*, and in particular in *Menuha VeSimha*, we speak of physical pleasures, with an emphasis on food: *Bemishneh lehem vekiddush rabba berov matamim*. Is that appropriate?

Rashi (ad loc.) connects the *neshama yeteira* to physical eating on Shabbat. He explains that eating on Shabbat is different due to our *neshama yeteira*.

נשמה יתירה – רוחב לב למנוחה ולשמחה ולהיות פתוח לרוחה ויאכל וישתה ואין נפשו קצה עליו.

Neshama Yeteira – breadth of heart for rest and joy and an open spirit, so that he can eat and drink and the soul will not be limited.

Through the Sabbath commandment
        God will give you strength,
Rise, pray to Him, and He will invigorate you.
Recite the Nishmat prayer, and the Kedusha,
Then eat with joy, for He is pleased with you.

With twin loaves, and wine for the Kiddush,
With many delicacies and a willing spirit;
Those who delight in it shall merit great reward:
The coming of the redeemer,
        and life in the World to Come.

---

stop and think, we can consider Hashem as the *tzur* (rock) and *tzayar* (artist) of the world and enhance both our love and awe toward our Creator.

מה ידידות

בְּמִצְוַת שַׁבָּת אֵל יַחֲלִיצָךְ
קוּם קְרָא אֵלָיו, יָחִישׁ לְאַמְּצָךְ
נִשְׁמַת כָּל חַי וְגַם נַעֲרִיצָךְ
אֱכֹל בְּשִׂמְחָה כִּי כְבָר רָצָךְ.

בְּמִשְׁנֶה לֶחֶם וְקִדּוּשׁ רַבָּה
בְּרֹב מַטְעַמִּים וְרוּחַ נְדִיבָה
יִזְכּוּ לְרַב טוּב הַמִּתְעַנְּגִים בָּהּ
בְּבִיאַת גּוֹאֵל לְחַיֵּי הָעוֹלָם הַבָּא.

---

and its perfection. At the same time, we are humbled by understanding our limitations in comparison to Hashem. On Shabbat, when we have time to

מַה־יְּדִידוּת How beloved is your rest, Sabbath Queen,
We run to greet you: Come, royal bride,
Dressed in fine robes. We light the light with blessing.
All labors end [as is said:] "You shall do no work."
To savor the delights of fowl, quail and fish.

In advance all kinds of tasty food have been prepared,
Fattened chickens made ready while it was still day.
Varied dishes set out, and fragrant wines to drink,
And special delicacies all three times.
To savor the delights of fowl, quail and fish.

They shall inherit Jacob's heritage, a heritage unbounded,
Rich and poor will honor [the Sabbath] and be worthy of redemption,
If you keep the Sabbath day you will be My special treasure,
Six days shall you labor – and on the seventh let us rejoice.
To savor the delights of fowl, quail and fish.

Similarly, the Torah refers to Rosh HaShana as a day of *terua* ("*yom terua*"), and therefore there is a minimum amount to fulfill the imperative to blow the shofar. Yet, the Levush (*Orah Hayim* 585) maintains that all additional blowing would also be part of the mitzva of the biblical imperative to blow the shofar.

In the same way, *Kiddush* is about sanctifying and praising the day of Shabbat. Every time we make a positive statement with respect to Shabbat, it is part of the mitzva of remembering the Shabbat: *Zakhor et yom haShabbat lekadsho*.

מה ידידות – MA YEDIDUT

Making Shabbat Special: Through Learning or Feasting?

We discuss the unique qualities of Shabbat. We distinguish it from the rest of the week by wearing different clothes, eating different delicacies, and walking and sleeping in a different manner (*vehasheina meshubahat*). This is due to the fact that Shabbat is *me'ein olam haba*, a taste of the next world.

The Talmud

מַה־יְּדִידוּת מְנוּחָתֵךְ, אַתְּ שַׁבָּת הַמַּלְכָּה
בְּכֵן נָרוּץ לִקְרָאתֵךְ, בּוֹאִי כַלָּה נְסוּכָה
לְבוּשׁ בִּגְדֵי חֲמוּדוֹת, לְהַדְלִיק נֵר בִּבְרָכָה
וַתֵּכֶל כָּל הָעֲבוֹדוֹת, לֹא תַעֲשׂוּ מְלָאכָה.
לְהִתְעַנֵּג בְּתַעֲנוּגִים בַּרְבּוּרִים וּשְׂלָו וְדָגִים.

מֵעֶרֶב מַזְמִינִים כָּל מִינֵי מַטְעַמִּים
מִבְּעוֹד יוֹם מוּכָנִים תַּרְנְגוֹלִים מְפֻטָּמִים
וְלַעֲרֹךְ בּוֹ כַּמָּה מִינִים, שְׁתוֹת יֵינוֹת מְבֻשָּׂמִים
וְתַפְנוּקֵי מַעֲדַנִּים בְּכָל שָׁלֹשׁ פְּעָמִים.
לְהִתְעַנֵּג בְּתַעֲנוּגִים בַּרְבּוּרִים וּשְׂלָו וְדָגִים.

נַחֲלַת יַעֲקֹב יִירָשׁ, בְּלִי מְצָרִים נַחֲלָה
וִיכַבְּדוּהוּ עָשִׁיר וָרָשׁ, וְתִזְכּוּ לִגְאֻלָּה
יוֹם שַׁבָּת אִם תְּכַבְּדוּ וִהְיִיתֶם לִי סְגֻלָּה
שֵׁשֶׁת יָמִים תַּעֲבֹדוּ וּבַשְּׁבִיעִי נָגִילָה.
לְהִתְעַנֵּג בְּתַעֲנוּגִים בַּרְבּוּרִים וּשְׂלָו וְדָגִים.

מה ידידות מנוחתך – MA YEDIDUT MENUHATEKH

Enhancing Kiddush with Zemirot

"How beloved is your rest" refers to Shabbat HaMalka. Rav Soloveitchik (*Birkon HaRav*) states that it is not just nice to sing *zemirot*; it is actually a fulfillment (*kiyum*) of the mitzva of *Kiddush*.

We often find that there is a minimal manner in which one can fulfill a mitzva, and then there is a more expanded manner in which the entire action is considered part of the fulfillment of the mitzva.

The Rambam in *Hilkhot Hametz UMatza* (6:1) writes that it is a mitzva to eat matza on the night of the *seder*. Once one has eaten a *kezayit* of matza, he has fulfilled his obligation. The Rambam could have simply said, "It is a mitzva to eat a *kezayit* of matza." From the Rambam's formulation, it is clear that any additional matza consumed is considered to be part of the mitzva.

Your secular concerns are forbidden; so too are
calculations.
Reflections are permitted, and arranging matches for girls,
And teaching a child a book, and singing songs of praise,
And meditating on fine words at every place and gathering.
To savor the delights of fowl, quail and fish.

Your walk shall be unhurried; you shall call the Sabbath
a delight.
Sleep too is praiseworthy, for it refreshes the spirit.
Therefore my soul yearns for you, to rest in you in love,
As if within a fence of roses: on it son and daughter rest.
To savor the delights of fowl, quail and fish.

A foretaste of the World to Come is the day of Sabbath rest.
All who take delight in it will be worthy of great joy.
They will be delivered with relief from the birthpangs
of the Messiah,
May our redemption spring forth, and sadness and sighing
flee away.
To savor the delights of fowl, quail and fish.

Meiri's introduction to *Shas*) suggests that people who are engaged in Torah all week should have some physical enjoyment on Shabbat, and someone who works all week should engage in spiritual pursuits through Torah on Shabbat. Shabbat should be different than the rest of the week, as the *zemer* clearly articulates.

חֲפָצֶיךָ אֲסוּרִים וְגַם לַחְשֹׁב חֶשְׁבּוֹנוֹת
הִרְהוּרִים מֻתָּרִים וּלְשַׁדֵּךְ הַבָּנוֹת
וְתִינוֹק לְלַמְּדוֹ סֵפֶר, לַמְנַצֵּחַ בִּנְגִינוֹת
וְלַהֲגוֹת בְּאִמְרֵי שֶׁפֶר בְּכָל פִּנּוֹת וּמַחֲנוֹת.
לְהִתְעַנֵּג בְּתַעֲנוּגִים בַּרְבּוּרִים וּשְׂלָו וְדָגִים.

הִלּוּכָךְ יְהֵא בְנַחַת, עֹנֶג קְרָא לַשַּׁבָּת
וְהַשֵּׁנָה מְשֻׁבַּחַת כְּדָת נֶפֶשׁ מְשִׁיבַת
בְּכֵן נַפְשִׁי לְךָ עָרְגָה וְלָנוּחַ בְּחִבַּת
כַּשּׁוֹשַׁנִּים סוּגָה, בּוֹ יָנוּחוּ בֵּן וּבַת.
לְהִתְעַנֵּג בְּתַעֲנוּגִים בַּרְבּוּרִים וּשְׂלָו וְדָגִים.

מֵעֵין עוֹלָם הַבָּא יוֹם שַׁבָּת מְנוּחָה
כָּל הַמִּתְעַנְּגִים בָּהּ יִזְכּוּ לְרֹב שִׂמְחָה
מֵחֶבְלֵי מָשִׁיחַ יֻצָּלוּ לִרְוָחָה
פְּדוּתֵנוּ תַצְמִיחַ, וְנָס יָגוֹן וַאֲנָחָה.
לְהִתְעַנֵּג בְּתַעֲנוּגִים בַּרְבּוּרִים וּשְׂלָו וְדָגִים.

The Talmud Yerushalmi (Shabbat 15:3) quotes two different opinions with respect to the manner of sanctifying Shabbat. One opinion suggests we should be *me'aneg Shabbat* (infuse Shabbat with enjoyment) through Torah and *tefilla,* and another suggests that we should honor it with food. The Gemara posits that the manner in which one sanctifies Shabbat may differ based on the individual. The Rama (*Orah Hayim* 290; see also the

יוֹם זֶה לְיִשְׂרָאֵל This day for Israel is light and joy,
a Sabbath of serenity.
At the assembly at Sinai You decreed the laws,
Sabbath and the festivals – to keep them all my years;
Setting a table before me with courses of fine food –
A Sabbath of serenity.
This day, for Israel, is light and joy, a Sabbath of serenity.

Heart's delight to a shattered people,
To suffering spirits, an extra soul.
From troubled hearts may it banish sighs –
A Sabbath of serenity.
This day, for Israel, is light and joy, a Sabbath of serenity.

You sanctified and blessed it above all other days.
In six days You finished the making of all worlds.
On it sad souls find quiet and safety –
A Sabbath of serenity.
This day, for Israel, is light and joy, a Sabbath of serenity.

All work is forbidden by the revered One's commandment,
I will merit royal glory if I keep the Sabbath day,
Bringing the awesome One a sweetly scented gift –
A Sabbath of serenity.
This day, for Israel, is light and joy, a Sabbath of serenity.

And I shall offer You verses, in melody and song.
Standing before Your great splendor, my soul longs for You.
Keep Your promise, to Your single-minded treasure –
A Sabbath of serenity.
This day, for Israel, is light and joy, a Sabbath of serenity.

יוֹם זֶה לְיִשְׂרָאֵל אוֹרָה וְשִׂמְחָה, שַׁבַּת מְנוּחָה.

צִוִּיתָ פִּקּוּדִים בְּמַעֲמַד סִינַי
שַׁבָּת וּמוֹעֲדִים לִשְׁמֹר בְּכָל שָׁנַי
לַעֲרֹךְ לְפָנַי מַשְׂאֵת וַאֲרוּחָה שַׁבַּת מְנוּחָה.

יוֹם זֶה לְיִשְׂרָאֵל אוֹרָה וְשִׂמְחָה, שַׁבַּת מְנוּחָה.

חֶמְדַּת הַלְּבָבוֹת לְאֻמָּה שְׁבוּרָה
לִנְפָשׁוֹת נִכְאָבוֹת נְשָׁמָה יְתֵרָה
לְנֶפֶשׁ מְצֵרָה יָסִיר אֲנָחָה שַׁבַּת מְנוּחָה.

יוֹם זֶה לְיִשְׂרָאֵל אוֹרָה וְשִׂמְחָה, שַׁבַּת מְנוּחָה.

קִדַּשְׁתָּ בֵּרַכְתָּ אוֹתוֹ מִכָּל יָמִים
בְּשֵׁשֶׁת כִּלִּיתָ מְלֶאכֶת עוֹלָמִים
בּוֹ מָצְאוּ עֲגוּמִים הַשְׁקֵט וּבִטְחָה שַׁבַּת מְנוּחָה.

יוֹם זֶה לְיִשְׂרָאֵל אוֹרָה וְשִׂמְחָה, שַׁבַּת מְנוּחָה.

לְאִסּוּר מְלָאכָה צִוִּיתָנוּ נוֹרָא
אֶזְכֶּה הוֹד מְלוּכָה אִם שַׁבָּת אֶשְׁמֹרָה
אַקְרִיב שַׁי לַמּוֹרָא, מִנְחָה מֶרְקָחָה שַׁבַּת מְנוּחָה.

יוֹם זֶה לְיִשְׂרָאֵל אוֹרָה וְשִׂמְחָה, שַׁבַּת מְנוּחָה.

וְשִׁיר אֶעֱרֹךְ לְךָ בְּנִגּוּן וּנְעִימָה
מוּל תִּפְאֶרֶת גָּדְלְךָ נַפְשִׁי לְךָ כָּמַהּ
לִסְגֻלָּה תְמִימָה קַיֵּם הַבְטָחָה שַׁבַּת מְנוּחָה.

יוֹם זֶה לְיִשְׂרָאֵל אוֹרָה וְשִׂמְחָה, שַׁבַּת מְנוּחָה.

Desire my prayers like the first offering of Nahshon,
And the day of my serenity with happiness and joy,
Beloved like the apple of one's eye, with all successes –
A Sabbath of serenity.
This day, for Israel, is light and joy, a Sabbath of serenity.

We still wait for You to save us, LORD, most glorious of the glorified,
Send, please, to the Hebrews, the child of David, our king.
And declare liberty, relief and respite – A Sabbath of serenity.
This day, for Israel, is light and joy, a Sabbath of serenity.

Please, Most High, held in awe, see our torments.
Redeem us quickly, be gracious to us, answer us.
Make our souls happy, in light and in joy – A Sabbath of serenity.
This day, for Israel, is light and joy, a Sabbath of serenity.

Renew our Sanctuary, remember the ruined city.
Bestow Your goodness, Savior, on one who is sad,
Yet still she spends the Sabbath in song and praise –
A Sabbath of serenity.
This day, for Israel, is light and joy, a Sabbath of serenity.

Remember us, Holy One, for the sake of the honored day,
Keep us, please, this day and every day.
My bright, formidable Beloved, bring relief – A Sabbath of serenity.
This day, for Israel, is light and joy, a Sabbath of serenity.

Let Israel hear a voice of joy and of salvation,
As the vision of redemption is fulfilled, our Rock, who makes
salvation flourish,
Make the light of my sun come and shine then always –
A Sabbath of serenity.
This day, for Israel, is light and joy, a Sabbath of serenity.

רְצֵה תְפִלָּתִי כְּמוֹ קָרְבַּן נַחְשׁוֹן
וְיוֹם מְנוּחָתִי בְּשִׂמְחָה וּבְשָׂשׂוֹן
חָבִיב כְּבַת אִישׁוֹן בְּרֹב הַצְלָחָה שַׁבָּת מְנוּחָה.
יוֹם זֶה לְיִשְׂרָאֵל אוֹרָה וְשִׂמְחָה, שַׁבַּת מְנוּחָה.

יֶשְׁעֲךָ קִוִּינוּ יָהּ אַדִּיר אַדִּירִים
בֶּן דָּוִד מַלְכֵּנוּ שְׁלַח נָא לְעִבְרִים
וְיִקְרָא לִדְרוֹרִים רֶוַח וַהֲנָחָה שַׁבָּת מְנוּחָה.
יוֹם זֶה לְיִשְׂרָאֵל אוֹרָה וְשִׂמְחָה, שַׁבַּת מְנוּחָה.

אָנָּא עֶלְיוֹן נוֹרָא הַבִּיטָה עָנֵינוּ
פְּדֵנוּ בִמְהֵרָה חָנֵּנוּ וַעֲנֵנוּ
שַׂמַּח נַפְשֵׁנוּ בְּאוֹר וְשִׂמְחָה שַׁבָּת מְנוּחָה.
יוֹם זֶה לְיִשְׂרָאֵל אוֹרָה וְשִׂמְחָה, שַׁבַּת מְנוּחָה.

חַדֵּשׁ מִקְדָּשֵׁנוּ זָכְרָה נֶחֱרֶבֶת
טוּבְךָ, מוֹשִׁיעֵנוּ תְּנָה לַנֶּעֱצֶבֶת
בְּשַׁבָּת יוֹשֶׁבֶת בְּזֶמֶר וּשְׁבָחָה שַׁבַּת מְנוּחָה.
יוֹם זֶה לְיִשְׂרָאֵל אוֹרָה וְשִׂמְחָה, שַׁבַּת מְנוּחָה.

זְכֹר, קָדוֹשׁ, לָנוּ בִּזְכוּת יִקְרַת הַיּוֹם
שְׁמָר נָא אוֹתָנוּ בְּיוֹם זֶה וּבְכָל יוֹם
דּוֹדִי צַח וְאָיֹם תָּבִיא רְוָחָה שַׁבָּת מְנוּחָה.
יוֹם זֶה לְיִשְׂרָאֵל אוֹרָה וְשִׂמְחָה, שַׁבַּת מְנוּחָה.

קוֹל רִנָּה וִישׁוּעָה לְיִשְׂרָאֵל הַשְׁמִיעָה
בְּבֹא חֶזְיוֹן תְּשׁוּעָה צוּר, מַצְמִיחַ יְשׁוּעָה
אוֹר שִׁמְשִׁי הוֹפִיעָה תָּמִיד הַזְרִיחָה
שַׁבָּת מְנוּחָה.
יוֹם זֶה לְיִשְׂרָאֵל אוֹרָה וְשִׂמְחָה, שַׁבַּת מְנוּחָה.

יָהּ רִבּוֹן Master of all worlds, our God, adored,
King of kings, over all the LORD:
Your wondrous deeds to applaud
We sing to You with one accord.

God of all worlds, our God, adored;
King of kings, over all, the LORD.

Early and late my praise shall ring,
To You, holy Author of every thing:
Beasts of the field, birds that take wing.
Angels and mortals to You shall sing.

God of all worlds, our God, adored;
King of kings, over all, the LORD.

Your great good deeds are vast in scale,
You humble the proud, You lift the frail.
A thousand years would not avail
Of Your works to tell the tale.

God of all worlds, our God, adored;
King of kings, over all, the LORD.

---

month later, he met a crowd at Niagra Falls and told them he would cross on a tightrope, blindfolded, and while pushing a wheelbarrow. Then he asked, "Who believes in the Great Blondini?" The crowd applauded and again repeated, "We believe in the Great Blondini!" He made it across. Finally, a few months later, he again appeared at Niagra Falls and asked, "Who believes in the Great Blondini?" Once more, they all applauded with a resounding "We believe in the Great Blondini!" He then asked, "If you all believe in me, which of you is going to get into the wheelbarrow that I'm going to push across the tightrope, while blindfolded, to the other side of Niagra Falls?" Everyone was silent! Did they really believe in the Great Blondini?

לא יעול גבורתך בחושבניא – LA YE'OL GEVURTEIKH BEHUSHBANYA

Understanding the Master Plan

Y-a Ribon Ribbon, one of the only *zemirot* written in Aramaic, was composed by Rav Yisrael Najara, who was born in Damascus, later moved to Tzfat, and

became

יָהּ רִבּוֹן עָלַם וְעָלְמַיָּא
אַנְתְּ הוּא מַלְכָּא מֶלֶךְ מַלְכַיָּא
עוֹבַד גְּבוּרְתָּךְ וְתִמְהַיָּא
שְׁפַר קֳדָמָךְ לְהַחֲוָיָא.
יָהּ רִבּוֹן עָלַם וְעָלְמַיָּא
אַנְתְּ הוּא מַלְכָּא מֶלֶךְ מַלְכַיָּא.

שְׁבָחִין אֲסַדֵּר צַפְרָא וְרַמְשָׁא
לָךְ אֱלָהָא קַדִּישָׁא דִּי בְרָא כָּל נַפְשָׁא
עִירִין קַדִּישִׁין וּבְנֵי אֱנָשָׁא
חֵיוַת בְּרָא וְעוֹפֵי שְׁמַיָּא.
יָהּ רִבּוֹן עָלַם וְעָלְמַיָּא
אַנְתְּ הוּא מַלְכָּא מֶלֶךְ מַלְכַיָּא.

רַבְרְבִין עוֹבְדָיךְ וְתַקִּיפִין
מָכֵךְ רָמַיָּא וְזָקֵף כְּפִיפִין
לוּ יְחֵי גְבַר שְׁנִין אַלְפִין
לָא יֵעֹל גְּבוּרְתָּךְ בְּחֻשְׁבְּנַיָּא.
יָהּ רִבּוֹן עָלַם וְעָלְמַיָּא
אַנְתְּ הוּא מַלְכָּא מֶלֶךְ מַלְכַיָּא.

Y-A RIBON

די ברא כל נפשא – DI VARA KOL NAFSHA

Believing in the Creator

This *zemer* relates not only to Shabbat, but also to the awesomeness of God. It describes God as creator. Around 120 years ago, someone tried to cross parts of Niagara Falls on a tightrope. He stood up and said, "Who believes in the Great Blondini?" The crowd applauded in recognition and repeated, "We believe in the Great Blondini!" He then proceeded to cross successfully. A few weeks later, he again stood up before a crowd and called out, "Who believes in the Great Blondini?" The crowd applauded and repeated, "We believe in the Great Blondini!" in recognition of this hero before them. Once again, he crossed Niagra Falls on a tightrope, but this time, he was also blindfolded. A

Yours is the glory, the greatness too,
From the lion's jaw, Your flock rescue.
Bring Your exiles home to You:
The people You chose, deliver anew.

God of all worlds, our God, adored;
King of kings, over all, the LORD.

Come back to Your Temple, Your sacred shrine,
That there in joy our souls may entwine.
In song our voices to combine,
When Jerusalem's beauty again will shine.

God of all worlds, our God, adored;
King of kings, over all, the LORD.

This expresses the hope for the *geula* (redemption). Just as a sheep is saved from being eaten by a lion, Hashem will redeem us from exile. The Smak (mitzva 1) wonders what the source is for the mitzva to believe in the *geula*. He quotes the *gemara* (Shabbat 31a) that lists the six questions that each individual will be asked after having lived for 120 years and proceeding to the next world. Question number four is "*Tzipita leyeshua*? Did you anticipate salvation, the *Mashiah*?" The Smak asks a seemingly simple but intriguing question. Each of the six questions listed in the Gemara have a source in the Torah. These questions include whether one was honest in business, engaged in Torah study, had children, and more. They are all explicitly mentioned as mitzvot, and some appear more than once in the Torah. But from where do we derive the mitzva to anticipate salvation? Can one be a good, God-fearing Jew, perform all the mitzvot, and not believe in *Mashiah* and the final redemption?

The Smak posits that the requirement to anticipate salvation is actually part of the mitzva to believe in Hashem. We believe that *HaKadosh Barukh Hu* controls the world now, just as He controlled it when He took us out of Egypt. Just as He redeemed us in the past, so too He will redeem us in the future. This paragraph in the *zemer* thus reflects the fact that we believe and recognize that Hashem will redeem us once again and bring us back to *Yerushalayim habenuya*.

צמאה נפשי

אֱלָהָא דִּי לֵהּ יְקָר וּרְבוּתָא
פְּרֹק יָת עָנָךְ מִפֻּם אַרְיְוָתָא
וְאַפֵּק יָת עַמָּךְ מִגּוֹ גָלוּתָא
עַמָּא דִּי בְחַרְתְּ מִכָּל אֻמַּיָּא.
יָהּ רִבּוֹן עָלַם וְעָלְמַיָּא
אַנְתְּ הוּא מַלְכָּא מֶלֶךְ מַלְכַיָּא.

לְמִקְדְּשָׁךְ תּוּב וּלְקֹדֶשׁ קֻדְשִׁין
אֲתַר דִּי בֵהּ יֶחֱדוּן רוּחִין וְנַפְשִׁין
וִיזַמְּרוּן לָךְ שִׁירִין וְרַחֲשִׁין
בִּירוּשְׁלֵם קַרְתָּא דְשׁוּפְרַיָּא.
יָהּ רִבּוֹן עָלַם וְעָלְמַיָּא
אַנְתְּ הוּא מַלְכָּא מֶלֶךְ מַלְכַיָּא.

---

then became the chief rabbi of Gaza in the 1600s. In the *zemer* we are told that *lu yihyeh gvir shanin alfin*, even if someone were to live for a thousand years, *lo ye'ol gevurteikh behushbanya*, one would still be unable to understand God's ways. What is so difficult to comprehend?

In his *birkon*, Rav Asher Weiss refers to the *asara harugei malkhut*, the ten martyrs. God says, "If you dare ask why I am doing this, I will return the world to *tohu vavohu* (pandemonium)." Why is that the response? To understand, Rav Weiss offers a *mashal*: A king asks his servants to make him a robe. One of them sews a beautiful robe. The others complain that he did not use all of the thread and that he cut corners. The individual responds, "If you want to see what I used and how I sewed it all together, you need to totally unravel it." So it is with the world. If we want to understand God's ways, we need to go back to the beginning, to when there was *tohu vavohu* – because everything in history is horizontally and vertically connected, like *had gadya*. It is not a threat, but rather a response to explain that it is incomprehensible to man, since everything is connected and cannot be viewed in a vacuum.

Ka Ribon reminds us that Hashem is the creator of all mankind, and that we need to have sincere faith and belief in Him.

Hoping for Redemption

פרוק ית ענך מפום אריותא ואפיק ית עמך מגו גלותא.

From the lion's jaw, Your flock rescue. Bring Your exiles home to You.

צָמְאָה נַפְשִׁי My soul thirsts for God, the living God Ps. 42
My heart and flesh will sing joyfully to the living God. Ps. 84
The One God created me, and said "As I live,
No one shall see Me and live."
My soul thirsts for God, the living God
My heart and flesh will sing joyfully to the living God.

He created all with wisdom, design and deliberation,
Deeply hidden though it is from the eyes of all that live.
His glory is high above all, every mouth makes known His splendor,
Blessed is He in whose hands is the life-force of all that lives.
My soul thirsts for God, the living God
My heart and flesh will sing joyfully to the living God.

He set apart the quiet one's offspring, to teach them decrees,
Which if one performs them, thereby he shall live.
Who can vindicate himself? We are like specks of dust,
Truly none can vindicate itself before You, nothing that lives.
My soul thirsts for God, the living God
My heart and flesh will sing joyfully to the living God.

> you today shall be upon your heart" (*Devarim* 6:6) – that through this, you will recognize the One who spoke and the world came into being."

However, in *Hilkhot Yesodei HaTorah* (2:1), the Rambam tells us there is another means of getting close to Hashem – by observing the world and the amazing creations and by recognizing the infinite wisdom of Hashem. As David HaMelekh says, "*Tzama nafshi leElokim*" (*Tehillim* 42:3). In the Rambam's words:

> **והיאך היא הדרך לאהבתו ויראתו? בשעה שיתבונן האדם במעשיו וברואיו הנפלאים הגדולים, ויראה מהם חכמתו שאין לה ערך ולא קץ, מיד הוא אוהב ומשבח ומפאר ומתאווה תאווה גדולה לידע השם הגדול, כמו שאמר דוד: "צמאה נפשי לאלוהים לאל חי".**

> What is the path [to attain] love and fear of God? When a person contemplates His wondrous and great deeds and creations and appreciates His infinite wisdom that surpasses all comparison, he will immediately love, praise, and glorify [Him], yearning with tremendous desire to know

[God's]

צָמְאָה נַפְשִׁי לֵאלֹהִים לְאֵל חָי: לִבִּי וּבְשָׂרִי יְרַנְּנוּ אֶל אֵל־חָי: תהלים מב / תהלים פד
אֵל אֶחָד בְּרָאַנִי, וְאָמַר חַי אָנִי כִּי לֹא יִרְאַנִי הָאָדָם וָחָי.

צָמְאָה נַפְשִׁי לֵאלֹהִים לְאֵל חָי
לִבִּי וּבְשָׂרִי יְרַנְּנוּ אֶל אֵל־חָי.

בָּרָא כֹל בְּחָכְמָה, בְּעֵצָה וּבִמְזִמָּה מְאֹד נֶעְלָמָה מֵעֵינֵי כָּל חָי.
רָם עַל כֹּל כְּבוֹדוֹ, כָּל פֶּה יְחַוֶּה הוֹדוֹ בָּרוּךְ אֲשֶׁר בְּיָדוֹ נֶפֶשׁ כָּל חָי.

צָמְאָה נַפְשִׁי לֵאלֹהִים לְאֵל חָי
לִבִּי וּבְשָׂרִי יְרַנְּנוּ אֶל אֵל־חָי.

הִבְדִּיל נִינֵי תָם, חֻקִּים לְהוֹרוֹתָם אֲשֶׁר יַעֲשֶׂה אוֹתָם הָאָדָם וָחָי.
מִי זֶה יִצְטַדָּק, נִמְשַׁל לְאָבָק דָּק אֱמֶת, כִּי לֹא יִצְדַּק לְפָנֶיךָ כָּל חָי.

צָמְאָה נַפְשִׁי לֵאלֹהִים לְאֵל חָי
לִבִּי וּבְשָׂרִי יְרַנְּנוּ אֶל אֵל־חָי.

צמאה נפשי – TZAMA NAFSHI

Cultivating a Desire for Hashem

This *zemer* was authored by Rav Avraham Ibn Ezra. The beginning of each stanza starts with the corresponding letter of his name.

The Rambam in *Sefer HaMitzvot* (mitzva 3) tells us that the manner in which to achieve *ahavat Hashem* is through studying the Torah, Hashem's "autobiography," and understanding how He acts and what He likes. In the Rambam's words:

לשון ספרי: לפי שנאמר "ואהבת את ה׳ אלוהיך" איני יודע כיצד אוהב את המקום, תלמוד לומר: "והיו הדברים האלה אשר אנכי מצוך היום על לבבך" שמתוך כך אתה מכיר את מי שאמר והיה העולם.

And the language of the *Sifrei* (*Sifrei Devarim* 33:1) is: Since it is stated, "And you shall love the Lord your God," I would not know how a man is to love the Omnipresent. [Hence] we learn, "And these things that I command

In the heart, the inclination is like a viper's poison,
How then can we return, and be like flesh that lives?
Those who have gone astray, if they wished, could turn from their way,
Before they go to their rest in the place destined for all that lives.
My soul thirsts for God, the living God
My heart and flesh will sing joyfully to the living God.

For everything, I shall thank You, every mouth shall declare Your oneness,
You who open Your hand and satisfy all that lives.
Recall the love of ancient times, and revive those who slumber,
Bring near the days when the Messiah shall live.
My soul thirsts for God, the living God
My heart and flesh will sing joyfully to the living God.

See who is the true mistress, when the handmaid says,
"No, your son is dead while my son lives."
I will bow face down and spread my hands toward you,
When I open my mouth to say: "The soul of all that lives."
My soul thirsts for God, the living God
My heart and flesh will sing joyfully to the living God.

---

the *ol mitzvot*. Each day, we can have a new recognition of wanting to get close to Hashem. Each day, we can have a new *kabbalat mitzvot*.

A story is told of Rav Saadia Gaon, that highlights how one can obtain a deeper understanding and appreciation of how remarkable Hashem is on a daily basis. Rav Saadia once returned from a trip, crying and engaging in elements of *teshuva*. When his students asked what he was doing, Rav Saadia replied that when he was traveling, he stayed at an inn. On his last day, someone recognized him and greeted him with great respect. The innkeeper started apologizing that he had not given him the finest suite, saying that had he known the *gadol hador* was at the inn, he would have given him presidential treatment. Rav Saadia then told his *talmidim* that he took the innkeeper's words to heart. "Each day I recognize God's awesomeness on a greater level," he explained. "Then I realized that had I known this yesterday, I would have acted differently. That is why I need to do *teshuva*." That is what Rav Asher Weiss suggests. We need to have a new attitude each day to get even closer to *Hakadosh Barukh Hu*, to fulfill the needs of our thirsting soul.

בְּלֵב יֵצֶר חָשׁוּב כִּדְמוּת חֲמַת עַכְשׁוּב   וְאֵיכָכָה יָשׁוּב הַבָּשָׂר הֶחָי.
נְסוֹגִים אִם אָבוֹ, וּמַדְרְכָם שָׁבוּ   טֶרֶם יִשְׁכָּבוּ בֵּית מוֹעֵד לְכָל חָי.

צָמְאָה נַפְשִׁי לֵאלֹהִים לְאֵל חָי
לִבִּי וּבְשָׂרִי יְרַנְּנוּ אֶל אֵל־חָי.

עַל כֹּל אֲהוֹדֶךָ, כָּל פֶּה תְּיַחֲדֶךָ   פּוֹתֵחַ אֶת יָדֶךָ וּמַשְׂבִּיעַ לְכָל חָי.
זְכֹר אַהֲבַת קְדוּמִים, וְהַחֲיֵה נִרְדָּמִים   וְקָרֵב הַיָּמִים אֲשֶׁר בֶּן יִשַׁי חָי.

צָמְאָה נַפְשִׁי לֵאלֹהִים לְאֵל חָי
לִבִּי וּבְשָׂרִי יְרַנְּנוּ אֶל אֵל־חָי.

רְאֵה לִגְבֶרֶת אֱמֶת, שִׁפְחָה נוֹאֶמֶת   לֹא כִי, בְּנֵךְ הַמֵּת וּבְנִי הֶחָי.
אֶקֹּד עַל אַפִּי, וְאֶפְרֹשׂ לְךָ כַּפִּי   עֵת אֶפְתַּח פִּי בְּנִשְׁמַת כָּל חָי.

צָמְאָה נַפְשִׁי לֵאלֹהִים לְאֵל חָי
לִבִּי וּבְשָׂרִי יְרַנְּנוּ אֶל אֵל־חָי.

[God's] great name, as David stated: "My soul thirsts for the Lord, for the living God" (*Tehillim* 42:3).

On Shabbat we have an opportunity to think about and appreciate God's creation. This leads to love, appreciation, and awe of God, satiating our thirst to be connected to God.

Increasing Our Connection to Hashem Each Day

In Rav Kalonymus Kalman Shapira's *Tzav VeZiruz,* he writes: "I want to come close to You, but what can I do? I learn – can I learn more? I *daven* – can I *daven* more? I wish I could convert, but I am Jewish. So what can I do?"

Rav Asher Weiss (*Sihot,* Shavuot 68) suggests that there might actually be a way for a Jew to "convert." He cannot redo *tevila* or *mila,* but he can re-accept

יָהּ אֶכְסֹף Lord, I yearn the grace of Sabbath, perfectly fitting,
one with Your treasured ones.
Draw the grace of Your reverence to a people that seeks Your desire.
Make them holy in the holiness of Shabbat, which is one with Your Torah;
Open up for them the grace and desire to open the gates of Your desire.

He Who Was and Is, keep those who keep and watch for Your holy Shabbat:
As a deer longs for springs of water,
so their soul longs to receive the grace of Shabbat,
which is one with Your holy Name.
Shade those who linger before parting from Shabbat,
so that You will not be closed off from them in the six days
that take holiness from Your holy Shabbat.
And purify their hearts in truth and in faithfulness, to serve You.

(And let Your compassion ripple down through all Your aspects)
Let Your compassion ripple down to Your holy people,
To quench those thirsting for Your kindness
from the river that flows from Eden,
To ornament Israel in the splendor of those
who glorify You in Your holy Shabbat,
To leave them, all six days, the heritage of Jacob whom You chose.

Shabbat, grace of souls; the seventh day, delight of spirits and Eden of life,
where they delight in Your love and in Your awe.
Holy Shabbat, my soul is sick with love for You;
Holy Shabbat, the souls of Israel shall shelter in the shade of Your wings,
Shall be nourished in the plenty of Your house.

Melakhim 10:9) places them together and links them with the conjunctive "*vekhen*":

> **עכו"ם שעסק בתורה חייב מיתה. לא יעסוק אלא בשבע מצות שלהן בלבד. וכן עכו"ם ששבת אפילו ביום מימות החול אם עשאהו לעצמו כמו שבת חייב מיתה.**
>
> A gentile who studies the Torah deserves the death penalty. They should only be involved in the study of their seven mitzvot. Similarly, a gentile who rests, even on a weekday, observing that day as a Sabbath, deserves death.

What do Shabbat and Torah study have in common? The Rambam is teaching us that a non-Jew who performs almost all mitzvot is still defined as a non-Jew.

But Torah

יָהּ אֶכְסֹף נֹעַם שַׁבָּת הַמַּתְאֶמֶת וּמִיֻחֶדֶת בִּסְגֻלָּתֶךָ
מְשֹׁךְ נֹעַם יִרְאָתְךָ לְעַם מְבַקְשֵׁי רְצוֹנֶךָ
קַדְּשֵׁם בִּקְדֻשַּׁת הַשַּׁבָּת הַמִּתְאַחֶדֶת בְּתוֹרָתֶךָ
פְּתַח לָהֶם נֹעַם וְרָצוֹן לִפְתֹּחַ שַׁעֲרֵי רְצוֹנֶךָ

הָיָה הֹוֶה, שְׁמֹר שׁוֹמְרֵי וּמְצַפִּים שַׁבַּת קָדְשֶׁךָ
כְּאַיָּל תַּעֲרֹג עַל אֲפִיקֵי מָיִם
כֵּן נַפְשָׁם תַּעֲרֹג לְקַבֵּל נֹעַם שַׁבָּת הַמִּתְאַחֶדֶת בְּשֵׁם קָדְשֶׁךָ
הַצֵּל מְאַחֲרֵי לִפְרֹשׁ מִן הַשַּׁבָּת, לְבִלְתִּי תִהְיֶה סָגוּר מֵהֶם שִׁשָּׁה יָמִים
הַמְקַבְּלִים קְדֻשָּׁה מִשַּׁבַּת קָדְשֶׁךָ
וְטַהֵר לִבָּם בֶּאֱמֶת וּבֶאֱמוּנָה לְעָבְדֶךָ

(וִיהִיוּ רַחֲמֶיךָ מִתְגּוֹלְלִים עַל מִדּוֹתֶיךָ)
וִיהִיוּ רַחֲמֶיךָ מִתְגּוֹלְלִים עַל עַם קָדְשֶׁךָ
לְהַשְׁקוֹת צְמֵאֵי חַסְדֶּךָ מִנָּהָר הַיּוֹצֵא מֵעֵדֶן
לְעַטֵּר אֶת יִשְׂרָאֵל בְּתִפְאֶרֶת, הַמְפָאֲרִים אוֹתְךָ עַל יְדֵי שַׁבַּת קָדְשֶׁךָ
כָּל שִׁשָּׁה יָמִים, לְהַנְחִילָם נַחֲלַת יַעֲקֹב בְּחִירֶךָ

הַשַּׁבָּת נֹעַם הַנְּשָׁמוֹת, וְהַשְּׁבִיעִי עֹנֶג הָרוּחוֹת וְעֵדֶן הַנְּפָשׁוֹת
לְהִתְעַדֵּן בְּאַהֲבָתְךָ וְיִרְאָתֶךָ
שַׁבַּת קֹדֶשׁ, נַפְשִׁי חוֹלַת אַהֲבָתֶךָ
שַׁבַּת קֹדֶשׁ, נַפְשׁוֹת יִשְׂרָאֵל בְּצֵל כְּנָפֶיךָ יֶחֱסָיוּן יִרְוְיֻן מִדֶּשֶׁן בֵּיתֶךָ.

י־ה אכסוף – Y-A EKHSOF

SHABBAT AND TORAH DEFINE A JEW

This *zemer* was written by Rav Aharon MiKarlin, one of the Hasidic masters. In the second line, we ask Hashem to sanctify the Jewish People with the sanctity of Shabbat and Torah:

קדשם בקדושת השבת המתאחדת בתורתך.

The Gemara tells us that there are two mitzvot that non-Jews may not fulfill – Shabbat (Sanhedrin 58b) and Torah (Sanhedrin 59a). The Rambam (*Hilkhot*

בַּר יוֹחַאי Bar Yoḥai,
you are annointed, happy man!
With oil of joy,
more than all your friends.

Bar Yoḥai, with holy anointing oil, holiness anointed you.
You have worn the high priest's headpiece,
marked "holy"; your crown
is dressed with your splendor.

Bar Yoḥai, you settled in a good place
on the day of your flight, when you ran away
to the cave of rocks; there you stood,
and there you gained your glory and honor.

Bar Yoḥai, of the [Tabernacle's] standing acacia planks
do the learned of the Lord learn from you.
It is enchanted light, the altar-light your teachers
burn; is it not they who teach your words?

Bar Yoḥai, you came to the apple orchard
and climbed up to gather sweet spices,
the secrets of the Torah among the buds and the flowers –
"Let Us make man" was said for your sake.

Bar Yoḥai, you dressed yourself in might,
and forced the battle of the Law's fire back to the gate.
You drew your sword out from its sheath
and brandished it against your tormentors.

---

two options for every human being: being a righteous Jew or a righteous gentile, but not blurring the lines. You can be a Jew or a *Ben Noah,* but you cannot be a non-Jew who learns Torah or keeps Shabbat. These mitzvot redefine a person and are unique to the Jewish religion. Rav Aharon MiKarlin is asking that we be sanctified by these two distinctive mitzvot.

בַּר יוֹחַאי, נִמְשַׁחְתָּ, אַשְׁרֶיךָ
שֶׁמֶן שָׂשׂוֹן מֵחֲבֵרֶיךָ

בַּר יוֹחַאי, שֶׁמֶן מִשְׁחַת קֹדֶשׁ
נִמְשַׁחְתָּ מִמִּדַּת הַקֹּדֶשׁ
נָשָׂאתָ צִיץ נֵזֶר הַקֹּדֶשׁ
חָבוּשׁ עַל רֹאשְׁךָ, פְּאֵרֶךָ

בַּר יוֹחַאי, מוֹשַׁב טוֹב יָשַׁבְתָּ
יוֹם נַסְתָּ, יוֹם אֲשֶׁר בָּרַחְתָּ
בִּמְעָרַת צוּרִים שֶׁעָמַדְתָּ
שָׁם קָנִיתָ הוֹדְךָ וַהֲדָרֶךָ

בַּר יוֹחַאי, עֲצֵי שִׁטִּים עוֹמְדִים
לִמּוּדֵי יהוה הֵם לוֹמְדִים
אוֹר מֻפְלָא, אוֹר הַיְקוֹד הֵם יוֹקְדִים
הֲלֹא הֵמָּה יוֹרוּךָ, מוֹרֶיךָ

בַּר יוֹחַאי, בָּאתָ לִשְׂדֵה תַּפּוּחִים
וְעָלִיתָ לִלְקֹט בּוֹ מֶרְקָחִים
סוֹד תּוֹרָה בְּצִיצִים וּפְרָחִים
"נַעֲשֶׂה אָדָם" נֶאֱמַר בַּעֲבוּרֶךָ

בַּר יוֹחַאי, נֶאֱזַרְתָּ בִּגְבוּרָה
וּבְמִלְחֶמֶת אֵשׁ דַּת הַשְּׁעָרָה
וְחֶרֶב הוֹצֵאתָ מִתַּעְרָהּ
שָׁלַפְתָּ נֶגֶד צוֹרְרֶיךָ

But Torah and Shabbat are definitional. A non-Jew keeping Shabbat or learning Torah is in effect creating a new religion, which is forbidden. There are

Bar Yoḥai, to a place of marble stones
you came. to the presence of a lion,
and even the globes atop the pillars above the Great Bear
you saw – but who shall ever see you?

Bar Yoḥai, in the Holy of Holies
stretches the green horizon, the beginning of new things;
seven Sabbaths, the secrets of all fifty [gates of wisdom]
you bound; your knots are the *shin*
knots [of God's tefillin].

Bar Yoḥai, you saw the *yod* of ancient Wisdom,
with its innermost honor,
the thirty-two paths [of creation],
beginning of the offering –
you are the cherub anointed
with the brilliance of your light.

Bar Yoḥai, at the wondrous light which is highest of all,
you were afraid to look, for it is too much,
this mystery – it is called Nothingness –
you, like it, shall be seen by no eye.

Bar Yoḥai, happy the one who gave birth to you,
happy the people who learn from you,
happy those who can reach your secrets,
wearing the priest's breast-plate
of your truth-telling stones.

בַּר יוֹחַאי, לִמְקוֹם אַבְנֵי שַׁיִשׁ
הִגַּעְתָּ, וּפְנֵי אַרְיֵה לַיִשׁ
גַּם גֻּלַּת כּוֹתֶרֶת עַל עַיִשׁ
תָּשׁוּרִי, וּמִי יְשׁוּרֶךָ

בַּר יוֹחַאי, בְּקֹדֶשׁ הַקֳּדָשִׁים
קַו יָרֹק מְחַדֵּשׁ חֳדָשִׁים
שֶׁבַע שַׁבָּתוֹת, סוֹד חֲמִשִּׁים
קָשַׁרְתָּ קִשְׁרֵי שי״ן קְשָׁרֶיךָ

בַּר יוֹחַאי, יו״ד חָכְמָה קְדוּמָה
הִשְׁקַפְתָּ, לִכְבוֹדוֹ פְּנִימָה
ל״ב נְתִיבוֹת, רֵאשִׁית תְּרוּמָה
אַתְּ כְּרוּב מִמְשַׁח זִיו אוֹרֶךָ

בַּר יוֹחַאי, אוֹר מֻפְלָא, רוּם מַעְלָה
יָרֵאתָ מִלְּהַבִּיט, כִּי רַב לָהּ
תַּעֲלוּמָה, וְאַיִן קוֹרָא לָהּ
נַמְתָּ: עַיִן לֹא תְשׁוּרֶךָ

בַּר יוֹחַאי, אַשְׁרֵי יוֹלַדְתֶּךָ
אַשְׁרֵי הָעָם, הֵם לוֹמְדֶיךָ
אַשְׁרֵי הָעוֹמְדִים עַל סוֹדֶךָ
לְבוּשֵׁי חֹשֶׁן תֻּמֶּיךָ וְאוּרֶיךָ.

צוּר מִשֶּׁלּוֹ The Rock from whom we have eaten:
Bless Him, my faithful friends;
we have sufficed, we have left over,
just as the LORD said.

He feeds His world – our Shepherd, our Father,
we have eaten of His bread, His wine we have drunk.
So let us thank His name, let us praise Him with our mouths,
saying, singing: None is holy like the LORD.

The Rock from whom we have eaten: Bless Him, my faithful friends;
we have sufficed, we have left over, just as the LORD said.

With song and sound of thanks, we shall bless our God,
for the gift He gave our fathers: A lovely land.
With food and sustenance He has satisfied our souls.
His kindness overwhelms us: True is the LORD.

The Rock from whom we have eaten: Bless Him, my faithful friends;
we have sufficed, we have left over, just as the LORD said.

Have compassion in Your love for Your people, our Rock,
for Zion, Your home of glory, Temple of our splendor.
The son of David Your servant: may he come and redeem us,
breath of our life, anointed of the LORD.

The Rock from whom we have eaten: Bless Him, my faithful friends;
we have sufficed, we have left over, just as the LORD said.

---

stanza, "*Rahem*," is similar to the third paragraph of *bentching*, "*Rahem na*." The last line, "*Al kos*," reflects the *kos shel berakha* that is recited after *bentching*.

It is told that Rav Haim of Volozhin avoided reciting the *zemer* of *Tzur Mishelo*, as he felt that one may fulfill the obligation to *bentch* by reciting this *zemer*. The *minhag* of *Klal Yisrael*, however, is to recite the *zemer*.

Even though it is parallel to *bentching*, the *kos yayin malei* may be referring to the cup of wine that will be drunk during the times of *Mashiah*. The Gemara (Pesahim 119b) speaks of the meal in the times of *Mashiah*. Present

צוּר מִשֶּׁלּוֹ אָכַלְנוּ בָּרְכוּ אֱמוּנַי
שָׂבַעְנוּ וְהוֹתַרְנוּ כִּדְבַר יהוה.

הַזָּן אֶת עוֹלָמוֹ רוֹעֵנוּ אָבִינוּ
אָכַלְנוּ אֶת לַחְמוֹ וְיֵינוֹ שָׁתִינוּ
עַל כֵּן נוֹדֶה לִשְׁמוֹ וּנְהַלְלוֹ בְּפִינוּ
אָמַרְנוּ וְעָנִינוּ אֵין קָדוֹשׁ כַּיהוה.
צוּר מִשֶּׁלּוֹ אָכַלְנוּ, בָּרְכוּ אֱמוּנַי, שָׂבַעְנוּ וְהוֹתַרְנוּ כִּדְבַר יהוה.

בְּשִׁיר וְקוֹל תּוֹדָה נְבָרֵךְ אֱלֹהֵינוּ
עַל אֶרֶץ חֶמְדָּה שֶׁהִנְחִיל לַאֲבוֹתֵינוּ
מָזוֹן וְצֵידָה הִשְׂבִּיעַ לְנַפְשֵׁנוּ
חַסְדּוֹ גָּבַר עָלֵינוּ וֶאֱמֶת יהוה.
צוּר מִשֶּׁלּוֹ אָכַלְנוּ, בָּרְכוּ אֱמוּנַי, שָׂבַעְנוּ וְהוֹתַרְנוּ כִּדְבַר יהוה.

רַחֵם בְּחַסְדֶּךָ עַל עַמְּךָ צוּרֵנוּ
עַל צִיּוֹן מִשְׁכַּן כְּבוֹדֶךָ זְבוּל בֵּית תִּפְאַרְתֵּנוּ
בֶּן דָּוִד עַבְדֶּךָ יָבוֹא וְיִגְאָלֵנוּ
רוּחַ אַפֵּינוּ מְשִׁיחַ יהוה.
צוּר מִשֶּׁלּוֹ אָכַלְנוּ, בָּרְכוּ אֱמוּנַי, שָׂבַעְנוּ וְהוֹתַרְנוּ כִּדְבַר יהוה.

צור משלו אכלנו – TZUR MISHELO AKHALNU

על כוס יין מלא – AL KOS YAYIN MALEI

Bentching at the Seuda of Mashiah

This *zemer* seems like a prelude to *bentching*. The first paragraph is parallel to *Hazan et haolam*, the first paragraph of *bentching*. The second paragraph referring to *toda* is similar to "*Nodeh*," the second paragraph of *bentching*. The third

May the Temple be rebuilt, Zion's city full again;
there we will sing a new song as we go up in joy,
to the Compassionate, the Holy One –
may He be blessed and raised on high –
with a full cup of wine, sign of the blessing of the LORD.

The Rock from whom we have eaten: Bless Him, my faithful friends;
we have sufficed, we have left over, just as the LORD said.

Birkat HaMazon can be found on page 149.

---

because he never had a son. Dovid Hamelekh agrees to *bentch*, even though he does not have a perfect record, perhaps because he was able to do *teshuva* and overcome his shortfall. It is Dovid who we recall will take center stage in the times of *Mashiah* and lead the *bentching* – *al kos yayin malei*!

יִבָּנֶה הַמִּקְדָּשׁ	עִיר צִיּוֹן תְּמַלֵּא
וְשָׁם נָשִׁיר שִׁיר חָדָשׁ	וּבִרְנָנָה נַעֲלֶה
הָרַחֲמָן הַנִּקְדָּשׁ	יִתְבָּרַךְ וְיִתְעַלֶּה
עַל כּוֹס יַיִן מָלֵא	כְּבִרְכַּת יהוה.

צוּר מִשֶּׁלּוֹ אָכַלְנוּ, בָּרְכוּ אֱמוּנַי, שָׂבַעְנוּ וְהוֹתַרְנוּ כִּדְבַר יהוה.

ברכת המזון *can be found on page 149.*

---

are our forefathers, and a determination needs to be made as to who will lead the *zimun*. Avraham declines *bentching* because he had a Yishmael. Yitzhak declines because he had an Esav. Yaakov declines because he married two sisters, and it is a stain on his record even though it was only prohibited later. Moshe declines because he never entered *Eretz Yisrael*. Yehoshua declines

יום שבת

SHABBAT DAY

Kiddush for Shabbat Morning

Some say:

אִם־תָּשִׁיב If you keep your feet from breaking the Sabbath, and from pursuing your affairs on My holy day, if you call the Sabbath a delight, and the LORD's holy day honorable, and if you honor it by not going your own way or attending to your own affairs, or speaking idle words, then you will find joy in the LORD, and I will cause you to ride on the heights of the earth and to feast on the inheritance of your father Jacob, for the mouth of the LORD has spoken. *Is. 58*

Most begin Kiddush here.
On Yom Tov, say the Kiddush on page 78 and on Rosh HaShana, on page 80.

וְשָׁמְרוּ The children of Israel must keep the Sabbath, *Ex. 31*
observing the Sabbath in every generation
as an everlasting covenant.
It is a sign between Me and the children of Israel for ever,
for in six days the LORD made the heavens and the earth,
but on the seventh day He ceased work
and refreshed Himself.

---

now Shabbat has concluded, woe [*vai*] for the additional soul [*nefesh*] that is lost.

Once Shabbat leaves, we lose this additional soul.

What is a *neshama yeteira*? Rashi believes it has to do with physical aspects, i.e., eating and drinking, as food tastes different on Shabbat (see "The Spice of Shabbat," above.) The *Shita Mekubetzet* explains that the *neshama yeteira* relates to the *shefa Eloki*, the spiritual aspects of Shabbat.

It is interesting to note that the source for the *neshama yeteira* cited in the Gemara above is learned from the end of Shabbat, when the additional soul leaves us.

"שבת וינפש", כיון ששבת ווי אבדה נפש.

"He ceased from work and was refreshed [*vayinafash*]" (*Shemot* 31:17). Since he ceased from work, and now Shabbat has concluded, woe [*vai*] for the additional soul [*nefesh*] that is lost.

Often

קידושא רבה לשבת

Some say:

אִם־תָּשִׁיב מִשַּׁבָּת רַגְלֶךָ עֲשׂוֹת חֲפָצֶךָ בְּיוֹם קָדְשִׁי, וְקָרָאתָ לַשַּׁבָּת עֹנֶג ישעיה נח
לִקְדוֹשׁ יהוה מְכֻבָּד, וְכִבַּדְתּוֹ מֵעֲשׂוֹת דְּרָכֶיךָ מִמְּצוֹא חֶפְצְךָ וְדַבֵּר דָּבָר:
אָז תִּתְעַנַּג עַל־יהוה, וְהִרְכַּבְתִּיךָ עַל־בָּמֳתֵי אָרֶץ, וְהַאֲכַלְתִּיךָ נַחֲלַת
יַעֲקֹב אָבִיךָ, כִּי פִּי יהוה דִּבֵּר:

Most begin קידוש *here.*
On יום טוב *say the* קידוש *on page 79 and on* ראש השנה*, on page 81*

וְשָׁמְרוּ בְנֵי־יִשְׂרָאֵל אֶת־הַשַּׁבָּת שמות לא
לַעֲשׂוֹת אֶת־הַשַּׁבָּת לְדֹרֹתָם בְּרִית עוֹלָם:
בֵּינִי וּבֵין בְּנֵי יִשְׂרָאֵל אוֹת הִוא לְעֹלָם
כִּי־שֵׁשֶׁת יָמִים עָשָׂה יהוה אֶת־הַשָּׁמַיִם וְאֶת־הָאָרֶץ
וּבַיּוֹם הַשְּׁבִיעִי שָׁבַת וַיִּנָּפַשׁ:

קידושא רבה – KIDDUSHA RABBA

שבת וינפש – SHABBAT VAYINAFASH

Appreciating the Neshama Yeteira When We Have It

Although the obligation of *Kiddush* on Shabbat morning may be fulfilled by merely reciting the *berakha* of "*borei pri hagafen,*" it is the custom to recite certain *pesukim* prior to reciting the blessing over the wine. Many include the paragraph of *VeShamru Bnei Yisrael et HaShabbat*. This paragraph ends with the term "*shavat vayinafash.*" The simple interpretation is that Hashem rested and was refreshed. The Gemara in Beitza (16a) cites this as the source for the idea of the *neshama yeteira*.

> **דאמר רבי שמעון בן לקיש: נשמה יתירה נותן הקדוש ברוך הוא באדם ערב שבת, ולמוצאי שבת נוטלין אותה הימנו, שנאמר: "שבת וינפש", כיון ששבת ווי אבדה נפש.**
>
> As R. Shimon ben Lakish said: The Holy One, blessed be He, gives a person an additional soul on Shabbat eve, and at the conclusion of Shabbat removes it from him, as it is stated: "He ceased from work and was refreshed [*vayinafash*]" (*Shemot* 31:17). Since he ceased from work, and

זָכוֹר Remember the Sabbath day to keep it holy. *Ex. 20*
Six days you shall labor and do all your work,
but the seventh day is a Sabbath of the Lord your God;
on it you shall not do any work –
you, your son or daughter, your male or female slave,
or your cattle, or the stranger within your gates.
For in six days the Lord made heaven and earth
and sea and all that is in them,
and rested on the seventh day;
therefore the Lord blessed the Sabbath day
and declared it holy.

When saying Kiddush for others, add:
Please pay attention, my masters.

בָּרוּךְ Blessed are You, Lord our God, King of the Universe,
who creates the fruit of the vine.

On Shabbat Ḥol HaMo'ed Sukkot, if Kiddush is made in the sukka, add:
Blessed are You, Lord our God, King of the Universe,
who has made us holy through His commandments,
and has commanded us to dwell in the sukka.

זָכוֹר אֶת־יוֹם הַשַּׁבָּת לְקַדְּשׁוֹ: שמות כ
שֵׁשֶׁת יָמִים תַּעֲבֹד, וְעָשִׂיתָ כָּל־מְלַאכְתֶּךָ:
וְיוֹם הַשְּׁבִיעִי שַׁבָּת לַיהוה אֱלֹהֶיךָ
לֹא־תַעֲשֶׂה כָל־מְלָאכָה אַתָּה וּבִנְךָ וּבִתֶּךָ
עַבְדְּךָ וַאֲמָתְךָ וּבְהֶמְתֶּךָ
וְגֵרְךָ אֲשֶׁר בִּשְׁעָרֶיךָ:
כִּי שֵׁשֶׁת־יָמִים עָשָׂה יהוה אֶת־הַשָּׁמַיִם וְאֶת־הָאָרֶץ
אֶת־הַיָּם וְאֶת־כָּל־אֲשֶׁר־בָּם
וַיָּנַח בַּיּוֹם הַשְּׁבִיעִי
עַל־כֵּן בֵּרַךְ יהוה אֶת־יוֹם הַשַּׁבָּת וַיְקַדְּשֵׁהוּ:

When saying קידוש *for others, add:*

סַבְרִי מָרָנָן

בָּרוּךְ אַתָּה יהוה אֱלֹהֵינוּ מֶלֶךְ הָעוֹלָם
בּוֹרֵא פְּרִי הַגָּפֶן.

On שבת חול המועד סוכות *if* קידוש *is made in the* סוכה *add:*

בָּרוּךְ אַתָּה יהוה אֱלֹהֵינוּ מֶלֶךְ הָעוֹלָם
אֲשֶׁר קִדְּשָׁנוּ בְּמִצְוֹתָיו וְצִוָּנוּ לֵישֵׁב בַּסֻּכָּה.

Often, we don't appreciate what we have until it is lacking. Let us try to appreciate the *neshama yeteira* and enjoy both the unique physical and spiritual aspects of Shabbat.

Kiddush for Yom Tov Morning

On Shabbat Ḥol HaMo'ed, turn to page 74.

On a Yom Tov that falls on Shabbat, start Kiddush here:

וְשָׁמְרוּ The children of Israel must keep the Sabbath, observing the Sabbath in every generation as an everlasting covenant. It is a sign between Me and the children of Israel for ever, for in six days the LORD made the heavens and the earth, but on the seventh day He ceased work and refreshed Himself. *Ex. 31*

זָכוֹר Remember the Sabbath day to keep it holy. Six days you shall labor and do all your work, but the seventh day is a Sabbath of the LORD your God; on it you shall not do any work – you, your son or daughter, your male or female slave, or your cattle, or the stranger within your gates. For in six days the LORD made heaven and earth and sea and all that is in them, and rested on the seventh day; *Ex. 20*

On a Yom Tov that falls on Shabbat, some start Kiddush here instead:

Therefore the LORD blessed the Sabbath day and declared it holy.

On a Yom Tov that falls on a weekday, start here:

אֵלֶּה These are the appointed times of the LORD, *Lev. 23*
sacred assemblies, which you shall announce in their due season.
Thus Moses announced the LORD's appointed seasons
to the children of Israel.

When saying Kiddush for others, add: Please pay attention, my masters.

בָּרוּךְ Blessed are You, LORD our God, King of the Universe,
who creates the fruit of the vine.

On Sukkot, if Kiddush is made in the sukka, add:

בָּרוּךְ Blessed are You, LORD our God, King of the Universe,
who has made us holy through His commandments
and has commanded us to dwell in the sukka.

קידושא רבה לשלוש רגלים

On שבת חול המועד *turn to page 75.*

On יום טוב *that falls on* שבת*, start* קידוש *here:*

וְשָׁמְרוּ בְנֵי־יִשְׂרָאֵל אֶת־הַשַּׁבָּת, לַעֲשׂוֹת אֶת־הַשַּׁבָּת לְדֹרֹתָם בְּרִית עוֹלָם: בֵּינִי וּבֵין בְּנֵי יִשְׂרָאֵל אוֹת הִוא לְעֹלָם, כִּי־שֵׁשֶׁת יָמִים עָשָׂה יהוה אֶת־הַשָּׁמַיִם וְאֶת־הָאָרֶץ וּבַיּוֹם הַשְּׁבִיעִי שָׁבַת וַיִּנָּפַשׁ: שמות לא

זָכוֹר אֶת־יוֹם הַשַּׁבָּת לְקַדְּשׁוֹ: שֵׁשֶׁת יָמִים תַּעֲבֹד, וְעָשִׂיתָ כָּל־מְלַאכְתֶּךָ: וְיוֹם הַשְּׁבִיעִי שַׁבָּת לַיהוה אֱלֹהֶיךָ, לֹא־תַעֲשֶׂה כָל־מְלָאכָה אַתָּה וּבִנְךָ וּבִתֶּךָ, עַבְדְּךָ וַאֲמָתְךָ וּבְהֶמְתֶּךָ, וְגֵרְךָ אֲשֶׁר בִּשְׁעָרֶיךָ: כִּי שֵׁשֶׁת־יָמִים עָשָׂה יהוה אֶת־הַשָּׁמַיִם וְאֶת־הָאָרֶץ אֶת־הַיָּם וְאֶת־כָּל־אֲשֶׁר־בָּם, וַיָּנַח בַּיּוֹם הַשְּׁבִיעִי שמות כ

On יום טוב *that falls on* שבת*, some start* קידוש *here instead:*

עַל־כֵּן בֵּרַךְ יהוה אֶת־יוֹם הַשַּׁבָּת וַיְקַדְּשֵׁהוּ:

On יום טוב *that falls on a weekday, start here:*

אֵלֶּה מוֹעֲדֵי יהוה מִקְרָאֵי קֹדֶשׁ אֲשֶׁר־תִּקְרְאוּ אֹתָם בְּמוֹעֲדָם: וַיְדַבֵּר מֹשֶׁה אֶת־מֹעֲדֵי יהוה אֶל־בְּנֵי יִשְׂרָאֵל: ויקרא כג

When saying קידוש *for others, add* סַבְרִי מָרָנָן

בָּרוּךְ אַתָּה יהוה אֱלֹהֵינוּ מֶלֶךְ הָעוֹלָם
בּוֹרֵא פְּרִי הַגָּפֶן.

On סוכות *if* קידוש *is made in the* סוכה *add:*

בָּרוּךְ אַתָּה יהוה אֱלֹהֵינוּ מֶלֶךְ הָעוֹלָם
אֲשֶׁר קִדְּשָׁנוּ בְּמִצְוֹתָיו וְצִוָּנוּ לֵישֵׁב בַּסֻּכָּה.

Kiddush for Rosh HaShana Day

On a Rosh HaShana that falls on Shabbat, start Kiddush here:

וְשָׁמְרוּ The children of Israel must keep the Sabbath, observing the Sabbath in every generation as an everlasting covenant. It is a sign between Me and the children of Israel for ever, for in six days the LORD made the heavens and the earth, but on the seventh day He ceased work and refreshed Himself. *Ex. 31*

זָכוֹר Remember the Sabbath day to keep it holy. Six days you shall labor and do all your work, but the seventh day is a Sabbath of the LORD your God; on it you shall not do any work – you, your son or daughter, your male or female slave, or your cattle, or the stranger within your gates. For in six days the LORD made heaven and earth and sea and all that is in them, and rested on the seventh day; *Ex. 20*

On a Yom Tov that falls on Shabbat, some start Kiddush here instead:

Therefore the LORD blessed the Sabbath day and declared it holy.

On a Yom Tov that falls on a weekday, some start here:

אֵלֶּה These are the appointed times of the LORD, sacred assemblies, which you shall announce in their due season. *Lev. 23*
Thus Moses announced the LORD's appointed seasons
to the children of Israel.

On a Yom Tov that falls on a weekday, start here:

תִּקְעוּ Sound the shofar on the new moon, *Ps. 81*
on our feast day when the moon is hidden.
For it is a statute for Israel, an ordinance of the God of Jacob.

When saying Kiddush for others: Please pay attention, my masters.

בָּרוּךְ Blessed are You, LORD our God, King of the Universe,
who creates the fruit of the vine.

קידושא רבה לראש השנה

On ראש השנה *that falls on* שבת*, start* קידוש *here:*

שמות לא וְשָׁמְרוּ בְנֵי־יִשְׂרָאֵל אֶת־הַשַּׁבָּת, לַעֲשׂוֹת אֶת־הַשַּׁבָּת לְדֹרֹתָם
בְּרִית עוֹלָם: בֵּינִי וּבֵין בְּנֵי יִשְׂרָאֵל אוֹת הִוא לְעֹלָם, כִּי־שֵׁשֶׁת
יָמִים עָשָׂה יהוה אֶת־הַשָּׁמַיִם וְאֶת־הָאָרֶץ וּבַיּוֹם הַשְּׁבִיעִי שָׁבַת
וַיִּנָּפַשׁ:

שמות כ זָכוֹר אֶת־יוֹם הַשַּׁבָּת לְקַדְּשׁוֹ: שֵׁשֶׁת יָמִים תַּעֲבֹד, וְעָשִׂיתָ כָּל־
מְלַאכְתֶּךָ: וְיוֹם הַשְּׁבִיעִי שַׁבָּת לַיהוה אֱלֹהֶיךָ, לֹא־תַעֲשֶׂה כָל־
מְלָאכָה אַתָּה וּבִנְךָ וּבִתֶּךָ, עַבְדְּךָ וַאֲמָתְךָ וּבְהֶמְתֶּךָ, וְגֵרְךָ אֲשֶׁר
בִּשְׁעָרֶיךָ: כִּי שֵׁשֶׁת־יָמִים עָשָׂה יהוה אֶת־הַשָּׁמַיִם וְאֶת־הָאָרֶץ
אֶת־הַיָּם וְאֶת־כָּל־אֲשֶׁר־בָּם, וַיָּנַח בַּיּוֹם הַשְּׁבִיעִי

On ראש השנה *that falls on* שבת*, some start* קידוש *here instead:*

עַל־כֵּן בֵּרַךְ יהוה אֶת־יוֹם הַשַּׁבָּת וַיְקַדְּשֵׁהוּ:

On ראש השנה *that falls on a weekday, some start here:*

ויקרא כג אֵלֶּה מוֹעֲדֵי יהוה מִקְרָאֵי קֹדֶשׁ
אֲשֶׁר־תִּקְרְאוּ אֹתָם בְּמוֹעֲדָם:
וַיְדַבֵּר מֹשֶׁה אֶת־מֹעֲדֵי יהוה אֶל־בְּנֵי יִשְׂרָאֵל:

On יום טוב *that falls on a weekday, start here:*

תהלים פא תִּקְעוּ בַחֹדֶשׁ שׁוֹפָר, בַּכֶּסֶה לְיוֹם חַגֵּנוּ:
כִּי חֹק לְיִשְׂרָאֵל הוּא, מִשְׁפָּט לֵאלֹהֵי יַעֲקֹב:

When saying קידוש *for others* סַבְרִי מָרָנָן

בָּרוּךְ אַתָּה יהוה אֱלֹהֵינוּ מֶלֶךְ הָעוֹלָם
בּוֹרֵא פְּרִי הַגָּפֶן.

Zemirot for Shabbat Day

בָּרוּךְ Blessed be the LORD who, day by day, carries our burden with salvation and redemption. We will rejoice in His name all day long, and raise our head high in His salvation. For He is a stronghold for the poor and a refuge for the needy.

The LORD's tribes are Israel's testimony: He was distressed in their distress, in their suffering and slavery. Through a pavement of sapphire He showed them the strength of His love, He revealed Himself, lifting them from the depths of the pit. For with the LORD is loving-kindness; He abounds in redemption. *Ps. 130*

How precious is His loving-kindness; He shelters them under His shade. For their sake He went with them into exile in Babylon. When they went down in ships, He was counted among them. He ensured that they were treated mercifully by those who took them captive. For the LORD will not forsake His people, for the sake of His great name.

In Eilam He placed His throne, to rescue His beloved, to remove from them the stronghold of His rebels. He redeemed His servants from passing under the sword. He raised the pride of His people, for the glory of all His devoted ones. For though He afflicts, He also shows compassion and loving-kindness. *Lam. 3*

When the he-goat [Greece] extended its power, and the vision of the four ascended to the heights, And in their hearts they intended to destroy those He loved, through His priests He laid low those who rose against Him: The LORD's *Lam. 3*
kindness has not ended nor His compassion ceased.

---

the Sea, or *Matan Torah*, but the mere existence of the Jewish nation throughout the generations of exile.

That perhaps relates to the covenant between Avraham and Hashem at the *brit bein hebetarim*. Rashi (*Bereshit* 15:10) explains that the convention of covenants was to split an animal in half, after which the two parties would walk between the two parts; hence the name "covenant between the parts." What is the symbolism of such a strange ceremony? The *Sefer Ikkarim* (*maamar* 4, chapter 45) suggests that before the covenant, there were two parties who were to become one. They take a whole item that was one and split it in half so as to portray that the parties are now each half of a whole, and they have to keep their commitment to each other. That is what Hashem

זמירות ליום שבת

בָּרוּךְ אֲדֹנָי יוֹם יוֹם, יַעֲמָס לָנוּ יֶשַׁע וּפִדְיוֹם
וּבִשְׁמוֹ נָגִיל כָּל הַיּוֹם, וּבִישׁוּעָתוֹ נָרִים רֹאשׁ עֶלְיוֹן.
כִּי הוּא מָעוֹז לַדָּל וּמַחְסֶה לָאֶבְיוֹן.

שִׁבְטֵי יָהּ לְיִשְׂרָאֵל עֵדוּת, בְּצָרָתָם לוֹ צָר בְּסִבְלוּת וּבְעַבְדוּת
בִּלְבְנַת הַסַּפִּיר הֶרְאָם עֹז יְדִידוּת, וְנִגְלָה לְהַעֲלוֹתָם מֵעֹמֶק בּוֹר וָדוּת.
כִּי־עִם־יהוה הַחֶסֶד, וְהַרְבֵּה עִמּוֹ פְדוּת: תהלים קל

מַה יָּקָר חַסְדּוֹ בְּצִלּוֹ לְגוֹנְנֵמוֹ, בְּגָלוּת בָּבֶלָה שֻׁלַּח לְמַעַנְמוֹ
לְהוֹרִיד בָּרִיחִים נִמְנָה בֵינֵימוֹ, וַיִּתְּנֵם לְרַחֲמִים לִפְנֵי שׁוֹבֵימוֹ.
כִּי לֹא יִטֹּשׁ יהוה אֶת עַמּוֹ, בַּעֲבוּר הַגָּדוֹל שְׁמוֹ.

עֵילָם שָׁת כִּסְאוֹ לְהַצִּיל יְדִידָיו, לְהַאֲבִיד מִשָּׁם מָעֻזְנֵי מוֹרְדָיו
מֵעֲבוֹר בַּשֶּׁלַח פָּדָה אֶת עֲבָדָיו, קֶרֶן לְעַמּוֹ יָרִים, תְּהִלָּה לְכָל חֲסִידָיו.
כִּי אִם־הוֹגָה, וְרִחַם כְּרֹב חֲסָדָו: איכה ג

וּצְפִיר הָעִזִּים הִגְדִּיל עֲצוּמָיו, וְגַם חָזוּת אַרְבַּע עָלוּ לִמְרוֹמָיו
וּבְלִבָּם דִּמּוּ לְהַשְׁחִית אֶת רְחוּמָיו, עַל יְדֵי כֹהֲנָיו מִגֵּר מִתְקוֹמְמָיו.
חַסְדֵי יהוה כִּי לֹא־תָמְנוּ, כִּי לֹא כָלוּ רַחֲמָיו: איכה ג

ברוך ה׳ יום יום – BARUKH HASHEM YOM YOM

Hashem is with Us Throughout the Exiles

In most *birkonim,* the first *zemer* listed for Shabbat morning is *Barukh Hashem Yom Yom,* written by Rav Shimon bar Yitzhak (whose name appears as an acrostic). He was an early *Rishon* and a student of the Rif. The *zemer* is similar to *Maoz Tzur,* sung on Hanukka, in that it refers to the various exiles (*galuyot*) that we have experienced over the centuries: Bavel, Yavan, the Roman exile, etc. Hashem is with us throughout each of the exiles. Although we lack the *Beit HaMikdash,* He is with us in the *galut.*

Rav Yaakov Emden, in his commentary on the siddur, writes that the greatest miracle in the history of the world is not the ten plagues, the Splitting of

I was handed over to Edom [Rome] by my quarrelsome friends, who daily sated their appetite with my treasures. His help was with me, supporting my foundations, He will not forsake me all the days of my age. For the LORD does not reject forever. *Lam. 3*

When He comes from Edom with garments stained crimson, there will be slaughter in Botzra, and an execution of traitors, their blood will turn His garments red, in His great strength He will bring the leaders low. With His mighty blast like a day of the east wind. *Is. 27*

When the oppressor from Edom sees how it will be, He will think Botzra to be a refuge like Betzer, giving protection to angels and men, willful and accidental sinners alike. Love the LORD, all His devoted ones: all His faithful ones He will guard. *Ps. 31*

The Rock in His kindness will command His communities to gather, coming together from the four winds, He will settle them upon the high mountains, He will return with us, gathering the dispersed, for it does not say, "He will bring back" but "He will return" and gather.

Blessed is our God who has bestowed good upon us. In His compassion and abundant kindness, He has done great things for us. Like these and those, may He do yet more for us, to magnify His great, mighty and awesome name, by which we are called.

Blessed is our God who created us for His glory, To praise and laud Him and tell of His majesty, His loving-kindness is greater to us than to any other nation. Therefore with all our heart and soul and might, let us proclaim His kingship and His unity.

May He to whom peace belongs, send us blessing and peace. From left and right, may Israel have peace. May the Compassionate One bless His people with peace, and may they merit to see children and children's children, occupied with Torah and the commandments, bringing Israel peace. Wondrous Counselor, mighty God, everlasting Father, Prince of peace. *Is. 9*

---

to a *talmid* of mine who was present, "I don't see any Phoenicians, ancient Egyptians, or Romans in this room, but the Hebrews are still around!" That is the message of this *zemer* – that throughout the exile we may be persecuted, but Hashem is by our side. We will persevere.

ברוך

נִסְגַּרְתִּי לֶאֱדוֹם בְּיַד רֵעַי מְדָנַי, שֶׁבְּכָל יוֹם מְמַלְּאִים כְּרֵסָם מֵעֲדָנַי
עֶזְרָתוֹ עִמִּי לִסְמֹךְ אֶת אֲדָנַי, וְלֹא נְטַשְׁתַּנִי כָּל יְמֵי עִדָּנַי.
כִּי לֹא יִזְנַח לְעוֹלָם אֲדֹנָי: איכה ג

בְּבוֹאוֹ מֵאֱדוֹם חֲמוּץ בְּגָדִים, זֶבַח לוֹ בְּבָצְרָה וְטֶבַח לוֹ בְּבוֹגְדִים
וְיֵז נִצְחָם מַלְבּוּשָׁיו לְהַאְדִּים, בְּכֹחוֹ הַגָּדוֹל יִבְצֹר רוּחַ נְגִידִים.
הָגָה בְּרוּחוֹ הַקָּשָׁה בְּיוֹם קָדִים: ישעיה כז

רְאוֹתוֹ כִּי כֵן אֲדוֹמִי הָעוֹצֵר, יַחְשָׁב לוֹ בָּצְרָה תִּקְלֹט כְּבֶצֶר
וּמַלְאָךְ כְּאָדָם בְּתוֹכָהּ יִנָּצֵר, וּמֵזִיד כַּשּׁוֹגֵג בְּמִקְלָט יֵעָצֵר.
אֶהֱבוּ אֶת־יהוה כָּל־חֲסִידָיו, אֱמוּנִים נֹצֵר: תהלים לא

יְצַוֶּה צוּר חַסְדּוֹ קְהִלּוֹתָיו לְקַבֵּץ, מֵאַרְבַּע רוּחוֹת עָדָיו לְהִקָּבֵץ
וּבְהַר מְרוֹם הָרִים אוֹתָנוּ לְהַרְבֵּץ, וְאִתָּנוּ יָשׁוּב נִדָּחִים קוֹבֵץ.
יָשִׁיב לֹא נֶאֱמַר, כִּי אִם וְשָׁב וְקִבֵּץ.

בָּרוּךְ הוּא אֱלֹהֵינוּ אֲשֶׁר טוֹב גְּמָלָנוּ, כְּרַחֲמָיו וּכְרֹב חֲסָדָיו הִגְדִּיל לָנוּ
אֵלֶּה וְכָאֵלֶּה יוֹסֵף עִמָּנוּ
לְהַגְדִּיל שְׁמוֹ הַגָּדוֹל הַגִּבּוֹר וְהַנּוֹרָא, שֶׁנִּקְרָא עָלֵינוּ.

בָּרוּךְ הוּא אֱלֹהֵינוּ שֶׁבְּרָאָנוּ לִכְבוֹדוֹ, לְהַלְלוֹ וּלְשַׁבְּחוֹ וּלְסַפֵּר הוֹדוֹ
מִכָּל אֹם גָּבַר עָלֵינוּ חַסְדּוֹ
לָכֵן בְּכָל לֵב וּבְכָל נֶפֶשׁ וּבְכָל מְאוֹדוֹ, נַמְלִיכוֹ וּנְיַחֲדוֹ.

שֶׁהַשָּׁלוֹם שֶׁלּוֹ יָשִׂים עָלֵינוּ בְּרָכָה וְשָׁלוֹם, מִשְּׂמֹאל וּמִיָּמִין עַל יִשְׂרָאֵל שָׁלוֹם
הָרַחֲמָן הוּא יְבָרֵךְ אֶת עַמּוֹ בַשָּׁלוֹם
וְיִזְכּוּ לִרְאוֹת בָּנִים וּבְנֵי בָנִים, עוֹסְקִים, בַּתּוֹרָה וּבְמִצְוֹת, עַל יִשְׂרָאֵל שָׁלוֹם.
פֶּלֶא יוֹעֵץ אֵל גִּבּוֹר אֲבִי־עַד שַׂר־שָׁלוֹם: ישעיה ט

---

promised Avraham: “No matter what, I will be with you.” Throughout every *galut*, Hashem is with us.

I was in the British Museum in England a number of years ago, looking at an Egyptian exhibit. There was a sign that stated that these artifacts were crafted during the time that the Egyptians persecuted the Hebrews. I said

בָּרוּךְ אֵל עֶלְיוֹן Blessed is God Most High who has given us rest,
To relieve our souls from distress and pain.
May He seek the good of Zion, the outcast city.
How long must she grieve, her spirits downcast?

All who keep the Sabbath, man and woman alike,
find favor like an offering made to God.

He who rides the heavens, King of worlds,
Gently told His people to rest,
With tasty food and delicacies of all kinds,
With elegant dress, as at a family feast.

All who keep the Sabbath, man and woman alike,
find favor like an offering made to God.

Happy are all who await a double reward
From the One who sees all, though He dwells in dense dark.
He will grant him a heritage in hill and valley,
A heritage and resting place like [Jacob] on whom the sun shone.

All who keep the Sabbath, man and woman alike,
find favor like an offering made to God.

---

offers a sacrifice in the *Mikdash*, a feeling of newness and excitement. Similarly, every Shabbat is new, and we ought to feel the newness and excitement like that unique *korban*. Perhaps that is why the *korban minha* is referenced in the *zemer* in relation to Shabbat. In addition, that is why it refers to a young boy and girl; it highlights the youthful excitement one should experience on Shabbat. No two *Shabbatot* are the same. Each is special and unique.

ואשרי כל חוכה לתשלומי כפל – VEASHREI KOL HOKHEH LETASHLUMEI KHEFEL

Announcing Hashem's Providence in This World

"Happy are all who await a double reward." This seems to be referring to the double portion of *mann* that fell on Friday so that there would be adequate food for Shabbat. Rav Biderman, in his *birkon*, offers an alternate suggestion. The word *kefel* (double) reminds us of the double payment that a thief is to

pay his

בָּרוּךְ אֵל עֶלְיוֹן, אֲשֶׁר נָתַן מְנוּחָה לְנַפְשֵׁנוּ פִדְיוֹן מִשֵּׂאת וַאֲנָחָה
וְהוּא יִדְרֹשׁ לְצִיּוֹן, עִיר הַנִּדָּחָה עַד אָנָה תּוּגְיוֹן נֶפֶשׁ נֶאֱנָחָה.

הַשּׁוֹמֵר שַׁבָּת הַבֵּן עִם הַבַּת
לָאֵל יֵרָצוּ כְּמִנְחָה עַל מַחֲבַת.

רוֹכֵב בָּעֲרָבוֹת, מֶלֶךְ עוֹלָמִים אֶת עַמּוֹ לִשְׁבֹּת אִזֵּן בַּנְּעִימִים
בְּמַאֲכָלוֹת עֲרֵבוֹת בְּמִינֵי מַטְעַמִּים בְּמַלְבּוּשֵׁי כָבוֹד זֶבַח מִשְׁפָּחָה.

הַשּׁוֹמֵר שַׁבָּת הַבֵּן עִם הַבַּת
לָאֵל יֵרָצוּ כְּמִנְחָה עַל מַחֲבַת.

וְאַשְׁרֵי כָּל חוֹכֶה לְתַשְׁלוּמֵי כֵפֶל מֵאֵת כֹּל סוֹכֶה, שׁוֹכֵן בָּעֲרָפֶל
נַחֲלָה לוֹ יִזְכֶּה בָּהָר וּבַשָּׁפֶל נַחֲלָה וּמְנוּחָה כַּשֶּׁמֶשׁ לוֹ זָרְחָה.

הַשּׁוֹמֵר שַׁבָּת הַבֵּן עִם הַבַּת
לָאֵל יֵרָצוּ כְּמִנְחָה עַל מַחֲבַת.

ברוך א־ל עליון – BARUKH E-L ELYON

The Excitement of Every Shabbat

This *zemer* was written by Rav Barukh Ben Shmuel, one of the Baalei HaTosafot (whose name is alluded to in the acrostic in the *zemer*). After each stanza, we recite, "*Hashomer Shabbat haben im habat* – He who observes the Shabbat, the son with the daughter." If we are referring to men and women observing the Shabbat, why not state "man with wife" rather than "son with daughter"? Second, we say our observance of Shabbat will be like bringing a sacrifice of a *korban minha* on a pan: "*LaE-l yeiratzu keminha al mahavat.*" Why is the observance of Shabbat compared to a sacrifice?

The Sfat Emet (*Tzav* 5647/1887) says that the sacrifice offered by the *Kohen Gadol* every single day – *minhat havitin* – is the same sacrifice that a regular *kohen* offers the first time he performs the *avoda* (service) in the *Mikdash*. The *Kohen Gadol* brings the same sacrifice each day, while the regular *kohen* brings it only the first time he works in the *Mikdash*. Why is this so?

There is a special feeling one has the first time that one engages in something new. That is the feeling the *Kohen Gadol* is to experience each time he

Whoever keeps the Sabbath fully, not profaning it,
Shows that he is worthy; holy is his lot.
Happy is he who fulfills the day's duty;
It is like a gift presented to God who fashioned him.

All who keep the Sabbath, man and woman alike,
find favor like an offering made to God.

The Rock, my God, called it "Beloved of days."
Happy are the faithful if it is kept intact.
He will set on their head a close-fitting crown.
On them the Rock of Eternity will make His spirit rest.

All who keep the Sabbath, man and woman alike,
find favor like an offering made to God.

He who remembers the Sabbath day to keep it holy
Will gain high honor like a diadem on his head.
Therefore let each give to his soul
Delight and joy with which to be exalted.

All who keep the Sabbath, man and woman alike,
find favor like an offering made to God.

Let her be holy to you – Sabbath the queen –
Placing a blessing in your home.
In all your dwellings, do no work,
Nor your sons and daughters, your servant or maid.

All who keep the Sabbath, man and woman alike,
find favor like an offering made to God.

---

punishments." Rav Biderman suggests that if a thief is punished double for failing to recognize that God witnesses everything, then through our actions that portray God's presence, we will surely get a double reward. Individuals who observe the Shabbat and thereby testify to God's dominion despite His hidden nature – *shokhen baarafel* – will be rewarded double for the fulfillment and observance of Shabbat.

כָּל שׁוֹמֵר שַׁבָּת כַּדָּת מֵחַלְּלוֹ הֵן הֶכְשֵׁר חִבַּת קֹדֶשׁ גּוֹרָלוֹ
וְאִם יֵצֵא חוֹבַת הַיּוֹם, אַשְׁרֵי לוֹ אֶל אֵל אָדוֹן מְחוֹלְלוֹ מִנְחָה הִיא שְׁלוּחָה.

הַשּׁוֹמֵר שַׁבָּת הַבֵּן עִם הַבַּת
לָאֵל יֵרָצוּ כְּמִנְחָה עַל מַחֲבַת.

חֶמְדַּת הַיָּמִים קְרָאוֹ אֵלִי צוּר וְאַשְׁרֵי לִתְמִימִים אִם יִהְיֶה נָצוּר
כֶּתֶר הִלּוּמִים עַל רֹאשָׁם יָצוּר צוּר הָעוֹלָמִים, רוּחוֹ בָּם נָחָה.

הַשּׁוֹמֵר שַׁבָּת הַבֵּן עִם הַבַּת
לָאֵל יֵרָצוּ כְּמִנְחָה עַל מַחֲבַת.

זָכוֹר אֶת יוֹם הַשַּׁבָּת לְקַדְּשׁוֹ קַרְנוֹ כִּי גָבְהָה נֵזֶר עַל רֹאשׁוֹ
עַל כֵּן יִתֵּן הָאָדָם לְנַפְשׁוֹ עֹנֶג וְגַם שִׂמְחָה בָּהֶם לְמָשְׁחָה.

הַשּׁוֹמֵר שַׁבָּת הַבֵּן עִם הַבַּת
לָאֵל יֵרָצוּ כְּמִנְחָה עַל מַחֲבַת.

קֹדֶשׁ הִיא לָכֶם שַׁבָּת הַמַּלְכָּה אֶל תּוֹךְ בָּתֵּיכֶם לְהָנִיחַ בְּרָכָה
בְּכָל מוֹשְׁבוֹתֵיכֶם לֹא תַעֲשׂוּ מְלָאכָה בְּנֵיכֶם וּבְנוֹתֵיכֶם עֶבֶד וְגַם שִׁפְחָה.

הַשּׁוֹמֵר שַׁבָּת הַבֵּן עִם הַבַּת
לָאֵל יֵרָצוּ כְּמִנְחָה עַל מַחֲבַת.

---

pay his victim. The Gemara in Bava Kamma (79b) explains why a *ganav* pays double and a *gazlan* does not. The *ganav* pretends that God does not see him. He acts at night in fear of man, but he lacks fear of God, and he is therefore punished for his act more severely. The *gazlan* acts in the daytime and fears neither man nor God. Since he does not distinguish between the two, his punishment is less harsh.

"*Midda tova meruba mimiddat puranut* – God's rewards are greater than His

יוֹם זֶה מְכֻבָּד This day is honored above all others,
For on it He who formed worlds found rest.

For six days, do your work
But the seventh day is God's:
On the Sabbath you shall do no work,
For in six days He made all.

> This day is honored above all others,
> for on it He who formed worlds found rest.

Foremost among sacred days
Is this day of rest, this holy Sabbath.
So let each say Kiddush over wine,
And break bread over two complete loaves.

> This day is honored above all others,
> for on it He who formed worlds found rest.

Eat choice food, drink sweet wine,
For God will give to those who cleave to Him
Clothes to wear, due portions of bread,
Meat and fish, and all tasty foods.

> This day is honored above all others,
> for on it He who formed worlds found rest.

The siddur of the Gra (*Keter Rosh*) states that the Gemara and Zohar never argued. The Gra therefore resolves the apparent conflict in a very creative manner.

The Gemara in Shabbat (117b) tells us:

רבי זירא הוה בצע אכולה שירותיה.

R. Zeira would break off a piece that would suffice for his entire meal.

Rashi interprets this to mean that R. Zeira would cut large pieces of *halla* so that all those around the table would have a sufficient piece to eat.

The Gra cites the Rashba (Shabbat ibid.), who interprets the statement about R. Zeira to mean that he cut *both hallot* on Shabbat. If one cuts both

hallot

יוֹם זֶה מְכֻבָּד מִכָּל יָמִים, כִּי בוֹ שָׁבַת צוּר עוֹלָמִים.

שֵׁשֶׁת יָמִים תַּעֲשֶׂה מְלַאכְתֶּךָ
וְיוֹם הַשְּׁבִיעִי לֵאלֹהֶיךָ
שַׁבָּת לֹא תַעֲשֶׂה בוֹ מְלָאכָה
כִּי כֹל עָשָׂה שֵׁשֶׁת יָמִים.

יוֹם זֶה מְכֻבָּד מִכָּל יָמִים, כִּי בוֹ שָׁבַת צוּר עוֹלָמִים.

רִאשׁוֹן הוּא לְמִקְרָאֵי קֹדֶשׁ
יוֹם שַׁבָּתוֹן יוֹם שַׁבַּת קֹדֶשׁ
עַל כֵּן כָּל אִישׁ בְּיֵינוֹ יְקַדֵּשׁ
עַל שְׁתֵּי לֶחֶם יִבְצְעוּ תְמִימִים.

יוֹם זֶה מְכֻבָּד מִכָּל יָמִים, כִּי בוֹ שָׁבַת צוּר עוֹלָמִים.

אֱכֹל מַשְׁמַנִּים, שְׁתֵה מַמְתַּקִּים
כִּי אֵל יִתֵּן לְכֹל בּוֹ דְבֵקִים
בֶּגֶד לִלְבֹּשׁ, לֶחֶם חֻקִּים
בָּשָׂר וְדָגִים וְכָל מַטְעַמִּים.

יוֹם זֶה מְכֻבָּד מִכָּל יָמִים, כִּי בוֹ שָׁבַת צוּר עוֹלָמִים.

יום זה מכובד – YOM ZEH MEKHUBAD

על שתי לחם יבצעו תמימים – AL SHTEI LEHEM YIVTZE'U TEMIMIM

How Many Hallot Do We Cut?

"And break bread over two complete loaves." There seems to be a contradiction between the Gemara and a statement of the Ari z"l with respect to the number of *hallot* one needs to have on Shabbat. The Gemara (Shabbat 117b) says one should have two *hallot*, while the Ari z"l, based on the Zohar, posits that one must have twelve *hallot* (from the word *zeh*, which has a *gematria* of twelve).

On it you shall lack nothing – so eat,
Be satisfied and bless
The Lord your God, whom you love,
For He has blessed you from all peoples.

This day is honored above all others,
for on it He who formed worlds found rest.

The heavens declare His glory
And the earth is full of His loving-kindness.
See all these things His hand has made
For He is the Rock, His work is perfect.

This day is honored above all others,
for on it He who formed worlds found rest.

> love, praise, and glorify [Him], yearning with tremendous desire to know [God's] great name.

The Rambam explains that when one sees God's amazing creations and recognizes how awesome He is, it draws one closer to God.

However, in the next line, the Rambam states:

וכשמחשב בדברים האלו עצמן, מיד הוא נרתע לאחוריו, ויירא ויפחד וידע שהוא בריה קטנה שפלה אפלה.

> When he [continues] to reflect on these same matters, he will immediately recoil in awe and fear, appreciating how he is a tiny, lowly, and dark creature.

The Rambam says that when one looks at the world, he has two feelings, one of love and one of awe. At the same time that we are drawn to love and admire God, we take a step back in awe, recognizing how small we are in the universe.

This dual recognition is alluded to in this *zemer*: The heavens depict His *kavod*, awe, and the earth reveals His *hesed*, which we love and which causes us to be drawn to Him. Both are legitimate reactions to God's awesomeness.

לֹא תֶחְסַר כֹּל בּוֹ, וְאָכַלְתָּ
וְשָׂבַעְתָּ וּבֵרַכְתָּ
אֶת יהוה אֱלֹהֶיךָ אֲשֶׁר אָהַבְתָּ
כִּי בֵרַכְךָ מִכָּל הָעַמִּים.
יוֹם זֶה מְכֻבָּד מִכָּל יָמִים, כִּי בוֹ שָׁבַת צוּר עוֹלָמִים.

הַשָּׁמַיִם מְסַפְּרִים כְּבוֹדוֹ
וְגַם הָאָרֶץ מָלְאָה חַסְדּוֹ
רְאוּ כָּל אֵלֶּה עָשְׂתָה יָדוֹ
כִּי הוּא הַצּוּר פָּעֳלוֹ תָמִים.
יוֹם זֶה מְכֻבָּד מִכָּל יָמִים, כִּי בוֹ שָׁבַת צוּר עוֹלָמִים.

---

hallot at each meal, he will end up having cut six *hallot* in half, leaving him with twelve pieces of *halla*. What the Ari seemed to refer to was twelve parts that resulted from cutting each *halla* in half. That resolves the apparent conflict between the Gemera and the Zohar.

השמים מספרים כבודו וגם הארץ מלאה חסדו – HASHAMAYIM MESAPRIM KEVODO VEGAM HAARETZ MALA HASDO

To Fear and to Love

What is significance of the double language of the heavens and the earth essentially praising Hashem? Perhaps this is alluded to in the Rambam (*Hilkhot Yesodei HaTorah*, ch. 2), who states the following:

> והיאך היא הדרך לאהבתו ויראתו. בשעה שיתבונן האדם במעשיו וברואיו הנפלאים הגדולים ויראה מהן חכמתו שאין לה ערך ולא קץ, מיד הוא אוהב ומשבח ומפאר ומתאוה תאוה גדולה לידע השם הגדול.

> What is the path [to attain] love and fear of Him? When a person contemplates His wondrous and great deeds and creations and appreciates His infinite wisdom that surpasses all comparison, he will immediately

יוֹם שַׁבָּתוֹן The day of rest should not be forgotten,
Its memory is like sweet fragrance,
On it the dove found rest, And in it the exhausted rest.

This day is honored by the people of faith.
Parents and children guard it with care.
It was engraved on two tablets of stone,
By the greatness of His power and His unfailing strength.
On it the dove found rest, And in it the exhausted rest.

And out of the mist, the darkness shone,
And He lifted the dwellers in low places onto cloud,
And I shall see the tower of my tormentors fall,
But I shall be filled with strength.
On it the dove found rest, And in it the exhausted rest.

Tread on the shoes of enemies and tormentors,
And make the ankles of strangers stumble,
And then my people will answer You with songs,
O God who travels on the wings of the wind.
On it the dove found rest, And in it the exhausted rest.

All came together in a covenant: "We will do and we will obey," they said as one.
Then they responded, saying, "The Lord is One" –
Blessed is He who gives the weary strength.
On it the dove found rest, And in it the exhausted rest.

He spoke in His holiness on the Mount of Myrrh [Sinai]:
"Remember and observe the seventh day."
And learn together all His commands: Gird your loins and muster strength.
On it the dove found rest, And in it the exhausted rest.

---

declaration at Har Sinai, but with a significant difference. In *Parashat Yitro* (19:8), the nation uses the term "*naaseh* – we will fulfill." Yet in *Parashat Mishpatim* (24:7), the term used is "*naaseh venishma* – we will do and we will listen." In *Yitro* the word "*yahad*" (together) also appears, while it is absent in *Mishpatim*.

ויענו כל העם יחדו ויאמרו כל אשר דִבר ה' נעשה...

And all the people replied in unison and said, "All that Hashem has spoken we shall do!" (*Shemot* 19:8)

ויקח

יוֹם שַׁבָּתוֹן אֵין לִשְׁכֹּחַ, זִכְרוֹ כְּרֵיחַ הַנִּיחֹחַ
יוֹנָה מָצְאָה בוֹ מָנוֹחַ וְשָׁם יָנוּחוּ יְגִיעֵי כֹחַ.

הַיּוֹם נִכְבָּד לִבְנֵי אֱמוּנִים, זְהִירִים לְשָׁמְרוֹ אָבוֹת וּבָנִים
חָקוּק בִּשְׁנֵי לוּחוֹת אֲבָנִים, מֵרֹב אוֹנִים וְאַמִּיץ כֹּחַ.
יוֹנָה מָצְאָה בוֹ מָנוֹחַ וְשָׁם יָנוּחוּ יְגִיעֵי כֹחַ.

וּמִתּוֹךְ עֲרָפֶל הָאִיר אֹפֶל, וְעַל עָב, הָרִים יֹשְׁבֵי שֶׁפֶל
וּמִגְדָּל צָרֵי אֶרְאֶה נוֹפֵל, אַךְ אָנֹכִי מָלֵאתִי כֹחַ.
יוֹנָה מָצְאָה בוֹ מָנוֹחַ וְשָׁם יָנוּחוּ יְגִיעֵי כֹחַ.

דְּרֹךְ בַּנֶּעַל אוֹיְבִים וְצָרִים, וְגַם הַמֵּעֵד קַרְסֻלֵּי זָרִים
וְאָז יַעֲנוּ לְךָ עַמִּי, בְּשִׁירִים, אֵל, הַמְהַלֵּךְ עַל כַּנְפֵי רוּחַ.
יוֹנָה מָצְאָה בוֹ מָנוֹחַ וְשָׁם יָנוּחוּ יְגִיעֵי כֹחַ.

וּבָאוּ כֻלָּם בִּבְרִית יַחַד, נַעֲשֶׂה וְנִשְׁמַע אָמְרוּ כְּאֶחָד
וּפָתְחוּ וְעָנוּ יהוה אֶחָד, בָּרוּךְ נֹתֵן לַיָּעֵף כֹּחַ.
יוֹנָה מָצְאָה בוֹ מָנוֹחַ וְשָׁם יָנוּחוּ יְגִיעֵי כֹחַ.

דִּבֶּר בְּקָדְשׁוֹ בְּהַר הַמֹּר, יוֹם הַשְּׁבִיעִי זָכוֹר וְשָׁמוֹר
וְכָל פִּקּוּדָיו יַחַד לִגְמֹר, חַזֵּק מָתְנַיִם וְאַמֵּץ כֹּחַ.
יוֹנָה מָצְאָה בוֹ מָנוֹחַ וְשָׁם יָנוּחוּ יְגִיעֵי כֹחַ.

יום שבתון – YOM SHABBATON

וכל פיקודיו יחד לגמור – VEKHOL PEKUDAV YAHAD LIGMOR

Everyone is a Partner in Torah

The *zemer* of *Yom Shabbaton* was composed by Rabbi Yehuda HaLevi, the author of the *Kuzari* as well as several *piyyutim* that are recited throughout the year. It talks about Har Sinai and states that the Torah was given on Shabbat. The mitzva of Shabbat is included on the *luhot* as well.

What is the meaning of the phrase "*Vekhol pekudav yahad ligmor* – And learn together all its commands"? It could be a reference to the observance of Shabbat, as the previous line references *zakhor veshamor,* symbolizing the positive and negative commandments associated with Shabbat.

Perhaps we can offer another interpretation based on the Meshekh Hokhma in *Shemot* (19:8). There are two similar *pesukim* describing our

The people who have wandered like a straying flock –
May He remember the covenant and the oath,
So that no harm should happen to them, As You swore at the end of
Noaḥ's flood.
On it the dove found rest, And in it the exhausted rest.

Maybe "*Naaseh venishma amru k'ehad*" is referring to the second method, while "*vekhol pekudav yahad ligmor*" is referring to the first method. Embedded in this *zemer* are the ways in which one can fulfill *kol haTorah kula*.

מי נח – MEI NOAH

Never Give Up

Why was the rainbow chosen as the symbol to teach Noah that there will be no future flood like the one that previously destroyed the world? Rav Meir Shapiro explains this with another question: How is it that during the more than one hundred years that it took to build the ark, Noah was unable to influence even one individual to do *teshuva*?

Apparently, Noah's heart was not in the task. He had given up on the people of his generation. When a *rebbi* (teacher) does not have faith in his students, they will certainly not succeed. The rainbow is a bright burst of color on an otherwise dreary, rainy day. It is symbolic of *not* giving up on others, no matter how dark the situation may seem. Out of the darkest, bleakest point in nature comes the most beautiful array of color. If we keep trying, we might be able to suddenly see our influence on our students and witness them beginning to shine. We need to believe in them and encourage them to expose their true colors. That is the symbolism of a rainbow.

הָעָם אֲשֶׁר נָע, כַּצֹּאן תָּעָה, יִזְכֹּר לְפָקְדוֹ בְּרִית וּשְׁבוּעָה
לְבַל יַעֲבָר בָּם מִקְרֵה רָעָה, כַּאֲשֶׁר נִשְׁבַּעְתָּ עַל מֵי נֹחַ.
יוֹנָה מָצְאָה בוֹ מָנוֹחַ וְשָׁם יָנוּחוּ יְגִיעֵי כֹחַ.

ויקח ספר הברית ויקרא באזני העם ויאמרו כל אשר דִבר ה׳ נעשה ונשמע.

> And he took the Book of the Covenant and read it within the hearing of the people, and they said, "All that Hashem spoke we will do and we will hear." (*Shemot* 24:7)

How are we to understand the discrepancies between these two *pesukim*, which describe the same event? The Meshekh Hokhma explains as follows. How is it possible for a single individual to fulfill all of the mitzvot? Some are only relevant for a Kohen, some only for a king, and others limited in their scope. There are two manners in which to fulfill all of the mitzvot:

1. If everyone performs the mitzvot applicable to them – he does what he is supposed to do and she does what she is supposed to do – then together as a unit, *yahad ligmor*, we can fulfill all of the taryag mitzvot. That is why in *Yitro* there is the addition of "*yahdav*" referring to collectively fulfilling the mitzvot.
2. When one learns about those mitzvot that he cannot pesonally fulfill, it is as if he has fulfilled those mitzvot. That is why there is no "*yahdav*" when *Am Yisrael* state "*Naaseh venishma*" – we will fulfill what we can, and we will listen and learn about those mitzvot that we cannot personally observe.

שַׁבָּת הַיּוֹם Today is the Sabbath of the LORD.
Celebrate greatly with my songs,
Multiply my delicacies,
Keep it like the LORD's command.
Today is the Sabbath of the LORD.

Do not travel beyond boundaries,
Do not labor on this day:
Eat, drink, make merry.
This is the day the LORD has made.
Today is the Sabbath of the LORD.

If you keep it God will guard you like the pupil of His eye,
You, your son and daughter too.
If you call the Sabbath a delight
Then you will find delight before the LORD.
Today is the Sabbath of the LORD.

Eat rich foods and delicacies,
Tasty dishes of many kinds,
Soft-shelled nuts and pomegranates:
Eat, be satisfied and bless the LORD.
Today is the Sabbath of the LORD.

Make ready on the table delicious bread,
And make, this day, three meals.
Bless and thank His glorious name.
Take care, observe and do, my sons.
Today is the Sabbath of the LORD.

שַׁבָּת הַיּוֹם לַיהוה
מְאֹד צַהֲלוּ בְּרִנּוּנַי
וְגַם הַרְבּוּ מַעֲדָנַי
אוֹתוֹ לִשְׁמֹר כְּמִצְוַת יהוה.
שַׁבָּת הַיּוֹם לַיהוה.

מֵעֲבֹר דֶּרֶךְ וּגְבוּלִים
מֵעֲשׂוֹת הַיּוֹם פְּעָלִים
לֶאֱכֹל וְלִשְׁתּוֹת בְּהִלּוּלִים
זֶה הַיּוֹם עָשָׂה יהוה.
שַׁבָּת הַיּוֹם לַיהוה.

וְאִם תִּשְׁמְרֶנּוּ
יָהּ יִנְצָרְךָ כְּבָבַת
אַתָּה וּבִנְךָ וְגַם הַבַּת
וְקָרָאתָ עֹנֶג לַשַּׁבָּת
אָז תִּתְעַנַּג עַל יהוה.
שַׁבָּת הַיּוֹם לַיהוה.

אֱכֹל מַשְׁמַנִּים וּמַעֲדַנִּים
וּמַטְעַמִּים הַרְבֵּה מִינִים
אֱגוֹזֵי פֶרֶךְ וְרִמּוֹנִים
וְאָכַלְתָּ וְשָׂבָעְתָּ וּבֵרַכְתָּ אֶת יהוה.
שַׁבָּת הַיּוֹם לַיהוה.

לַעֲרֹךְ בְּשֻׁלְחָן לֶחֶם חֲמוּדוֹת
לַעֲשׂוֹת הַיּוֹם שָׁלֹשׁ סְעוּדוֹת
אֶת הַשֵּׁם הַנִּכְבָּד לְבָרֵךְ וּלְהוֹדוֹת
שִׁקְדוּ וְשִׁמְרוּ וַעֲשׂוּ בָנַי.
שַׁבָּת הַיּוֹם לַיהוה.

שִׁמְרוּ שַׁבְּתוֹתַי Observe My Sabbaths,
so that you are nourished and sated,
From the radiance of My blessings,
when you come to rest.
Borrow on My account, My children,
Delight in My pleasures:
Today is the Sabbath of the LORD.

Borrow on My account, My children,
Delight in My pleasures:
Today is the Sabbath of the LORD.

Proclaim freedom from toil,
then I will grant My blessing,
joining one to the next,
bringing gladness on My day of joy.
Wear clothes of fine linen and wool.
And learn from My elders:
Today is the Sabbath of the LORD.

Borrow on My account, My children,
Delight in My pleasures:
Today is the Sabbath of the LORD.

Quickly bring the portion,
obey Esther's command.
Make a reckoning with the Creator,
He will repay you for the food, and more.
Trust in Me, My faithful ones,
And drink wine from My plentiful supply.
Today is the Sabbath of the LORD.

Borrow on My account, My children,
Delight in My pleasures:
Today is the Sabbath of the LORD.

What is the connection between observing Shabbat and the redemption? The Gemara (Shabbat 118b) states that the *geula* will come if all the Jews observe two *Shabbatot* (according to some manuscripts, one Shabbat). Why

is specifically

שִׁמְרוּ שַׁבְּתוֹתַי
לְמַעַן תִּינְקוּ וּשְׂבַעְתֶּם
מִזִּיו בִּרְכוֹתַי
אֶל הַמְּנוּחָה כִּי בָאתֶם
וּלְווּ עָלַי בָּנַי
וְעִדְנוּ מַעֲדָנַי שַׁבָּת הַיּוֹם לַיהוה.

וּלְווּ עָלַי בָּנַי, וְעִדְנוּ מַעֲדָנַי, שַׁבָּת הַיּוֹם לַיהוה.

לְעָמֵל קִרְאוּ דְרוֹר
וְנָתַתִּי אֶת בִּרְכָתִי
אִשָּׁה אֶל אֲחוֹתָהּ לִצְרֹר
לְגַלּוֹת עַל יוֹם שִׂמְחָתִי
בִּגְדֵי שֵׁשׁ עִם שָׁנִי
וְהִתְבּוֹנְנוּ מִזְּקֵנַי שַׁבָּת הַיּוֹם לַיהוה.

וּלְווּ עָלַי בָּנַי, וְעִדְנוּ מַעֲדָנַי, שַׁבָּת הַיּוֹם לַיהוה.

מַהֲרוּ אֶת הַמָּנֶה
לַעֲשׂוֹת אֶת דְּבַר אֶסְתֵּר
וְחִשְׁבוּ עִם הַקּוֹנֶה
לְשַׁלֵּם אָכוֹל וְהוֹתֵר
בִּטְחוּ בִי אֱמוּנַי
וּשְׁתוּ יֵין מִשְׁמַנַּי שַׁבָּת הַיּוֹם לַיהוה.

וּלְווּ עָלַי בָּנַי, וְעִדְנוּ מַעֲדָנַי, שַׁבָּת הַיּוֹם לַיהוה.

שמרו שבתותי – SHIMRU SHABBTOTAI

Shabbat and the Geula

"*Hinei yom geula yom Shabbat im tishmoru* – Today is a day of redemption, if you observe the Shabbat."

Today is a day of redemption,
if you observe the Sabbath;
Then you will be My special treasure.
Stay [for the night of exile], then pass on.
Then you will live before Me.
And be filled from My hidden store.
Today is the Sabbath of the LORD.

Borrow on My account, My children,
Delight in My pleasures:
Today is the Sabbath of the LORD.

Make my city strong,
God, the God most high.
Bring back my Temple,
With joy and words of song.
There may my singers chant,
My Levites and my priests.
Then you will delight in the LORD.
Today is the Sabbath of the LORD.

Borrow on My account, My children,
Delight in My pleasures:
Today is the Sabbath of the LORD.

---

beShabbat – One who prepares on Erev Shabbat will be able to eat on Shabbat" (Avoda Zara 3a). If all the Jews observe Shabbat, that means they prepared in advance. In a similar vein, this whole world is preparation for the World to Come. If the message of preparation is understood and fulfilled, we will be worthy of the *geula*.

כי אשמרה

הִנֵּה יוֹם גְּאֻלָּה
יוֹם שַׁבָּת אִם תִּשְׁמֹרוּ
וִהְיִיתֶם לִי סְגֻלָּה
לִינוּ וְאַחַר תַּעֲבֹרוּ
וְאָז תִּחְיוּ לְפָנַי
וּתְמַלְאוּ צְפוּנַי שַׁבָּת הַיּוֹם לַיהוה.

וּלְווּ עָלַי בָּנַי, וְעִדְנוּ מַעֲדָנַי, שַׁבָּת הַיּוֹם לַיהוה.

חֲזֵק קִרְיָתִי
אֵל אֱלֹהִים עֶלְיוֹן
וְהָשֵׁב אֶת נָוָתִי
בְּשִׂמְחָה וּבְהִגָּיוֹן
יְשׁוֹרְרוּ שָׁם רְנָנַי
לְוִיַּי וְכֹהֲנַי
אָז תִּתְעַנַּג עַל יהוה שַׁבָּת הַיּוֹם לַיהוה.

וּלְווּ עָלַי בָּנַי, וְעִדְנוּ מַעֲדָנַי, שַׁבָּת הַיּוֹם לַיהוה.

---

is specifically observing Shabbat equated with bringing the *geula*? Why not observing the laws of *kashrut* or *mezuza*? What is the unique connection between Shabbbat and the *geula*?

Rav Aryeh Kaplan, in his *sefer* on Shabbat, explains that Shabbat is about preparation. The Gemara states, "*Mi shetarah b'erev Shabbat yokhal*

כִּי אֶשְׁמְרָה If I keep the Sabbath, God will keep me,
It is an eternal sign between God and me.
It is an eternal sign between God and me.

It is forbidden to engage in business or to travel,
Even to speak about the things we need,
or about matters of trade or state.
Instead I will study God's Torah and it will make me wise.
It is an eternal sign between God and me.

On it I always find refreshment for my soul.
See: My Holy One gave the first generation,
A sign, by giving them a double portion on the sixth day.
So may my food be doubled every sixth day!
It is an eternal sign between God and me.

Torah we fulfill the mitzva of engaging in Torah study. The Rambam adds (*Sefer HaMitzvot* 3) that it is also a fulfillment of loving God. We learn to be close to Him.

The Ramban (*Shemot* 20:8) suggests a third facet of learning Torah on Shabbat. Shabbat is a day to provide *oneg* to our souls and to engage in the study of Torah:

> והטעם, שתהא השביתה בעינינו בעבור שהוא יום קדוש, להפנות בו מעסקי המחשבות והבלי הזמנים, ולתת בו עונג לנפשנו בדרכי ה׳, וללכת אל החכמים ואל הנביאים לשמוע דברי ה׳.
>
> And the reason is that the rest should be in our eyes because it is a holy day, to turn away on it from involvement in our plans and the vanities of the time, and to provide pleasure to our souls in the ways of God, and to go to the sages and the prophets to hear the words of God.

Based on the Ramban, Rav Soloveitchik claims that learning on Shabbat is a fulfillment of *zekhor et yom haShabbat lekadsho*. The Zohar (cited in *Mishna Berura* 290:3) states that when our *neshama yeteira* goes back to heaven, it is asked, "What *hiddushim* (new words of Torah) did you hear in that world?" Therefore, it is essential that we engage in Torah study on Shabbat.

כִּי אֶשְׁמְרָה שַׁבָּת אֵל יִשְׁמְרֵנִי.
אוֹת הִיא לְעוֹלְמֵי עַד בֵּינוֹ וּבֵינִי.
אוֹת הִיא לְעוֹלְמֵי עַד בֵּינוֹ וּבֵינִי.

אָסוּר מְצֹא חֵפֶץ, עֲשׂוֹת דְּרָכִים
גַּם מִלְּדַבֵּר בּוֹ דִּבְרֵי צְרָכִים
דִּבְרֵי סְחוֹרָה אַף דִּבְרֵי מְלָכִים
אֶהְגֶּה בְּתוֹרַת אֵל וּתְחַכְּמֵנִי.
אוֹת הִיא לְעוֹלְמֵי עַד בֵּינוֹ וּבֵינִי.

בּוֹ אֶמְצָא תָמִיד נֹפֶשׁ לְנַפְשִׁי
הִנֵּה לְדוֹר רִאשׁוֹן נָתַן קְדוֹשִׁי
מוֹפֵת, בְּתֵת לֶחֶם מִשְׁנֶה בַּשִּׁשִּׁי
כָּכָה בְּכָל שִׁשִּׁי יַכְפִּיל מְזוֹנִי.
אוֹת הִיא לְעוֹלְמֵי עַד בֵּינוֹ וּבֵינִי.

כי אשמרה שבת א־ל ישמרני – KI ESHMERA SHABBAT E-L YISHMEREINI

אהגה בתורת א־ל ותחכמני – EGHEH BETORAT E-L UTEHAKMEINI

Engaging in Torah Study on Shabbat

This *zemer* was written by the Rav Avraham Ibn Ezra, one of the *Rishonim*. The first word of each stanza begins with the letters that form his name.

The chorus is *Ot hi l'olmei ad* – Shabbat is an *ot* (eternal sign) between *Am Yisrael* and Hashem. The Hafetz Hayim (*Al HaTorah, Parashat Ki Tisa*; and *Mishna Berura*, introduction to *helek* 3) offers a *mashal* to explain the term "*ot.*" When a shoemaker has a store, there is a sign above the door with the name of the store. The sign remains there even when the store is closed. Once the sign is removed, we know the store is no longer there. Similarly, when someone is *shomer Shabbat*, they are identified as observant Jews, as *ovdei Hashem*. If we observe Shabbat, then we are known as *shomer Shabbat* Jews even during the week. It is a part of our identity. That is the symbol of Shabbat – it reflects our connection to Hashem on all days of the week. It is an *ot*.

Learning Torah on Shabbat has an added element. Usually, when we learn

Engraved in God's law is His priests' decree,
To prepare the Show-Bread in His presence.
So, His sages ruled, on it fasting is forbidden,
except on sins' Atonement Day.
It is an eternal sign between God and me.

It is a day of honor, a day of delight,
with bread and fine wine, meat and fish.
On it those who mourn are turned around,
For it is a joyous day and it will bring me joy.
It is an eternal sign between God and me.

Those who desecrate it by working will, in the end, be cut off.
Therefore I cleanse my heart with it as if with soap.
Evening and morning I will pray to God,
Additional and afternoon prayer also, and He will answer me.
It is an eternal sign between God and me.

רָשַׁם בְּדָת הָאֵל חֹק אֶל סְגָנָיו
בּוֹ לַעֲרֹךְ לֶחֶם פָּנִים בְּפָנָיו
עַל כֵּן לְהִתְעַנּוֹת בּוֹ עַל פִּי נְבוֹנָיו
אָסוּר, לְבַד מִיּוֹם כִּפּוּר עֲוֹנִי.
אוֹת הִיא לְעוֹלְמֵי עַד בֵּינוֹ וּבֵינִי.

הוּא יוֹם מְכֻבָּד, הוּא יוֹם תַּעֲנוּגִים
לֶחֶם וְיַיִן טוֹב, בָּשָׂר וְדָגִים
הַמִּתְאַבְּלִים בּוֹ אָחוֹר נְסוֹגִים
כִּי יוֹם שְׂמָחוֹת הוּא וּתְשַׂמְּחֵנִי.
אוֹת הִיא לְעוֹלְמֵי עַד בֵּינוֹ וּבֵינִי.

מֵחֵל מְלָאכָה בּוֹ סוֹפוֹ לְהַכְרִית
עַל כֵּן אֲכַבֵּס בּוֹ לִבִּי כְּבוֹרִית
וְאֶתְפַּלְלָה אֶל אֵל עַרְבִית וְשַׁחְרִית
מוּסָף וְגַם מִנְחָה הוּא יַעֲנֵנִי.
אוֹת הִיא לְעוֹלְמֵי עַד בֵּינוֹ וּבֵינִי.

דְּרוֹר יִקְרָא God proclaims freedom to boy and girl,
And guards you like the pupil of His eye.
Your name is pleasant, never will it cease.
Rest and be at ease on the Sabbath day.

Seek my Temple and my hall,
And show me a sign of salvation.
Plant a shoot in my vineyard.
Hear the cry of my people.

Tread the winepress in Botzra,
And in Babylon which overpowered.
Crush my foes in anger and wrath,
Hear my voice on the day I cry.

God, let there be on the desert mountain,
Myrtle, acacia, cypress and box tree.
To one who warns and one who is warned,
Let peace flow like river waters.

---

didn't understand what scared them off. The Gra explained that it was because he was wearing *tefillin*, as the Gemara (Berakhot 6a) states:

"וראו כל עמי הארץ כי שם ה' נקרא עליך ויראו ממך" ותניא ר' אליעזר הגדול אומר, אלו תפילין שבראש.

> "The nations of the world will see God's name upon you." R. Eliezer HaGadol said: That refers to seeing the *tefillin* that is placed on one's head.

The nations will fear us when they see our *tefillin*. The *talmidim* responded, "But we too were wearing *tefillin*, and that did not scare off the enemy." The Gra explained that R. Eliezer does not refer to "*tefillin al harosh*" but rather "*tefillin shebarosh*" – *tefillin* in the head, not on the head. One must be a person who lives his life in accordance with the word of God, one who totally internalizes the mitzvot. Only then will the nations be in awe of us.

In a

דְּרוֹר יִקְרָא לְבֵן עִם בַּת
וְיִנְצָרְכֶם כְּמוֹ בָבַת
נְעִים שִׁמְכֶם וְלֹא יֻשְׁבַּת
שְׁבוּ נוּחוּ בְּיוֹם שַׁבָּת

דְּרֹשׁ נָוִי וְאוּלַמִּי
וְאוֹת יֶשַׁע עֲשֵׂה עִמִּי
נְטַע שׂוֹרֵק בְּתוֹךְ כַּרְמִי
שְׁעֵה שַׁוְעַת בְּנֵי עַמִּי.

דְּרֹךְ פּוּרָה בְּתוֹךְ בָּצְרָה
וְגַם בָּבֶל אֲשֶׁר גָּבְרָה
נְתֹץ צָרַי בְּאַף עֶבְרָה
שְׁמַע קוֹלִי בְּיוֹם אֶקְרָא.

אֱלֹהִים תֵּן בְּמִדְבָּר הָר
הֲדַס שִׁטָּה בְּרוֹשׁ תִּדְהָר
וְלַמַּזְהִיר וְלַנִּזְהָר
שְׁלוֹמִים תֵּן כְּמֵי נָהָר.

דרור יקרא – DROR YIKRA

Internalizing the Torah

This is one of the oldest *zemirot* that we have. It was written by Dunush Ben Labrat, one of the *Ge'onim* who lived in the 900s. He was a *talmid* and nephew of Rav Saadia Gaon, and he is also quoted by Rashi. His name is spelled out in certain stanzas (first, second, third, and the last stanza). The *zemer* is about *davening* to Hashem and asking for peace.

"*Ne'im shimkhem velo yushbat* – Your name is pleasant, never will it cease." In other words, one who observes Shabbat will have a good reputation. What is the connection between observing Shabbat and a good reputation?

A story is told about the Gra: His enemies ran into his room intending to ransack the place, but when they saw the Gra they retreated. His students

Crush those who rise against me, zealous God,
Melting their heart with grief.
Then we will open and fill our mouths,
And tongues with songs of joy to You.

Know what is wisdom for your soul,
And it will be a crown for your head.
Keep your Holy One's command,
Observe your holy Sabbath day.

Birkat HaMazon can be found on page 149.

(thirty matzot and ten loaves of bread). No other *korban shelamim* is accompanied by so many additional breads. At the same time, the *korban toda* has the shortest window in which to be eaten – only until the next morning, unlike other *korbanot shelamim,* which can be eaten over the course of two days and the night in between. When it comes to a *korban toda,* there is so much to consume in such a short period. This highlights the need to publicize it, inviting others to share in the occasion to spread one's appreciation of Hashem. Similarly, in this *zemer,* we ask Him to knock down our enemies, and then we will tell everyone how awesome are the ways of *HaKadosh Barukh Hu. VeNarhiv peh* – we will spread the word!

הֲדֹךְ קָמַי, אֵל קַנָּא
בְּמוֹג לֵבָב וּבִמְגִנָּה
וְנַרְחִיב פֶּה וּנְמַלְאֶנָּה
לְשׁוֹנֵנוּ לְךָ רִנָּה.

דְּעֵה חָכְמָה לְנַפְשֶׁךָ
וְהִיא כֶתֶר לְרֹאשֶׁךָ
נְצֹר מִצְוַת קְדוֹשֶׁךָ
שְׁמֹר שַׁבַּת קָדְשֶׁךָ.

ברכת המזון *can be found on page 149.*

In a similar manner, we are to live our lives based on the message of Shabbat – that everything comes from Hashem. If one lives a *shomer Shabbat* life, his reputation will proceed him. His *emuna* and *bitahon* will be reflected and admired by others.

ונרחיב פה ונמלאנה – VENARHIV PEH UNEMALENA

Spreading the Word

We ask Hashem to destroy our enemies, saying that then we will share the good news with many others. This might hint to the Netziv's explanation of a *korban toda* (*Vayikra* 7:15). The *korban toda* is brought with forty loaves

סעודה שלישית
SEUDA SHELISHIT

SEUDA SHELISHIT

Why do we colloquially refer to this meal as "*shalosh seudos*" (three meals), given that it is actually a single meal? The Hida explains that the first two Shabbat meals are eaten when we are hungry, but we often squeeze in the third meal, as we are not so hungry at that time. We refer to it as "*shalosh seudos*" to highlight that just as this meal is being conducted as a fulfillment of the mitzva to have three meals, so too the previous two meals are viewed as a fulfillment of an obligation and not just as meals consumed out of necessity. It was all performed *leshem Shamayim*. The Gemara in Shabbat (118) cites R. Yossi, who stated that his portion should be shared with those who partake in *seuda shelishit*, as it is challenging. Truth be told, we know in advance that we are going to eat the third meal, so we should pace ourselves accordingly and eat a little less for lunch so that we have an appetite for *seuda shelishit*.

The Zohar refers to the time of *seuda shelishit* as *raava deraavin, ratzon shel ratzon*. Hashem has a tremendous *ratzon* (will) at this time. Where does it come from? The Bnei Yissakhar (*Maamarei Shabbatot* 8:22) explains that right before the creation of the world, Hashem had a great will to create the world. The will to create the world occurred prior to the first day of creation (Sunday), which means it essentially was late on what would have been the previous day (Shabbat). That *ratzon* returns each week close to Motza'ei Shabbat. It is why we desire to extend Shabbat.

Rav Yosef Dov Soloveitchik tells a story from his childhood: One Shabbat, he was at a certain *shteibel*. He asked Yankele the porter (whom he did not recognize in his distinguished Shabbat *kapata*), "What time will Shabbat be over?" Yankele replied, "Do you miss weekdays so much that you are eager to dismiss Shabbat?" The members of the *shteibel* extended Shabbat because of their love for the day. We ought to appreciate this special time as we usher out the Shabbat, taking care to do so in an honorable manner.

Zemirot for Seuda Shelishit

אַתְקִינוּ Prepare the feast of perfect faith, joy of the holy King.
Prepare the Royal feast,
this is the feast [mystically known as] "the Small Face,"
and "the Holy Ancient One" and "the Field of Holy Apples" [mystical terms for aspects of the Divine] come to partake in the feast with it.

Children of the palace
who yearn to see the radiance of "the Small Face,"
be here at this table in which the King is engraved.
Long to join this gathering together with the winged angels.
Rejoice now at this time of favor when there is no displeasure.
Come close to me, see my strength, for there are no harsh judgments:
Those brazen dogs are outside, unable to enter.
So I invite the holy Ancient of Days, His brow of desire
as the moment fades,
And His will is revealed, to annul all forces of impurity.
Hurl them into the abyss, hide them in the clefts of rocks,
For now, at Minḥa-time, is a time of joy for "the Small Face."

מִזְמוֹר לְדָוִד A psalm of David. *Ps. 23*
The Lord is my Shepherd, I shall not want.
He makes me lie down in green pastures.
He leads me beside the still waters.
He refreshes my soul.
He guides me in the paths of righteousness
for His name's sake.
Though I walk through the valley of the shadow of death,
I will fear no evil, for You are with me;
Your rod and Your staff, they comfort me.

---

shepherd merely walks around with his stick all day. He may have time for contemplation, but it is certainly not the most illustrious profession. Yet, as we know, many of our great ancestors were shepherds: Moshe, Dovid, our *avot*. A shepherd is not special job, and yet Dovid HaMelekh refers to Hashem as a shepherd. What, then, is its significance?

In *Parashat*

זמירות לסעודה שלישית

אַתְקִינוּ סְעוּדְתָא דִמְהֵימְנוּתָא שְׁלִימְתָא, חֶדְוָתָא דְמַלְכָּא קַדִּישָׁא.
אַתְקִינוּ סְעוּדְתָא דְמַלְכָּא.
דָּא הִיא סְעוּדְתָא דִזְעֵיר אַנְפִּין
וְעַתִּיקָא קַדִּישָׁא וַחֲקַל תַּפּוּחִין קַדִּישִׁין אָתַיִן לְסַעֲדָה בַּהֲדֵהּ.

בְּנֵי הֵיכְלָא, דִּכְסִיפִין לְמֶחֱזֵי זִיו זְעֵיר אַנְפִּין
יְהוֹן הָכָא, בְּהַאי תַּכָּא, דְּבֵהּ מַלְכָּא בְּגִלּוּפִין.
צְבוּ לַחֲדָא, בְּהַאי וַעֲדָא, בְּגוֹ עִירִין וְכָל גַּדְפִין.
חֲדוּ הַשְׁתָּא, בְּהַאי שַׁעְתָּא, דְּבֵהּ רַעֲוָא וְלֵית זַעְפִין.
קְרִיבוּ לִי, חֲזוּ חֵילִי, דְּלֵית דִּינִין דְּתַקִּיפִין.
לְבַר נָטְלִין, וְלָא עָלִין, הָנֵי כַּלְבִּין דַּחֲצִיפִין.
וְהָא אַזְמִין עַתִּיק יוֹמִין, לְמִצְחֵהּ עַד יְהוֹן חָלְפִין.
רְעוּ דִי לֵהּ, דְּגַלֵּי לֵהּ, לְבַטָּלָה בְּכָל קְלִיפִין.
יְשַׁוֵּי לוֹן, בְּנָקְבֵּהוֹן, וְיִטַמְרוּן בְּגוֹ כֵּפִין.
אֲרֵי הַשְׁתָּא, בְּמִנְחֲתָא, בְּחֶדְוָתָא דִזְעֵיר אַנְפִּין.

מִזְמוֹר לְדָוִד

תהלים כג

יהוה רֹעִי לֹא אֶחְסָר:
בִּנְאוֹת דֶּשֶׁא יַרְבִּיצֵנִי, עַל־מֵי מְנֻחוֹת יְנַהֲלֵנִי:
נַפְשִׁי יְשׁוֹבֵב, יַנְחֵנִי בְמַעְגְּלֵי־צֶדֶק לְמַעַן שְׁמוֹ:
גַּם כִּי־אֵלֵךְ בְּגֵיא צַלְמָוֶת לֹא־אִירָא רָע
כִּי־אַתָּה עִמָּדִי, שִׁבְטְךָ וּמִשְׁעַנְתֶּךָ הֵמָּה יְנַחֲמֻנִי:

מזמור לדוד ה׳ רועי – MIZMOR LEDOVID HASHEM RO'I

God is My Shepherd

Dovid refers to Hashem as a shepherd. In the *Yalkut Shimoni*, Rabbi Hama bar Hanina comments that there is no lower profession than a shepherd. A

You set a table before me in the presence of my enemies;
You anoint my head with oil; my cup is filled to overflowing.
May goodness and kindness follow me all the days of my life,
and may I live in the House of the LORD for evermore.

---

who follow their shepherd blindly, we have faith in Hashem and follow His path unequivocally.

שבטך ומשענתך המה ינחמוני – SHIVTEKHA UMISHANTEKHA HEMA YENAHAMUNI

"*Shivtetkha*" is a reference to the rod that a shepherd uses to hit the sheep to get them back in line. "*Mishantekha*" is a support. Why are both called comforting here? Getting hit by a rod can hurt. How is that comforting?

We recognize that *HaKadosh Barukh Hu* is always acting, at times behind the scenes. The *Sefer HaHinukh* (241) discusses the prohibition of taking revenge. Isn't it natural to want revenge? How is it possible to control oneself in such a situation? He explains that in life, we are both objects and subjects. We are subjects who make decisions, using our free choice to shape our religious personality. But we are also objects to factors out of our control. What happens to us was meant to happen. Any other person involved was just a pawn in the hand of God. Thus, we have to use our *behira hofshit* to withstand the temptation to take revenge, as after all, it was meant to happen.

We see a beautiful example of this in the story of Yosef and his brothers. Yosef tells his brothers not to worry about what happened between them. Hashem sent him to Mitzrayim through their actions, and so he has no authority to take revenge. Did Yosef just whitewash the entire course of events? Did the brothers actually perform a mitzva by selling him? Of course not! Yosef was simply expressing that as subjects, they are responsible for their actions and will be dealt with by Hashem. However, as an object, Yosef recognizes that their behavior was orchestrated from above. As such, he has no right to take revenge.

Even if I experience challenges and I feel like a rod is hitting me, I recognize that it has a greater purpose, and that is comforting. As Shabbat is coming to a close, we reflect upon these *pesukim* of *emuna* to strengthen us as we transition to a new week.

ידיד

תַּעֲרֹךְ לְפָנַי שֻׁלְחָן נֶגֶד צֹרְרָי
דִּשַּׁנְתָּ בַשֶּׁמֶן רֹאשִׁי, כּוֹסִי רְוָיָה:
אַךְ טוֹב וָחֶסֶד יִרְדְּפוּנִי כָּל־יְמֵי חַיָּי
וְשַׁבְתִּי בְּבֵית־יהוה לְאֹרֶךְ יָמִים:

In *Parashat Vayigash,* when Yaakov meets Pharaoh, the ruler inquires as to Yaakov's age. Yaakov responds:

ויאמר יעקב אל פרעה ימי שני מגורי שלשים ומאת שנה. מעט ורעים היו ימי שני חיי.

I am one hundred and thirty years old and I have had a short and bad life.

What exactly was Pharaoh asking? Is it polite to ask someone their age? In addition, how does Yaakov respond – by saying that he's had a rough life? No one can dispute the fact that Yaakov had a difficult life, but what exactly did he mean by his answer?

The word "*raa*" (bad) and the word "*ro'eh*" (shepherd) are spelled similarly. Rav Matisyahu Salomon (*Matnat Hayim, maamarim,* p. 79), answers our questions utilizing the similarity of these words. He suggests that Yaakov Avinu had a tough life and that he was a little bitter. Why did Pharaoh ask Yaakov how old he was? The Ramban explains that Yaakov looked even older than his one hundred and thirty years because of how he carried himself. Yaakov was punished for Pharaoh's question in addition to his own answer, because his demeanor caused Pharaoh's question in the first place. The question came about because of Yaakov's attitude of *me'at vera'im.*

Ideally, we should realize that what appears to be *raa* is not really bad; rather, there is a *ro'eh,* a shepherd in charge. Everything comes from *HaKadosh Baruch Hu.* It took Yaakov until the end of his life to realize that the *raa* is really *ro'eh.* In *Parashat Vayehi,* Yaakov finally states: "*HaElokim haro'eh oti*" (*Bereshit* 48:9). He finally realized that it wasn't *raa,* but *ro'eh*; the word in the *pasuk* is even spelled without a *vav,* so it can be read interchangeably.

The lesson we must learn from Yaakov is that even when one experiences difficulty, he must realize that it is never *raa,* bad, but always directed by the *Ro'eh,* the ultimate Shepherd. Hashem shepherds our lives, and like sheep

יְדִיד Beloved of the soul, Father of compassion,
draw Your servant close to Your will.
Like a deer will Your servant run
and fall prostrate before Your beauty.
To him Your love is sweeter
than honey from the comb, than any taste.

הָדוּר Glorious, beautiful, radiance of the world,
my soul is sick with love for You.
Please, God, heal her now
by showing her Your tender radiance.
Then she will recover her strength and be healed,
Be Your servant for eternity.

---

on Shabbat because during the week, we are unable to focus exclusively on strengthening our closeness to *HaKadosh Barukh Hu*. Perhaps that is why it is a custom to recite *Yedid Nefesh* both as Shabbat enters (before *Kabbalat Shabbat*) and again during *seuda shelishit* as Shabbat nears its end. It highlights the idea that Shabbat is a time that we can focus on our *ahavat Hashem*.

כי יערב לו ידידותך מנופת צוף וכל טעם – KI YAAREV LO YEDIDOTEKH MINOFET TZUF VEKHOL TAAM

Enjoyment from Learning Torah

"To him Your love is sweeter than honey from the comb, than any taste." Some suggest this is also a reference to the Torah. The Iglei Tal writes in his introduction that one should not feel as if he cannot enjoy learning Torah because it is a commandment. Quite the contrary. We are to enjoy and cherish every moment that we engage in learning Torah, and that is the highest level of *limud Torah*, as it brings us closer to Hashem.

Rav Avraham Min Hahar (Nedarim 48) explains the *mishna* that states that if one took upon himself not to obtain any enjoyment from a city, that individual is permitted to use a *lulav* or *etrog* that grew in that city. However, that individual would be prohibited from using a *sefer* from the city. There is a principle that appears throughout Shas: *Mitzvot lav leihanot nitnu* – mitzvot were not transmitted to us for our pleasure. But learning Torah is different. *Pikudei Hashem yesharim mesamhei lev* – Torah brings us enjoyment (*Tehillim* 19:9).

יְדִיד נֶפֶשׁ, אָב הָרַחֲמָן
מְשׁוֹךְ עַבְדְּךָ אֶל רְצוֹנָךְ.
יָרוּץ עַבְדְּךָ כְּמוֹ אַיָּל
יִשְׁתַּחֲוֶה מוּל הֲדָרָךְ.
כִּי יֶעֱרַב לוֹ יְדִידוּתָךְ
מִנֹּפֶת צוּף וְכָל טָעַם.

הָדוּר, נָאֶה, זִיו הָעוֹלָם
נַפְשִׁי חוֹלַת אַהֲבָתָךְ.
אָנָּא, אֵל נָא, רְפָא נָא לָהּ
בְּהַרְאוֹת לָהּ נֹעַם זִיוָךְ.
אָז תִּתְחַזֵּק וְתִתְרַפֵּא
וְהָיְתָה לָךְ שִׁפְחַת עוֹלָם.

ידיד נפש – YEDID NEFESH

נפשי חולת אהבתך – NAFSHI HOLAT AHAVATEKHA

Yedid Nefesh was written by the Baal HaHaredim, a contemporary of the Ari who lived in Tzfat. The Rambam, in the last *perek* of *Hilkhot Teshuva* (10:3), states that we ought to strive to attain a close connection to Hashem. The highest level of *teshuva* is *ahavat Hashem,* love of God.

> **הוא שיאהב את ה׳ אהבה גדולה יתרה עזה מאד, עד שתהא נפשו קשורה באהבת ה׳ ונמצא שוגה בה תמיד, כאלו חולה חולי האהבה שאין דעתו פנויה מאהבת אותה אשה והוא שוגה בה תמיד.**
>
> He shall love Hashem with an exceedingly great and very strong love, so that his soul is bound up in loving Hashem, finding himself in a constant tremor, as if he were suffering lovesickness, wherein his mind is not free because of his love for that woman. He is always preoccupied with her.

The Rambam compares man's feelings toward Hashem to the strong bond and desire one feels toward a person he loves. We mention this emotion

וָתִיק Ancient of Days, let Your mercy be aroused;
please have pity on Your beloved child.
How long have I yearned
to see the glory of Your strength.
Please, my God, my heart's desire –
hasten; do not hide Yourself.

הִגָּלֵה Reveal Yourself, beloved, and spread over me
the tabernacle of Your peace.
Let the earth shine with Your glory,
let us be overjoyed and rejoice in You.
Hurry, beloved, for the appointed time has come,
and be gracious to me as in the times of old.

Birkat HaMazon can be found on page 149.

---

acknowledging the sweetness of the Torah – *Vehaarev Na*. On Shabbat, when are free from the distractions of the week and have time to learn, we express our appreciation of having received the sweetest gift.

וָתִיק, יֶהֱמוּ רַחֲמֶיךָ
וְחוּס נָא עַל בֵּן אוֹהֲבָךְ
כִּי זֶה כַּמֶּה נִכְסֹף נִכְסַף
לִרְאוֹת בְּתִפְאֶרֶת עֻזָּךְ
אָנָּא, אֵלִי, מַחְמַד לִבִּי
חוּשָׁה נָּא, וְאַל תִּתְעַלָּם.

הִגָּלֶה נָא וּפְרֹשׂ, חָבִיב
עָלַי אֶת סֻכַּת שְׁלוֹמָךְ
תָּאִיר אֶרֶץ מִכְּבוֹדָךְ
נָגִילָה וְנִשְׂמְחָה בָךְ.
מַהֵר, אָהוּב, כִּי בָא מוֹעֵד
וְחָנֵּנִי כִּימֵי עוֹלָם.

ברכת המזון *can be found on page 149.*

19:9). That is why it is forbidden for someone who is sitting *shiva* to engage in Torah study, as they must refrain from participating in pleasurable endeavors.

We use the term *arev* in the *Birkat HaTorah* that we recite each morning,

הבדלה

HAVDALA

Seder Havdala

On Motza'ei Yom Tov that is not a Motza'ei Shabbat, the first paragraph and the blessings for the spices and flame are omitted. At the end of Yom Kippur, only the blessing for the spices is omitted.

Taking a cup of wine in the right hand, say:

הִנֵּה Behold, God is my salvation. I will trust and not be afraid. *Is. 12*
The LORD, the LORD, is my strength and my song.
He has become my salvation.
With joy you will draw water from the springs of salvation.
Salvation is the LORD's; on Your people is Your blessing, Selah. *Ps. 3*
The LORD of hosts is with us, *Ps. 46*
the God of Jacob is our stronghold, Selah.
LORD of hosts: happy is the one who trusts in You. *Ps. 84*
LORD, save! May the King answer us on the day we call. *Ps. 20*
For the Jews there was light and gladness, joy and honor – *Esther 8*
so may it be for us.
I will lift the cup of salvation and call on the name of the LORD. *Ps. 116*

When making Havdala for others, add:
Please pay attention, my masters.

Blessed are You, LORD our God, King of the Universe,
who creates the fruit of the vine.

Hold the spice box and say:

Blessed are You, LORD our God, King of the Universe,
who creates the various spices.

Smell the spices and put the spice box down.
Lift the hands toward the flame of the Havdala candle and say:

Blessed are You, LORD our God, King of the Universe,
who creates the lights of fire.

12:3). The Gemara (Sukka 48b) cites a heretic named Sasson who tells R. Abahu that in the future, R. Abahu will pour water for him, as it is stated, "*UShe'avtem mayim besasson.*" R. Abahu responds: "Had the *pasuk* stated '*lesasson,*' you may have been correct, as the letter *lamed* means 'to.' However,

since

סדר הבדלה

On מוצאי יום טוב *that is not a* מוצאי שבת*, the first paragraph and the blessings for the spices and flame are omitted. At the end of* יום כיפור*, only the blessing for the spices is omitted.*

Taking a cup of wine in the right hand, say:

הִנֵּה אֵל יְשׁוּעָתִי אֶבְטַח, וְלֹא אֶפְחָד ישעיה יב
כִּי־עָזִּי וְזִמְרָת יָהּ יהוה, וַיְהִי־לִי לִישׁוּעָה:
וּשְׁאַבְתֶּם־מַיִם בְּשָׂשׂוֹן, מִמַּעַיְנֵי הַיְשׁוּעָה:
לַיהוה הַיְשׁוּעָה, עַל־עַמְּךָ בִרְכָתֶךָ סֶּלָה: תהלים ג
יהוה צְבָאוֹת עִמָּנוּ, מִשְׂגָּב לָנוּ אֱלֹהֵי יַעֲקֹב סֶלָה: תהלים מו
יהוה צְבָאוֹת, אַשְׁרֵי אָדָם בֹּטֵחַ בָּךְ: תהלים פד
יהוה הוֹשִׁיעָה, הַמֶּלֶךְ יַעֲנֵנוּ בְיוֹם־קָרְאֵנוּ: תהלים כ
לַיְּהוּדִים הָיְתָה אוֹרָה וְשִׂמְחָה וְשָׂשֹׂן וִיקָר: כֵּן תִּהְיֶה לָּנוּ. אסתר ח
כּוֹס־יְשׁוּעוֹת אֶשָּׂא, וּבְשֵׁם יהוה אֶקְרָא: תהלים קטז

When making הבדלה *for others, add:*

סַבְרִי מָרָנָן

בָּרוּךְ אַתָּה יהוה אֱלֹהֵינוּ מֶלֶךְ הָעוֹלָם, בּוֹרֵא פְּרִי הַגָּפֶן.

Hold the spice box and say:

בָּרוּךְ אַתָּה יהוה אֱלֹהֵינוּ מֶלֶךְ הָעוֹלָם, בּוֹרֵא מִינֵי בְשָׂמִים.

Smell the spices and put the spice box down.
Lift the hands toward the flame of the הבדלה *candle and say:*

בָּרוּךְ אַתָּה יהוה אֱלֹהֵינוּ מֶלֶךְ הָעוֹלָם, בּוֹרֵא מְאוֹרֵי הָאֵשׁ.

הבדלה – HAVDALA

Serving Hashem Through Happiness

The *minhag* is to recite certain *pesukim* prior to making the blessings of *Havdala*. We state *UShe'avtem mayim besasson mimaayanei hayeshua* (*Yeshayahu*

Holding the cup of wine again in the right hand, say:

בָּרוּךְ Blessed are You, Lord our God, King of the Universe,
who distinguishes between sacred and secular,
between light and darkness,
between Israel and the nations,
between the seventh day and the six days of work.
Blessed are You, Lord,
who distinguishes between sacred and secular.

The Levush states that "*Ata honen*" refers to the wisdom to distinguish between elements of the physical world that anyone would be able to recognize, and that is why we recite that term all week. However, there is a different type of distinction that we make between the holy and mundane. This is related to the wisdom of the Torah, and it is unique to us and depicted by term "*Ata honantanu*." Perhaps this is also alluded to in the progression of the examples we use in *Havdala*, starting with distinguishing between *kodesh* and *hol*, which is unique to Jews, and then distinguishing between light and darkness, which is obvious to all.

It could also be that after experiencing a *neshama yeteira* for twenty-five hours, we have a deeper understanding and capability of distinguishing between *kodesh* and *hol*, and that is why we mention it in the *berakha* of *Havdala*.

Intellect and Torah

The Maharal, in his *hakdama* to *Pirkei Avot* (*Derekh Haim*), writes that Hashem gives us *sekhel* (intellect) and Torah. Intellect helps us act like a mensch, a moral and ethical person. That relates to the seven mitzvot given to *Bnei Noah*; these mitzvot can be appreciated logically as behavior necessary for society to function. However, Torah helps us to become more than just a functioning member of society. It helps us to be a Jew. To be a light unto the nations, we need the higher form of knowledge – Torah and mitzvot, which go beyond mere intellect. That is the distinction between "*Ata honen*" (intellect) and "*Ata honantanu*" (Torah).

Holding the cup of wine again in the right hand, say:

בָּרוּךְ אַתָּה יהוה אֱלֹהֵינוּ מֶלֶךְ הָעוֹלָם
הַמַּבְדִּיל בֵּין קֹדֶשׁ לְחֹל
בֵּין אוֹר לְחֹשֶׁךְ
בֵּין יִשְׂרָאֵל לָעַמִּים
בֵּין יוֹם הַשְּׁבִיעִי לְשֵׁשֶׁת יְמֵי הַמַּעֲשֶׂה.
בָּרוּךְ אַתָּה יהוה, הַמַּבְדִּיל בֵּין קֹדֶשׁ לְחֹל.

---

since the *pasuk* uses a *bet* – *besasson* – it means that with your skin we will make a bottle that will be used to pour water." What is the deeper meaning of this story?

This heretic thought that the pursuit of happiness (*sasson*) is the goal in life. R. Abahu corrects him and explains that happiness is a means by which to serve Hashem. *Ivdu et Hashem besimha* – serve God with happiness. Obtaining happiness is not a goal in itself, but a means through which to serve Hashem. As we conclude the Shabbat, we hope to extend the happiness and enjoyment that we experienced into the coming week so that it will enhance our *avodat Hashem.*

המבדיל בין קודש לחול – HAMAVDIL BEN KODESH LEHOL

Distinguishing Between Holy and Mundane

At the end of *Havdala* we have several examples of distinguishing between two items: *Hamavdil ben kodesh lehol, ben ohr lehoshekh, ben Yisrael laamim* – distinguishing holy from the mundane, light from darkness, *Am Yisrael* from the other nations.

This may relate to a discussion among the *Rishonim* (summarized by the Levush in *Hilkhot Havdala* 294) with respect to the recitation of *Ata honantanu* as a version of *Havdala* in the *Amida,* inserted in the *tefilla* of *Ata honen.* Several *Rishonim* ask why the double language is used – we start the paragraph with "*Ata honen*" and then insert "*Ata honantanu.*"

Zemirot for Havdala

הַמַּבְדִּיל He who distinguishes between sacred and secular,
may He forgive our sins.
May He multiply our offspring and wealth like the sand,
and like the stars at night.

The day has passed like a palm tree's shadow;
I call on God to fulfill what the watchman said: *Is. 21*
"Morning comes, though now it is night."

Your righteousness is as high as Mount Tabor.
May You pass high over my sins.
[Let them be] like yesterday when it has passed, *Ps. 90*
like a watch in the night.

Rav Nebenzahl (*Devarim*, p. 36) notes that every Shabbat afternoon at Minha, we read a portion of the next week's *sedra*. Why is that? Why not *lein* this week's *parasha*? This highlights the idea that no matter what challenges we may face during the week, we know that Shabbat awaits us. A Jew always looks ahead and knows that there will be a better tomorrow.

The Netivot Shalom (*Shemot*) writes that when Pharaoh's daughter Batya saw a child crying in a basket, she knew it was a Jew.

ותפתח ותראהו את הילד והנה נער בֹּכה, ותחמֹל עליו ותאמר מילדי העברים זה.

> She opened [it], and she saw him, the child, and behold, he was a weeping lad, and she had compassion on him, and she said, "This is [one] of the children of the Hebrews." (*Shemot* 2:6)

How did she know that the child was Jewish (see Rashi)? The Netivot Shalom explains that his crying was a different type of cry. A Jew cries out of hope, not despair: *bekhi shel tikva velo bekhi shel yeush*. We are yearning and looking ahead. A Jew always has Shabbat in mind and looks forward to once again rejoicing in its delight.

זמירות להבדלה

הַמַּבְדִּיל בֵּין קֹדֶשׁ לְחֹל
חַטֹּאתֵינוּ הוּא יִמְחֹל
זַרְעֵנוּ וְכַסְפֵּנוּ יַרְבֶּה כַּחוֹל
וְכַכּוֹכָבִים בַּלָּיְלָה.

יוֹם פָּנָה כְּצֵל תֹּמֶר
אֶקְרָא לָאֵל עָלַי גּוֹמֵר,
אָמַר שֹׁמֵר ישעיה כא
אָתָא בֹקֶר וְגַם־לָיְלָה:

צִדְקָתְךָ כְּהַר תָּבוֹר
עַל חֲטָאַי עָבוֹר תַּעֲבֹר
כְּיוֹם אֶתְמוֹל כִּי יַעֲבֹר תהלים צ
וְאַשְׁמוּרָה בַלָּיְלָה:

ZEMIROT FOR HAVDALA

Yearning for Next Shabbat

There is a custom to sing *HaMavdil ben kodesh lehol* after *Havdala*. One of the phrases we include is:

חלפה עונת מנחתי מי יתן מנוחתי.

The time of offerings has passed; would that I might rest.

This is a reference to Shabbat. The Shabbat has just passed, and I yearn for the next one. Right after Shabbat is over, we start looking forward to the next Shabbat. *Kavod Shabbat* begins on Motza'ei Shabbat, and it is reflected in the way we refer to the days of the week: *yom rishon leShabbat, yom sheni leShabbat,* and so on.

The time of offerings has passed.
    Would that I might rest.
I am weary with my sighing, every night I drench [with tears]. *Ps. 6*

Hear my voice; let it not be cast aside.
    Open for me the lofty gate.
My head is filled with the dew of dawn, *Song. 5*
    my hair with raindrops of the night.

Heed my prayer, revered and awesome God.
    When I cry, grant me deliverance at twilight, *Prov. 7*
as the day fades, or in the darkness of the night.

I call to You, LORD: Save me.
    Make known to me the path of life.
Rescue me from misery before day turns to night.

Cleanse the defilement of my deeds, lest those who torment me say,
    "Where is the God who made me, *Job 35*
who gives cause for songs in the night?"

We are in Your hands like clay: please forgive our sins, light and grave.
    Day to day they pour forth speech, *Ps. 19*
and night to night [they communicate knowledge].

חָלְפָה עוֹנַת מִנְחָתִי
מִי יִתֵּן מְנוּחָתִי
יָגַעְתִּי בְאַנְחָתִי תהלים ו
אַשְׂחֶה בְכָל־לַיְלָה:

קוֹלִי בַּל יֻנְטַל
פְּתַח לִי שַׁעַר הַמְנֻטָּל
שֶׁרֹּאשִׁי נִמְלָא טָל שיר השירים ה
קְוֻצּוֹתַי רְסִיסֵי לָיְלָה:

הֵעָתֵר נוֹרָא וְאָיֹם
אֲשַׁוֵּעַ, תְּנָה פִדְיוֹם
בְּנֶשֶׁף־בְּעֶרֶב יוֹם משלי ז
בְּאִישׁוֹן לָיְלָה:

קְרָאתִיךָ יָהּ, הוֹשִׁיעֵנִי
אֹרַח חַיִּים תּוֹדִיעֵנִי
מִדַּלָּה תְבַצְּעֵנִי
מִיּוֹם עַד לָיְלָה.

טַהֵר טִנּוּף מַעֲשַׂי
פֶּן יֹאמְרוּ מַכְעִיסַי
אַיֵּה אֱלוֹהַּ עֹשָׂי איוב לה
נֹתֵן זְמִרוֹת בַּלָּיְלָה:

נַחְנוּ בְיָדְךָ כַּחֹמֶר
סְלַח נָא עַל קַל וָחֹמֶר
יוֹם לְיוֹם יַבִּיעַ אֹמֶר תהלים יט
וְלַיְלָה לְלָיְלָה:

אֱלֹהִים יִסְעָדֵנוּ God sustain us
with blessing, in all we have,
and grant us goodness
in all we put our hands to,
God sustain us.

On Sunday as we set to work,
may He order blessing to us,
and so too on Monday,
may He sweeten the secret
hidden in wait for us.
God sustain us.

Multiply my hosts, Savior,
on Tuesday and on Wednesday.
On Thursday, without suffering,
may He send us our redeemer.
God sustain us.

Prepare fresh meat
on Friday for the sacred meal.
Holiness, praise, honor,
on all that we desire.
God sustain us.

We shall offer our souls
delights on our holy day,
and our couch is luscious with life,
and the night, lit up for us.
God sustain us.

אֱלֹהִים יִסְעָדֵנוּ
בְּרָכָה בִּמְאֹדֵנוּ
וְזֶבֶד טוֹב יִזְבְּדֵנוּ
בְּכָל מִשְׁלַח יָדֵינוּ.
אֱלֹהִים יִסְעָדֵנוּ.

בְּיוֹם רִאשׁוֹן לִמְלָאכָה
יְצַו אִתָּנוּ בְּרָכָה
וְיוֹם הַשֵּׁנִי כָּכָה
יַמְתִּיק אֶת סוֹדֵנוּ.
אֱלֹהִים יִסְעָדֵנוּ.

רַבֵּה צְבָאַי, יִשְׁעִי
בַּשְּׁלִישִׁי וּבָרְבִיעִי
בַּחֲמִישִׁי אַךְ לֹא בְעִי
יִשְׁלַח אֶת פּוֹדֵנוּ.
אֱלֹהִים יִסְעָדֵנוּ.

הָכֵן טְבֹחַ טֶבַח
בְּיוֹם הַשִּׁשִּׁי זֶבַח
קֹדֶשׁ הִלּוּל וָשֶׁבַח
עַל כָּל מַחְמַדֵּנוּ.
אֱלֹהִים יִסְעָדֵנוּ.

מַעֲדַנִּים לְנַפְשֵׁנוּ
נִתַּן בְּיוֹם קָדְשֵׁנוּ
וְרַעֲנָנָה עַרְשֵׂנוּ
וְלַיְלָה אוֹר בַּעֲדֵנוּ.
אֱלֹהִים יִסְעָדֵנוּ.

אִישׁ חָסִיד הָיָה Once upon a time there was a devoted man. So poor was he that he had no food or sustenance; and in his shame he stayed at home to study, for he had no clothes to wear either. What is more, he was responsible for the upkeep of his wife, an honorable woman, and five sons.

One day his wife said, "I cannot be distracted any longer. We have no bread to eat, no clothes, nothing at all to call our own. You have searched the Torah and found what you looked for – but what are we to eat now?

"Listen. Go out to the marketplace, fearless as a knight in arms. Gracious, compassionate God above might perhaps take pity on us with some act of kindness. He is a shelter for those who place trust in Him; He grants the wishes of those who fear Him."

"You advise me soundly and wisely," he said, "but I cannot agree to what you say. I cannot go out in shame and humiliation with nothing to cover me at all, with nothing in my hand to trade with, not even a penny."

But the woman hurried round to her neighbors and borrowed a fine set of handsome clothes. And her husband put them on and cast all his trust onto the God he loved so much. The children, in their prayers, said, "Please, do not make this poor man come home shamed."

Full of hope, he came to the marketplace. And who should be there to greet him but Elijah the prophet? The seer said to him, "Today you shall indeed become rich. Now command me, with all the honor you have: I am your slave.

"Call out to anyone who may have a mind to buy a slave unmatched in all the world." The man was disturbed: how could he overturn all the laws? How can a servant sell his own master? But Elijah placed his wisdom within the man, and he then held onto Elijah as if he were indeed the prophet's master.

A merchant eagerly bought the slave – for eight hundred thousand gold pieces. He demanded of Elijah what kind of work he did; asked whether he was skilled at building. "Build me a palace – a mansion," he said. "When it is finished – you are a free man."

אִישׁ חָסִיד הָיָה, בְּלִי מָזוֹן וּמִחְיָה.
בְּבֵיתוֹ עָסַק מִלְּבוּשׁ, וְאֵין בֶּגֶד לִלְבֹּשׁ.
גּוֹנֵן בַּחֲשׁוּבָה אִשָּׁה, וְגַם בְּבָנִים חֲמִשָּׁה.

דִּבְּרָה לוֹ הָאִשָּׁה, יוֹתֵר אֵין לְהִתְיָאֲשָׁה.
הֲמִבְּלִי לֶחֶם לֶאֱכֹל, בְּעֵרֹם וּבְחֹסֶר כֹּל.
וְתוֹרָה מָצָאתָ כִּי יָגַעְתָּ, מַה נֹּאכַל מֵעַתָּה.

זָהִיר כְּבַר נָשׁוּק, הֲלֹא תֵּצֵא לַשּׁוּק.
חַנּוּן וְרַחוּם בִּמְרוֹמָיו, אוּלַי יִגְמְלֵנוּ בְּרַחֲמָיו.
טוֹב לְקַוּוֹ מַחֲסֶה, רְצוֹן יְרֵאָיו יַעֲשֶׂה.

יָעַצְתְּ בְּדַעַת וּבְחָכְמָה, עֲצָתֵךְ בְּלִי לְהַסְכִּימָה.
כְּצֵאתִי לְבֹשֶׁת וְלִכְלִמָּה, מִבְּלִי כְסוּת וְשַׂלְמָה.
לְאֵין בְּיָדַי לְפָרְטָה, אֲפִלּוּ שָׁוֶה פְרוּטָה.

מִהֲרָה וְשָׁאֲלָה מִשְּׁכֵנִים, מַלְבּוּשִׁים נָאִים מְתֻקָּנִים.
נִלְבַּשׁ וְהִשְׁלִיךְ יְהָבוֹ, עַל יהוה אֲשֶׁר אֲהֵבוֹ.
סָחוּ יְלָדָיו בְּפִלּוּלָם, אַל יֵשֵׁב דַּךְ נִכְלָם.

עָבַר בַּשּׁוּק בְּשִׁבְרָתוֹ, וְהִנֵּה אֵלִיָּהוּ הַנָּבִיא לִקְרָאתוֹ.
פָּץ לוֹ הַמְבַשֵּׂר, בֶּאֱמֶת הַיּוֹם תִּתְעַשֵּׁר.
צַוֵּנִי בְּכָל כְּבוֹדֶךָ, כִּי הִנְנִי עַבְדֶּךָ.

קְרָא לְמִי בְדַעְתּוֹ, קְנוֹת עֶבֶד אֵין כְּמוֹתוֹ.
רָחַשׁ אֵיךְ יְשַׁנֶּה דִּינוֹ, עֶבֶד לִמְכֹּר אֶת אֲדוֹנוֹ.
שָׁת לוֹ חָכְמָתוֹ בְּקִרְבּוֹ, וְהֶחֱזִיק בּוֹ כְּמוֹ רַבּוֹ.

תַּגָּר קְנָאוֹ בַּאֲהָבִים, בִּשְׁמוֹנֶה מֵאוֹת אֶלֶף זְהוּבִים.
תְּבָעוֹ מַה מְּלַאכְתֶּךָ, אִם בְּבִנְיָן חָכְמָתֶךָ.
תַּכְלִית טְרַקְלִין וּפַלְטְרִין, הֲרֵי אַתָּה בֶּן חוֹרִין.

On the first day at work, Elijah toiled with all the other laborers. But at midnight he prayed, "Answer me, answer me, Performer of Wonders. I took this upon myself and had myself sold into slavery, not for my own honor's sake, but for Yours.

"Now, God who created Your whole world, finish off this building. As I entreat You, show Your mercy, for my intentions are good." Angels of Mercy from high above, then came down and began to build.

The children of Majesty were many and soon all the work was done. The merchant was overjoyed when he saw that the task was finished, the most beautiful of handsome towers, exactly as the architects had planned.

"Now," said Elijah, "Remember what you told me yesterday. Set me free, clearly and certainly, as you said you would when you spoke of liberty." The merchant was true to his word, and the man of truth, Elijah – vanished away.

יוֹם רִאשׁוֹן בְּמִפְעָלִים, פָּעַל עִם פּוֹעֲלִים.
שִׁוַּע בַּחֲצִי הַלַּיְלָה, עֲנֵנִי נוֹרָא עֲלִילָה.
יַזַּמְתִּי וְנִמְכַּרְתִּי לְהַעֲבִידִי, לִכְבוֹדְךָ וְלֹא לִכְבוֹדִי.

בּוֹרֵא עוֹלָם בְּקִנְיָן, הַשְׁלֵם זֶה הַבִּנְיָן.
רַחֲמֶיךָ יִכְמְרוּ בַּחֲנִינָתִי, כִּי לְטוֹבָה כִּוַּנְתִּי.
מַלְאֲכֵי רַחֲמִים מִמְּעוֹנָתוֹ, אָז הֵחֵלּוּ לִבְנוֹתוֹ.

רַבּוּ בְּנֵי הַמְּלוּכָה, וַתִּשְׁלַם כָּל הַמְּלָאכָה.
דָּץ הַסּוֹחֵר בִּרְאוֹתוֹ, כִּי נִגְמְרָה מְלַאכְתּוֹ.
כְּלוּלַת מִגְדָּלִים נָאִים, לְפִי עִנְיַן הַבַּנָּאִים.

יִזָּכֵר לְךָ עַתָּה, אֶתְמוֹל אֲשֶׁר דִּבַּרְתָּ.
חָפְשֵׁנִי בְּוַדַּאי וּבְבֵרוּר, כְּנַמְתָּ לְעִנְיַן שִׁחְרוּר.
זֶה קִיְּמוּ בֶּאֱמֶת, וּפָרַח לוֹ אִישׁ הָאֱמֶת.

אָמַר יהוה לְיַעֲקֹב The LORD said to Jacob,	"Do not be afraid, my servant Jacob."	
The LORD chose Jacob,	"Do not be afraid, my servant Jacob."	
The LORD redeemed Jacob,	"Do not be afraid, my servant Jacob."	
A star is to come forth from Jacob,	"Do not be afraid, my servant Jacob."	*Num. 24*
In coming times he shall take root, Jacob,	"Do not be afraid, my servant Jacob."	*Is. 27*
A ruler shall rise up from Jacob,	"Do not be afraid, my servant Jacob."	*Num. 24*
Remember but this of Jacob,	"Do not be afraid, my servant Jacob."	
The bliss of the salvation of Jacob,	"Do not be afraid, my servant Jacob."	
Goodly are your tents, O Jacob,	"Do not be afraid, my servant Jacob."	
They shall teach Your laws to Jacob,	"Do not be afraid, my servant Jacob."	*Deut. 33*
There is no sorcery in Jacob,	"Do not be afraid, my servant Jacob."	*Num. 23*
He has seen no sin in Jacob,	"Do not be afraid, my servant Jacob."	
Who can count the dust of Jacob?	"Do not be afraid, my servant Jacob."	
The LORD swore an oath to Jacob,	"Do not be afraid, my servant Jacob."	
Please, forgive the sins of Jacob,	"Do not be afraid, my servant Jacob."	
Restore the fortunes, now, of Jacob,	"Do not be afraid, my servant Jacob."	
The LORD has recalled Jacob,	"Do not be afraid, my servant Jacob."	
He ordered the salvations of Jacob,	"Do not be afraid, my servant Jacob."	
This voice, it is the voice of Jacob,	"Do not be afraid, my servant Jacob."	
Sing out in the joy of Jacob,	"Do not be afraid, my servant Jacob."	
LORD, restore the might of Jacob,	"Do not be afraid, my servant Jacob."	
You shall grant truth to Jacob.	"Do not be afraid, my servant Jacob."	*Micha 7*

אָמַר יהוה לְיַעֲקֹב, אַל תִּירָא עַבְדִּי יַעֲקֹב.

בָּחַר יהוה בְּיַעֲקֹב, אַל תִּירָא עַבְדִּי יַעֲקֹב.

גָּאַל יהוה אֶת יַעֲקֹב, אַל תִּירָא עַבְדִּי יַעֲקֹב.

דָּרַךְ כּוֹכָב מִיַּעֲקֹב, אַל תִּירָא עַבְדִּי יַעֲקֹב. במדבר כד

הַבָּאִים יַשְׁרֵשׁ יַעֲקֹב, אַל תִּירָא עַבְדִּי יַעֲקֹב. ישעיה כז

וְיֵרְדְּ מִיַּעֲקֹב, אַל תִּירָא עַבְדִּי יַעֲקֹב. במדבר כד

זְכֹר זֹאת לְיַעֲקֹב, אַל תִּירָא עַבְדִּי יַעֲקֹב.

חֶדְוַת יְשׁוּעוֹת יַעֲקֹב, אַל תִּירָא עַבְדִּי יַעֲקֹב.

טֹבוּ אֹהָלֶיךָ יַעֲקֹב, אַל תִּירָא עַבְדִּי יַעֲקֹב.

יוֹרוּ מִשְׁפָּטֶיךָ לְיַעֲקֹב, אַל תִּירָא עַבְדִּי יַעֲקֹב. דברים לג

כִּי לֹא נַחַשׁ בְּיַעֲקֹב, אַל תִּירָא עַבְדִּי יַעֲקֹב. במדבר כג

לֹא הִבִּיט אָוֶן בְּיַעֲקֹב, אַל תִּירָא עַבְדִּי יַעֲקֹב.

מִי מָנָה עֲפַר יַעֲקֹב, אַל תִּירָא עַבְדִּי יַעֲקֹב.

נִשְׁבַּע יהוה לְיַעֲקֹב, אַל תִּירָא עַבְדִּי יַעֲקֹב.

סְלַח נָא לַעֲוֹן יַעֲקֹב, אַל תִּירָא עַבְדִּי יַעֲקֹב.

עַתָּה הָשֵׁב שְׁבוּת יַעֲקֹב, אַל תִּירָא עַבְדִּי יַעֲקֹב.

פָּדָה יהוה אֶת יַעֲקֹב, אַל תִּירָא עַבְדִּי יַעֲקֹב.

צַוֵּה יְשׁוּעוֹת יַעֲקֹב, אַל תִּירָא עַבְדִּי יַעֲקֹב.

קוֹל קוֹל יַעֲקֹב, אַל תִּירָא עַבְדִּי יַעֲקֹב.

רָנּוּ שִׂמְחָה לְיַעֲקֹב, אַל תִּירָא עַבְדִּי יַעֲקֹב.

שָׁב יהוה אֶת גְּאוֹן יַעֲקֹב, אַל תִּירָא עַבְדִּי יַעֲקֹב.

תִּתֵּן אֱמֶת לְיַעֲקֹב, אַל תִּירָא עַבְדִּי יַעֲקֹב. מיכה ז

אֵלִיָּהוּ הַנָּבִיא Elijah the Prophet,
Elijah the Tishbite, Elijah the Gileadite –
he will come to us quickly with the Messiah, son of David.

The man who acted with zeal in God's name;
The man for whom Yekutiel [Moses] declared endless peace;
The man who stepped forward and atoned Israel's sin.

The man whose eyes saw twelve generations.
The man who was recognized as the "hairy one";
The man whose loins were girded with leather.

The man who raged against idol worshipers;
The man who swore that there would be no season's rain;
The man who stalled rain and dew for three whole years.

The man who went out to find his soul a hiding place,
The man sustained by ravens, the man who would not be killed;
The man for whose sake jug and flour-basket were blessed.

The man whose instruction was heard with yearning,
The man who was answered with fire from high heavens.
The man after whom they would say, "The Lord is God!" *1 Kings 18*

The man who will be sent from the highest heaven.
The man appointed over all good tidings.
The man trusted as mediator, to reconcile fathers with sons.

The man who cried gloriously, "I have been zealous for the Lord!" *1 Kings 19*
The man who rode horses of fire in the storm.
The man who never tasted death or burial.

Man of Tishbe, save us from the lion's mouth.
Bring us tidings of good things to come.
Make us happy, all, fathers with sons,
At the ends of our Sabbaths.

That man who is called "the Man of Tishbe,"
Let us prevail in the Torah with his aid.
Let us hear good tidings soon, from his mouth.
Bring us out of darkness into light.

Happy the one who saw his face in a dream.
Happy the one who has greeted or answered him, "Peace."
The Lord will bless His people with peace. *Ps. 29*

As is written, "I shall send Elijah the Prophet to you *Mal. 3*
before the coming of the great and terrifying day of the Lord.
And he shall reconcile fathers to sons and sons to fathers."

אֵלִיָּהוּ הַנָּבִיא

אֵלִיָּהוּ הַתִּשְׁבִּי, אֵלִיָּהוּ הַגִּלְעָדִי
בִּמְהֵרָה יָבוֹא אֵלֵינוּ עִם מָשִׁיחַ בֶּן דָּוִד.

אִישׁ אֲשֶׁר קִנֵּא לְשֵׁם הָאֵל
אִישׁ בֻּשַּׂר שָׁלוֹם עַל יַד יְקוּתִיאֵל
אִישׁ גַּשׁ וַיְכַפֵּר עַל בְּנֵי יִשְׂרָאֵל.
אֵלִיָּהוּ הַנָּבִיא

אִישׁ דּוֹרוֹת שְׁנֵים עָשָׂר רָאוּ עֵינָיו
אִישׁ הַנִּקְרָא בַּעַל שֵׂעָר בְּסִמָּנָיו
אִישׁ וְאֵזוֹר עוֹר אָזוּר בְּמָתְנָיו.
אֵלִיָּהוּ הַנָּבִיא

אִישׁ זָעַף עַל עוֹבְדֵי חַמָּנִים
אִישׁ חָשׁ וְנִשְׁבַּע מִהְיוֹת גִּשְׁמֵי מְעוֹנִים
אִישׁ טַל וּמָטָר עָצַר שָׁלֹשׁ שָׁנִים.
אֵלִיָּהוּ הַנָּבִיא

אִישׁ יָצָא לִמְצֹא לְנַפְשׁוֹ נַחַת
אִישׁ כִּלְכְּלוּהוּ הָעוֹרְבִים וְלֹא מֵת לַשַּׁחַת
אִישׁ לְמַעֲנוֹ נִתְבָּרְכוּ כַּד וְצַפַּחַת.
אֵלִיָּהוּ הַנָּבִיא

אִישׁ מוּסָרָיו הִקְשִׁיבוּ כְמֵהִים
אִישׁ נַעֲנָה בָאֵשׁ מִשְּׁמֵי גְבוֹהִים
אִישׁ סָחוּ אַחֲרָיו יהוה הוּא הָאֱלֹהִים.
אֵלִיָּהוּ הַנָּבִיא

אִישׁ עָתִיד לְהִשְׁתַּלֵּחַ מִשְּׁמֵי עֲרָבוֹת
אִישׁ פָּקִיד עַל כָּל בְּשׂוֹרוֹת טוֹבוֹת
אִישׁ צִיר נֶאֱמָן לְהָשִׁיב לֵב בָּנִים עַל אָבוֹת. מלכים א׳ יח
אֵלִיָּהוּ הַנָּבִיא

אִישׁ קָרָא קַנֹּא קִנֵּאתִי לַיהוה
בְּתִפְאָרָה
אִישׁ רָכַב עַל סוּסֵי אֵשׁ בִּסְעָרָה
אִישׁ שֶׁלֹּא טָעַם טַעַם מִיתָה וּקְבוּרָה.
אֵלִיָּהוּ הַנָּבִיא

אִישׁ תִּשְׁבִּי תַּצִּילֵנוּ מִפִּי אֲרָיוֹת מלכים א׳ יט
תְּבַשְּׂרֵנוּ בְּשׂוֹרוֹת טוֹבוֹת
תְּשַׂמְּחֵנוּ בָּנִים עַל אָבוֹת
בְּמוֹצָאֵי שַׁבָּתוֹת.
אֵלִיָּהוּ הַנָּבִיא

אִישׁ תִּשְׁבִּי עַל שְׁמוֹ נִקְרָא
תַּצְלִיחֵנוּ עַל יָדוֹ בַּתּוֹרָה
תַּשְׁמִיעֵנוּ מִפִּיו בְּשׂוֹרָה טוֹבָה בִּמְהֵרָה
תּוֹצִיאֵנוּ מֵאֲפֵלָה לְאוֹרָה.
אֵלִיָּהוּ הַנָּבִיא

אַשְׁרֵי מִי שֶׁרָאָה פָנָיו בַּחֲלוֹם
אַשְׁרֵי מִי שֶׁנָּתַן לוֹ שָׁלוֹם
וְהֶחֱזִיר לוֹ שָׁלוֹם
יהוה יְבָרֵךְ אֶת עַמּוֹ בַשָּׁלוֹם. תהלים כט
אֵלִיָּהוּ הַנָּבִיא

כַּכָּתוּב: הִנֵּה אָנֹכִי שֹׁלֵחַ לָכֶם אֵת אֵלִיָּה הַנָּבִיא מלאכי ג
לִפְנֵי בּוֹא יוֹם יהוה הַגָּדוֹל וְהַנּוֹרָא:
וְהֵשִׁיב לֵב־אָבוֹת עַל־בָּנִים, וְלֵב בָּנִים עַל־אֲבוֹתָם:

לָעַד Always it lived on in our hearts,
this loyal faith
That we shall return to our Holy Land,
the city where David camped.

> Always it lived on in our hearts, this loyal faith
> That we shall return to our Holy Land,
> the city where David camped.

There we shall serve our God
in happiness, in joy and in delight;
There we shall go up at feasts of pilgrimage,
three times a year.

> Always it lived on in our hearts, this loyal faith
> That we shall return to our Holy Land,
> the city where David camped.

There we shall stand up to meet our destiny,
that which the father of many received.
There we shall live out our lives,
the lives of the nation that cannot be counted.

> Always it lived on in our hearts, this loyal faith
> That we shall return to our Holy Land,
> the city where David camped.

The Torah of life is our desire,
given at the mouth of the Most High.
That is our inheritance always –
a gift of the desert.

> Always it lived on in our hearts, this loyal faith
> That we shall return to our Holy Land,
> the city where David camped.

לָעַד חַיָּה בִּלְבָבֵנוּ
הָאֱמוּנָה הַנֶּאֱמָנָה
לָשׁוּב לְאֶרֶץ קָדְשֵׁנוּ
עִיר בָּהּ דָּוִד חָנָה.

לָעַד חַיָּה בִּלְבָבֵנוּ, הָאֱמוּנָה הַנֶּאֱמָנָה
לָשׁוּב לְאֶרֶץ קָדְשֵׁנוּ, עִיר בָּהּ דָּוִד חָנָה.

שָׁמָּה נַעֲבֹד אֱלֹהֵינוּ
בְּחֶדְוָה בְּגִילָה וּבִרְנָנָה
שָׁמָּה נַעֲלֶה לִרְגָלֵינוּ
שָׁלֹשׁ פְּעָמִים בַּשָּׁנָה.

לָעַד חַיָּה בִּלְבָבֵנוּ, הָאֱמוּנָה הַנֶּאֱמָנָה
לָשׁוּב לְאֶרֶץ קָדְשֵׁנוּ, עִיר בָּהּ דָּוִד חָנָה.

שָׁמָּה נַעֲמֹד לְגוֹרָלֵנוּ
אַב הֲמוֹן קָנָה
שָׁמָּה נִחְיֶה חַיֵּינוּ
חַיֵּי עֲדַת מִי מָנָה.

לָעַד חַיָּה בִּלְבָבֵנוּ, הָאֱמוּנָה הַנֶּאֱמָנָה
לָשׁוּב לְאֶרֶץ קָדְשֵׁנוּ, עִיר בָּהּ דָּוִד חָנָה.

תּוֹרַת חַיִּים חֶמְדָּתֵנוּ
מִפִּי עֶלְיוֹן נִתָּנָה
נֶצַח הִיא נַחֲלָתֵנוּ
מִמִּדְבָּר מַתָּנָה.

לָעַד חַיָּה בִּלְבָבֵנוּ, הָאֱמוּנָה הַנֶּאֱמָנָה
לָשׁוּב לְאֶרֶץ קָדְשֵׁנוּ, עִיר בָּהּ דָּוִד חָנָה.

סעודה וברכותיה
THE MEAL AND ITS BLESSINGS

Birkat HaMazon / Grace After Meals

On days when Taḥanun is said, say the below.

עַל־נַהֲרוֹת By the rivers of Babylon we sat and wept Ps. 137
as we remembered Zion.
There on the willow trees we hung up our harps,
for there our captors asked us for songs, our tormentors, for amusement,
said: "Sing us one of the songs of Zion!"
How can we sing the LORD's song on foreign soil?
If I forget you, Jerusalem, may my right hand forget its skill.
May my tongue cling to the roof of my mouth if I do not remember you,
if I do not set Jerusalem above my highest joy.
Remember, LORD, what the Edomites did on the day Jerusalem fell.
They said, "Tear it down, tear it down to its very foundations!"
Daughter of Babylon, doomed to destruction,
happy is he who repays you for what you have done to us,
who seizes your infants and dashes them against the rocks.

---

another *siyum haShas*? Perhaps some act of kindness? The *rav* replied, "I will seek to recite *Birkat HaMazon* from a *bentcher*." Obviously, Rav Shach knew the *bentching* by heart, but he knew that without the use of a *bentcher,* it is possible to recite the *berakhot* improperly.

These tidbits illustrate the importance of *bentching*. Since according to many opinions, it is the only *berakha mid'oraita,* we should do our best to try to recite *Birkat HaMazon* with the proper *kavana*.

Birkat HaMazon and Tefilla

In *Masoret HaRav,* Rav Soloveitchik distinguishes between *bentching* and *davening*. The Gemara (Berakhot 34b) states that although we bow during *Modim* in the *Amida,* it is inappropriate to do so when we recite "*Nodeh*" in *benching*. This distinction is due to the fundamentally different modes of approaching Hashem that we experience in *tefilla* versus *Birkat HaMazon*.

As the Rav so beautifully declares: "Prayer is the act of insubstantial man lacking the wherewithal to subsist appearing before the all-powerful Being upon whom his existence depends. When one prays, one is afflicted with troubles and is unable to overcome them without the help of God." This is

ברכת המזון

On days when תחנון *is said, say the below.*

עַל־נַהֲרוֹת בָּבֶל, שָׁם יָשַׁבְנוּ גַּם־בָּכִינוּ, בְּזָכְרֵנוּ אֶת־צִיּוֹן: תהלים קלז
עַל־עֲרָבִים בְּתוֹכָהּ תָּלִינוּ כִּנֹּרוֹתֵינוּ:
כִּי שָׁם שְׁאֵלוּנוּ שׁוֹבֵינוּ דִּבְרֵי־שִׁיר וְתוֹלָלֵינוּ שִׂמְחָה
שִׁירוּ לָנוּ מִשִּׁיר צִיּוֹן:
אֵיךְ נָשִׁיר אֶת־שִׁיר־יהוה עַל אַדְמַת נֵכָר:
אִם־אֶשְׁכָּחֵךְ יְרוּשָׁלָםִ, תִּשְׁכַּח יְמִינִי:
תִּדְבַּק לְשׁוֹנִי לְחִכִּי אִם־לֹא אֶזְכְּרֵכִי
אִם־לֹא אַעֲלֶה אֶת־יְרוּשָׁלַםִ עַל רֹאשׁ שִׂמְחָתִי:
זְכֹר יהוה לִבְנֵי אֱדוֹם אֵת יוֹם יְרוּשָׁלָםִ
הָאֹמְרִים עָרוּ עָרוּ עַד הַיְסוֹד בָּהּ:
בַּת־בָּבֶל הַשְּׁדוּדָה, אַשְׁרֵי שֶׁיְשַׁלֶּם־לָךְ אֶת־גְּמוּלֵךְ שֶׁגָּמַלְתְּ לָנוּ:
אַשְׁרֵי שֶׁיֹּאחֵז, וְנִפֵּץ אֶת־עֹלָלַיִךְ אֶל־הַסָּלַע:

BENTCHING

Importance of Birkat HaMazon

Rav Shlomo Zalman Auerbach once said that it is harder to *bentch* properly than to *daven* properly. During *davening,* one is in shul and the atmosphere is conducive to concentrating. But when sitting around a table, with people talking or cleaning, it is more difficult to focus with the proper *kavana.*

Rav Schwab discussed the difficulty of how to best fulfill the mitzva of *seuda shelishit* when Erev Pesach is on Shabbat, given that one is restricted from eating bread from early in the morning. Many suggest that one should wash, eat a small amount, and *bentch* early in the morning, walk around the block, and then wash, eat, and *bentch* again. Rav Schwab claimed, however, that *bentching* twice in such close proximity is not acceptable. This highlights how much effort he put into *bentching,* to the extent that it was difficult to repeat it within such a short period of time.

It is told that on one of Rav Shach's later birthdays, his *talmidim* inquired as to what the *rav* would take upon himself in the coming year. Would it be

On days when Taḥanun is omitted, say the below:

שִׁיר הַמַּעֲלוֹת A song of ascents. Ps. 126
When the LORD brought back the exiles of Zion
we were like people who dream.
Then were our mouths filled with laughter,
and our tongues with songs of joy.
Then was it said among the nations,
"The LORD has done great things for them."
The LORD did do great things for us and we rejoiced.
Bring back our exiles, LORD, like streams in a dry land.
May those who sowed in tears, reap in joy.
May one who goes out weeping, carrying a bag of seed,
come back with songs of joy, carrying his sheaves.

Some say:

תְּהִלַּת My mouth shall speak the praise of God, Ps. 145
and all creatures shall bless His holy name for ever and all time.
We will bless God now and for ever. Ps. 115
Halleluya! Thank the LORD for He is good; Ps. 136
His loving-kindness is for ever.
Who can tell of the LORD's mighty acts and make all His praise be heard? Ps. 106

May we be blessed with material and spiritual blessings and be able to properly express our gratitude for all of God's gifts.

Recognizing the Source

Rav Yosef Dov Soloveitchik (*Mo'adei HaRav*, p. 170) compares the *berakha* we make after eating fruit to the *Birkat HaMazon* we recite after bread. After we eat fruit, which is easily obtained from a tree, we recite the short *berakha* of *borei nefashot*. However, bread required us to toil. It went through several processes of production, from cultivating the grain to producing flour and ultimately baking. Yet for bread, we recite a long *berakha, Birkat HaMazon.*

Given these differences, why do we recite a short *berakha* after the fruit and *Birkat HaMazon* after the bread?

One might have thought the opposite would be more appropriate. With respect to fruit, I had little to do with creating it. I simply picked it off the

On days when תחנון *is omitted, say the below:*

שִׁיר הַמַּעֲלוֹת, בְּשׁוּב יהוה אֶת־שִׁיבַת צִיּוֹן הָיִינוּ כְּחֹלְמִים: תהלים קכו
אָז יִמָּלֵא שְׂחוֹק פִּינוּ וּלְשׁוֹנֵנוּ רִנָּה
אָז יֹאמְרוּ בַגּוֹיִם הִגְדִּיל יהוה לַעֲשׂוֹת עִם־אֵלֶּה:
הִגְדִּיל יהוה לַעֲשׂוֹת עִמָּנוּ, הָיִינוּ שְׂמֵחִים:
שׁוּבָה יהוה אֶת־שְׁבִיתֵנוּ, כַּאֲפִיקִים בַּנֶּגֶב:
הַזֹּרְעִים בְּדִמְעָה בְּרִנָּה יִקְצֹרוּ:
הָלוֹךְ יֵלֵךְ וּבָכֹה נֹשֵׂא מֶשֶׁךְ־הַזָּרַע
בֹּא־יָבֹא בְרִנָּה נֹשֵׂא אֲלֻמֹּתָיו:

Some say:

תְּהִלַּת יהוה יְדַבֶּר פִּי, וִיבָרֵךְ כָּל־בָּשָׂר שֵׁם קָדְשׁוֹ לְעוֹלָם וָעֶד: תהלים קמה
וַאֲנַחְנוּ נְבָרֵךְ יָהּ מֵעַתָּה וְעַד־עוֹלָם, הַלְלוּיָהּ: תהלים קטו
הוֹדוּ לַיהוה כִּי־טוֹב, כִּי לְעוֹלָם חַסְדּוֹ: תהלים קלו
מִי יְמַלֵּל גְּבוּרוֹת יהוה, יַשְׁמִיעַ כָּל־תְּהִלָּתוֹ: תהלים קו

---

different from *Birkat HaMazon,* which is recited on a full stomach to express our gratitude to Hashem for the material blessings He has bestowed upon us.

There is a *mahloket* between the Rambam and the Ramban as to whether or not there is an obligation to *daven* daily. The Rambam believes that there is an obligation to pray each day (mitzva 5). The Ramban posits that the obligation to pray arises only when one is in an *et tzara,* a moment of danger or difficulty. The Rav explains elsewhere that conceptually, there is really no argument between the Rambam and the Ramban. According to the Rambam, every day is defined as an *et tzara.* We experience uncertainty on a daily basis.

There are various manners and emotions with which we approach Hashem. One engages in *tefilla* when one is uncomfortable. One recites *Birkat HaMazon* when one is satiated. Even within *tefilla,* there are blessings of *shevah, bakasha,* and *hodaa* – praise, requests, and gratitude. We ought to focus on what we are reciting and recognize the way in which we address our Creator.

Zimmun / Invitation

For the zimmun said at a wedding or during the week of Sheva Berakhot, *see page 180. At a Brit, see page 196.*

When three or more men say Birkat HaMazon together, the following zimmun is said. When three or more women say Birkat HaMazon, substitute "Friends" for "Gentlemen." The leader should ask permission from those with precedence to lead the Birkat HaMazon.

Leader Gentlemen, let us say grace.

Others May the name of the LORD be blessed from now and for ever. *Ps. 113*

Leader May the name of the LORD be blessed from now and for ever.
With your permission, (my father and teacher / my mother and teacher / the Kohanim present / our teacher the Rabbi / the master of this house / the mistress of this house)
my masters and teachers,
let us bless (*in a minyan:* our God,) the One
from whose food we have eaten.

Others Blessed be (*in a minyan:* our God,) the One
from whose food we have eaten, and by whose goodness we live.

**People present who have not taken part in the meal say:*
*Blessed be (*in a minyan:* our God,) the One
whose name is continually blessed for ever and all time.

Leader Blessed be (*in a minyan:* our God,) the One
from whose food we have eaten, and by whose goodness we live.
Blessed be He, and blessed be His name.

---

to Hashem for having provided us with the ingredients. Therefore, a much longer and more detailed *berakha* is required after eating bread. With respect to a fruit, it is crystal clear that it was provided by Hashem. As there is no risk of forgetting its source, a concise blessing is sufficient.

Another possibility is that the goal of life is to actually partner with Hashem in achieving accomplishments and not simply to receive divine gifts. Thus, when we merit to share in God's work, that is when we offer the most praise.

סדר הזימון

For the זימון said at a wedding or during the week of שבע ברכות, see page 181.
At a ברית, see page 197.

When three or more men say ברכת המזון together, the following זימון is said.
When three or more women say ברכת המזון, substitute חֲבֵרוֹתַי for רַבּוֹתַי.
The leader should ask permission from those with precedence to lead the ברכת המזון.

Leader רַבּוֹתַי, נְבָרֵךְ.

Others יְהִי שֵׁם יהוה מְבֹרָךְ מֵעַתָּה וְעַד־עוֹלָם: תהלים קיג

Leader יְהִי שֵׁם יהוה מְבֹרָךְ מֵעַתָּה וְעַד־עוֹלָם:
בִּרְשׁוּת (אָבִי מוֹרִי / אִמִּי מוֹרָתִי / כֹּהֲנִים / מוֹרֵנוּ הָרַב / בַּעַל הַבַּיִת הַזֶּה / בַּעֲלַת הַבַּיִת הַזֶּה)
מָרָנָן וְרַבָּנָן וְרַבּוֹתַי
נְבָרֵךְ (במנין: אֱלֹהֵינוּ) שֶׁאָכַלְנוּ מִשֶּׁלוֹ.

Others בָּרוּךְ (במנין: אֱלֹהֵינוּ) שֶׁאָכַלְנוּ מִשֶּׁלוֹ וּבְטוּבוֹ חָיִינוּ.

**People present who have not taken part in the meal say:*
*בָּרוּךְ (במנין: אֱלֹהֵינוּ) וּמְבֹרָךְ שְׁמוֹ תָּמִיד לְעוֹלָם וָעֶד.

Leader בָּרוּךְ (במנין: אֱלֹהֵינוּ) שֶׁאָכַלְנוּ מִשֶּׁלוֹ וּבְטוּבוֹ חָיִינוּ.
בָּרוּךְ הוּא וּבָרוּךְ שְׁמוֹ.

---

tree, and it was ready for me. Therefore, the blessing after eating fruit should be longer and more detailed, so I can express my gratitude to Hashem for doing the work for me. With respect to the bread, I worked hard to turn the grain into bread. Since I had to perform the activities that turned grain into bread, one would imagine the blessing could be shorter.

However, *Birkat HaMazon* is precisely where we need to be reminded to offer our appreciation to Hashem for having provided us with our food. We may erroneously take credit for creating our bread and lack true gratitude

BLESSING OF NOURISHMENT

בָּרוּךְ Blessed are You, LORD our God, King of the Universe,
who in His goodness feeds the whole world
with grace, kindness and compassion.
He gives food to all living things,
for His kindness is for ever.
Because of His continual great goodness,
we have never lacked food,
nor may we ever lack it, for the sake of His great name.
For He is God who feeds and sustains all, does good to all,
and prepares food for all creatures He has created.
Blessed are You, LORD, who feeds all.

BLESSING FOR THE LAND

נוֹדֶה We thank You, LORD our God,
for having granted as a heritage to our ancestors
a desirable, good and spacious land;
for bringing us out, LORD our God, from the land of Egypt,
freeing us from the house of slavery;
for Your covenant which You sealed in our flesh;
for Your Torah which You taught us;
for Your laws which You made known to us;
for the life, grace and kindness You have bestowed on us;
and for the food by which You continually feed and sustain us,
every day, every season, every hour.

The Rav explains that we need to have that same feeling regarding *Eretz Yisrael*. We have to figure out a way to feel its attraction, its inexplicable pull. Those in the Diaspora have to feel that they are lacking something by not being in *Eretz Yisrael*. Historically, we have constantly yearned to return to Israel. That bond shall never be severed.

First Person or Third Person?

The Beit Yaakov, the second Rav of Ishbitz, points out that the first *berakha* of *Birkat HaMazon* is written in the third person: "***Hu** noten lehem lekhol basar* – **He** gives bread to all." The second *berakha* is written in the first person:

"*Nodeh*

ברכת הזן

בָּרוּךְ אַתָּה יהוה אֱלֹהֵינוּ מֶלֶךְ הָעוֹלָם
הַזָּן אֶת הָעוֹלָם כֻּלּוֹ בְּטוּבוֹ, בְּחֵן בְּחֶסֶד וּבְרַחֲמִים
הוּא נוֹתֵן לֶחֶם לְכָל בָּשָׂר כִּי לְעוֹלָם חַסְדּוֹ.
וּבְטוּבוֹ הַגָּדוֹל, תָּמִיד לֹא חָסַר לָנוּ
וְאַל יֶחְסַר לָנוּ מָזוֹן לְעוֹלָם וָעֶד
בַּעֲבוּר שְׁמוֹ הַגָּדוֹל.
כִּי הוּא אֵל זָן וּמְפַרְנֵס לַכֹּל, וּמֵטִיב לַכֹּל
וּמֵכִין מָזוֹן לְכָל בְּרִיּוֹתָיו אֲשֶׁר בָּרָא.
בָּרוּךְ אַתָּה יהוה, הַזָּן אֶת הַכֹּל.

ברכת הארץ

נוֹדֶה לְּךָ, יהוה אֱלֹהֵינוּ
עַל שֶׁהִנְחַלְתָּ לַאֲבוֹתֵינוּ אֶרֶץ חֶמְדָּה טוֹבָה וּרְחָבָה
וְעַל שֶׁהוֹצֵאתָנוּ יהוה אֱלֹהֵינוּ מֵאֶרֶץ מִצְרַיִם
וּפְדִיתָנוּ מִבֵּית עֲבָדִים
וְעַל בְּרִיתְךָ שֶׁחָתַמְתָּ בִּבְשָׂרֵנוּ, וְעַל תּוֹרָתְךָ שֶׁלִּמַּדְתָּנוּ
וְעַל חֻקֶּיךָ שֶׁהוֹדַעְתָּנוּ, וְעַל חַיִּים חֵן וָחֶסֶד שֶׁחוֹנַנְתָּנוּ
וְעַל אֲכִילַת מָזוֹן שָׁאַתָּה זָן וּמְפַרְנֵס אוֹתָנוּ תָּמִיד
בְּכָל יוֹם וּבְכָל עֵת וּבְכָל שָׁעָה.

ארץ חמדה – ERETZ HEMDA

In *Birkat HaMazon* we use the phrase "*Eretz hemda tova urehava.*" What is the meaning of this phrase? "*Hemda*" means a desirous land. The word appears in the beginning of *Sefer Bereshit,* where the Tree of Knowledge was labeled as having a pleasing appearance, "*nehmad lemareh.*" Rav Yosef Dov Soloveitchik explains that Hava felt some kind of magnetic pull that drew her to the tree. She couldn't stop herself. When she saw the tree, she fell under a spell. Like a sleepwalker, she reached out for its fruit almost involuntarily.

On Ḥanukka:

עַל הַנִּסִּים [We thank You also] for the miracles, the redemption, the mighty deeds, the salvations, and the victories in battle which You performed for our ancestors in those days, at this time.

בִּימֵי מַתִּתְיָהוּ In the days of Mattityahu, son of Yoḥanan, the High Priest, the Hasmonean, and his sons, the wicked Greek kingdom rose up against Your people Israel to make them forget Your Torah and to force them to transgress the statutes of Your will. It was then that You in Your great compassion stood by them in the time of their distress. You championed their cause, judged their claim, and avenged their wrong. You delivered the strong into the hands of the weak, the many into the hands of the few, the impure into the hands of the pure, the wicked into the hands of the righteous, and the arrogant into the hands of those who were engaged in the study of Your Torah. You made for Yourself great and holy renown in Your world, and for Your people Israel You performed a great salvation and redemption as of this very day. Your children then entered the holiest part of Your House, cleansed Your Temple, purified Your Sanctuary, kindled lights in Your holy courts, and designated these eight days of Ḥanukka for giving thanks and praise to Your great name.

Continue with "For all this."

On Purim:

עַל הַנִּסִּים [We thank You also] for the miracles, the redemption, the mighty deeds, the salvations, and the victories in battle which You performed for our ancestors in those days, at this time.

בִּימֵי מָרְדְּכַי In the days of Mordekhai and Esther, in Shushan the capital,
the wicked Haman rose up against them and sought to destroy, slay and *Esther 3*
exterminate all the Jews, young and old, children and women, on one day, the thirteenth day of the twelfth month, which is the month of Adar, and to plunder their possessions. Then You in Your great compassion thwarted his counsel, frustrated his plans, and caused his scheme to recoil on his own head, so that they hanged him and his sons on the gallows.

Continue with "For all this."

וְעַל הַכֹּל For all this, Lord our God, we thank and bless You.
May Your name be blessed continually
by the mouth of all that lives, for ever and all time –

and recite "*Nodeh lekha,*" we should remember the special connection we have and the direct *hashgaha* we experience through the privilege to live in *Eretz Yisrael.*

בחנוכה:

עַל הַנִּסִּים וְעַל הַפֻּרְקָן וְעַל הַגְּבוּרוֹת וְעַל הַתְּשׁוּעוֹת וְעַל הַמִּלְחָמוֹת שֶׁעָשִׂיתָ לַאֲבוֹתֵינוּ בַּיָּמִים הָהֵם בִּזְּמַן הַזֶּה.

בִּימֵי מַתִּתְיָהוּ בֶּן יוֹחָנָן כֹּהֵן גָּדוֹל חַשְׁמוֹנַאי וּבָנָיו, כְּשֶׁעָמְדָה מַלְכוּת יָוָן הָרְשָׁעָה עַל עַמְּךָ יִשְׂרָאֵל לְהַשְׁכִּיחָם תּוֹרָתֶךָ וּלְהַעֲבִירָם מֵחֻקֵּי רְצוֹנֶךָ, וְאַתָּה בְּרַחֲמֶיךָ הָרַבִּים עָמַדְתָּ לָהֶם בְּעֵת צָרָתָם, רַבְתָּ אֶת רִיבָם, דַּנְתָּ אֶת דִּינָם, נָקַמְתָּ אֶת נִקְמָתָם, מָסַרְתָּ גִבּוֹרִים בְּיַד חַלָּשִׁים, וְרַבִּים בְּיַד מְעַטִּים, וּטְמֵאִים בְּיַד טְהוֹרִים, וּרְשָׁעִים בְּיַד צַדִּיקִים, וְזֵדִים בְּיַד עוֹסְקֵי תוֹרָתֶךָ, וּלְךָ עָשִׂיתָ שֵׁם גָּדוֹל וְקָדוֹשׁ בְּעוֹלָמֶךָ, וּלְעַמְּךָ יִשְׂרָאֵל עָשִׂיתָ תְּשׁוּעָה גְדוֹלָה וּפֻרְקָן כְּהַיּוֹם הַזֶּה. וְאַחַר כֵּן בָּאוּ בָנֶיךָ לִדְבִיר בֵּיתֶךָ, וּפִנּוּ אֶת הֵיכָלֶךָ, וְטִהֲרוּ אֶת מִקְדָּשֶׁךָ, וְהִדְלִיקוּ נֵרוֹת בְּחַצְרוֹת קָדְשֶׁךָ, וְקָבְעוּ שְׁמוֹנַת יְמֵי חֲנֻכָּה אֵלּוּ, לְהוֹדוֹת וּלְהַלֵּל לְשִׁמְךָ הַגָּדוֹל.

Continue with וְעַל הַכֹּל.

בפורים:

עַל הַנִּסִּים וְעַל הַפֻּרְקָן וְעַל הַגְּבוּרוֹת וְעַל הַתְּשׁוּעוֹת וְעַל הַמִּלְחָמוֹת שֶׁעָשִׂיתָ לַאֲבוֹתֵינוּ בַּיָּמִים הָהֵם בִּזְּמַן הַזֶּה.

בִּימֵי מָרְדְּכַי וְאֶסְתֵּר בְּשׁוּשַׁן הַבִּירָה, כְּשֶׁעָמַד עֲלֵיהֶם הָמָן הָרָשָׁע, בִּקֵּשׁ לְהַשְׁמִיד לַהֲרֹג וּלְאַבֵּד אֶת־כָּל־הַיְּהוּדִים מִנַּעַר וְעַד־זָקֵן טַף וְנָשִׁים בְּיוֹם אֶחָד, בִּשְׁלוֹשָׁה עָשָׂר לְחֹדֶשׁ שְׁנֵים־עָשָׂר, הוּא־חֹדֶשׁ אֲדָר, וּשְׁלָלָם לָבוֹז: (אסתר ג) וְאַתָּה בְּרַחֲמֶיךָ הָרַבִּים הֵפַרְתָּ אֶת עֲצָתוֹ, וְקִלְקַלְתָּ אֶת מַחֲשַׁבְתּוֹ, וַהֲשֵׁבוֹתָ לּוֹ גְּמוּלוֹ בְּרֹאשׁוֹ, וְתָלוּ אוֹתוֹ וְאֶת בָּנָיו עַל הָעֵץ.

Continue with וְעַל הַכֹּל.

וְעַל הַכֹּל, יהוה אֱלֹהֵינוּ, אֲנַחְנוּ מוֹדִים לָךְ וּמְבָרְכִים אוֹתָךְ, יִתְבָּרַךְ שִׁמְךָ בְּפִי כָּל חַי תָּמִיד לְעוֹלָם וָעֶד

"*Nodeh lekha* – We express gratitude to **You**." Why do we switch from third person to first person, starting off distant and then coming closer?

The Ishbitzer explains that there is a distinction based on the individual who authored each *berakha*. The first *berakha* was written by Moshe Rabbeinu in connection with the *mann*. The second *berakha* was written by Yehoshua bin Nun, when *Bnei Yisrael* entered *Eretz Yisrael*. There's a certain level of closeness with *HaKadosh Barukh Hu* that a Jew can have only in *Eretz Yisrael*, and Moshe Rabbeinu didn't merit that, as he never entered the land. Whenever we *bentch*,

for so it is written:
"You will eat and be satisfied, then you shall bless the LORD your God for the good land He has given you." *Deut. 8*
Blessed are You, LORD,
for the land and for the food.

BLESSING FOR JERUSALEM

רַחֶם נָא Have compassion, please, LORD our God,
on Israel Your people,
on Jerusalem Your city,
on Zion the dwelling place of Your glory,
on the royal house of David Your anointed,
and on the great and holy House that bears Your name.
Our God, our Father,
tend us, feed us, sustain us and support us,
relieve us and send us relief, LORD our God,
swiftly from all our troubles.
Please, LORD our God, do not make us dependent
on the gifts or loans of other people,
but only on Your full, open, holy and generous hand
so that we may suffer neither shame nor humiliation
for ever and all time.

סומא לעולם אינו שֹבֵע כיון שאינו רואה מאכלו.

A blind person is never satiated, because he cannot see his food.

With respect to delicacies, it's often all about the presentation. The Gemara cited above declares that one who cannot visualize the food before him cannot fully appreciate the taste and will not be fully satiated. When we ask Hashem to satiate us, we also request that we recognize all the good that Hashem is bestowing upon us so that we can express our gratitude for all of His *hesed*. Some people fail to see how blessed they are. May we be able to recognize and appreciate our blessings.

כַּכָּתוּב:

וְאָכַלְתָּ וְשָׂבָעְתָּ, וּבֵרַכְתָּ אֶת־יהוה אֱלֹהֶיךָ דברים ח
עַל־הָאָרֶץ הַטֹּבָה אֲשֶׁר נָתַן־לָךְ:
בָּרוּךְ אַתָּה יהוה, עַל הָאָרֶץ וְעַל הַמָּזוֹן.

ברכת ירושלים

רַחֶם נָא, יהוה אֱלֹהֵינוּ
עַל יִשְׂרָאֵל עַמֶּךָ
וְעַל יְרוּשָׁלַיִם עִירֶךָ
וְעַל צִיּוֹן מִשְׁכַּן כְּבוֹדֶךָ
וְעַל מַלְכוּת בֵּית דָּוִד מְשִׁיחֶךָ
וְעַל הַבַּיִת הַגָּדוֹל וְהַקָּדוֹשׁ שֶׁנִּקְרָא שִׁמְךָ עָלָיו.
אֱלֹהֵינוּ, אָבִינוּ
רְעֵנוּ, זוּנֵנוּ, פַּרְנְסֵנוּ וְכַלְכְּלֵנוּ
וְהַרְוִיחֵנוּ, וְהַרְוַח לָנוּ יהוה אֱלֹהֵינוּ מְהֵרָה מִכָּל צָרוֹתֵינוּ.
וְנָא אַל תַּצְרִיכֵנוּ, יהוה אֱלֹהֵינוּ
לֹא לִידֵי מַתְּנַת בָּשָׂר וָדָם
וְלֹא לִידֵי הַלְוָאָתָם
כִּי אִם לְיָדְךָ הַמְּלֵאָה, הַפְּתוּחָה, הַקְּדוֹשָׁה וְהָרְחָבָה
שֶׁלֹּא נֵבוֹשׁ וְלֹא נִכָּלֵם לְעוֹלָם וָעֶד.

ואכלת ושבעת – VEAKHALTA VESAVATA

Recognizing One's Blessings

In his *birkon* (*Minhat Asher*), Rav Asher Weiss cites an idea he heard from the Divrei Yatziv, the Klausenberger Rebbe. In the *Amida shel Shabbat*, we ask: "*Sabeinu mituvekha* – Satiate us with Your goodness." The Gemara (Yoma 74b) states:

On Shabbat, say:

רְצֵה Favor and strengthen us, Lord our God,
through Your commandments,
especially through the commandment of the seventh day,
this great and holy Sabbath.
For it is, for You, a great and holy day.
On it we cease work and rest in love
in accord with Your will's commandment.
May it be Your will, Lord our God,
to grant us rest without distress, grief, or lament on our day of rest.
May You show us the consolation of Zion Your city,
and the rebuilding of Jerusalem Your holy city,
for You are the Master of salvation and consolation.

On Rosh Ḥodesh and Festivals, say:

אֱלֹהֵינוּ Our God and God of our ancestors,
may there rise, come, reach, appear, be favored, heard, regarded
and remembered before You, our recollection and remembrance,
as well as the remembrance of our ancestors,
and of the Messiah son of David Your servant,
and of Jerusalem Your holy city,
and of all Your people the house of Israel –
for deliverance and well-being, grace,
loving-kindness and compassion, life and peace, on this day of:

On Rosh Ḥodesh: Rosh Ḥodesh.
On Rosh HaShana: the Day of Memorial.
On Pesaḥ: the Festival of Matzot.
On Shavuot: the Festival of Shavuot.
On Sukkot: the Festival of Sukkot.
On Shemini Atzeret & Simḥat Torah: the Festival of Shemini Atzeret.

On it remember us, Lord our God, for good;
recollect us for blessing, and deliver us for life.
In accord with Your promise of salvation and compassion,
spare us and be gracious to us;
have compassion on us and deliver us,
for our eyes are turned to You because You are God,
gracious and compassionate (*on Rosh HaShana:* King).

On שבת, say:

רְצֵה וְהַחֲלִיצֵנוּ, יהוה אֱלֹהֵינוּ, בְּמִצְוֹתֶיךָ
וּבְמִצְוַת יוֹם הַשְּׁבִיעִי הַשַּׁבָּת הַגָּדוֹל וְהַקָּדוֹשׁ הַזֶּה
כִּי יוֹם זֶה גָּדוֹל וְקָדוֹשׁ הוּא לְפָנֶיךָ
לִשְׁבָּת בּוֹ, וְלָנוּחַ בּוֹ בְּאַהֲבָה כְּמִצְוַת רְצוֹנֶךָ
וּבִרְצוֹנְךָ הָנִיחַ לָנוּ, יהוה אֱלֹהֵינוּ
שֶׁלֹּא תְהֵא צָרָה וְיָגוֹן וַאֲנָחָה בְּיוֹם מְנוּחָתֵנוּ
וְהַרְאֵנוּ, יהוה אֱלֹהֵינוּ, בְּנֶחָמַת צִיּוֹן עִירֶךָ
וּבְבִנְיַן יְרוּשָׁלַיִם עִיר קָדְשֶׁךָ
כִּי אַתָּה הוּא בַּעַל הַיְשׁוּעוֹת וּבַעַל הַנֶּחָמוֹת.

On ראש חודש and חגים, say:

אֱלֹהֵינוּ וֵאלֹהֵי אֲבוֹתֵינוּ, יַעֲלֶה וְיָבוֹא וְיַגִּיעַ, וְיֵרָאֶה וְיֵרָצֶה וְיִשָּׁמַע
וְיִפָּקֵד וְיִזָּכֵר זִכְרוֹנֵנוּ וּפִקְדוֹנֵנוּ, וְזִכְרוֹן אֲבוֹתֵינוּ
וְזִכְרוֹן מָשִׁיחַ בֶּן דָּוִד עַבְדֶּךָ
וְזִכְרוֹן יְרוּשָׁלַיִם עִיר קָדְשֶׁךָ
וְזִכְרוֹן כָּל עַמְּךָ בֵּית יִשְׂרָאֵל
לְפָנֶיךָ, לִפְלֵיטָה לְטוֹבָה, לְחֵן וּלְחֶסֶד וּלְרַחֲמִים
לְחַיִּים וּלְשָׁלוֹם בְּיוֹם

בראש חודש: רֹאשׁ הַחֹדֶשׁ הַזֶּה.

בראש השנה: הַזִּכָּרוֹן הַזֶּה.

בפסח: חַג הַמַּצּוֹת הַזֶּה.

בשבועות: חַג הַשָּׁבוּעוֹת הַזֶּה.

בסוכות: חַג הַסֻּכּוֹת הַזֶּה.

בשמיני עצרת ושמחת תורה: הַשְּׁמִינִי חַג הָעֲצֶרֶת הַזֶּה.

זָכְרֵנוּ יהוה אֱלֹהֵינוּ בּוֹ לְטוֹבָה
וּפָקְדֵנוּ בוֹ לִבְרָכָה, וְהוֹשִׁיעֵנוּ בוֹ לְחַיִּים.
וּבִדְבַר יְשׁוּעָה וְרַחֲמִים, חוּס וְחָנֵּנוּ וְרַחֵם עָלֵינוּ, וְהוֹשִׁיעֵנוּ
כִּי אֵלֶיךָ עֵינֵינוּ, כִּי אֵל (בראש השנה: מֶלֶךְ) חַנּוּן וְרַחוּם אָתָּה.

וּבְנֵה And may Jerusalem the holy city be rebuilt soon, in our time.
Blessed are You, LORD, who in His compassion
will rebuild Jerusalem. Amen.

BLESSING OF GOD'S GOODNESS

בָּרוּךְ Blessed are You, LORD our God, King of the Universe –
God our Father, our King, our Sovereign,
our Creator, our Redeemer, our Maker,
our Holy One, the Holy One of Jacob.
He is our Shepherd, Israel's Shepherd,
the good King who does good to all.
Every day He has done, is doing, and will do good to us.
He has acted, is acting, and will always act kindly
toward us for ever,
granting us grace, kindness and compassion, relief and rescue,
prosperity, blessing, redemption and comfort,
sustenance and support, compassion,
life, peace and all good things,
and of all good things may He never let us lack.

ADDITIONAL REQUESTS

הָרַחֲמָן May the Compassionate One
reign over us for ever and all time.
May the Compassionate One
be blessed in heaven and on earth.
May the Compassionate One
be praised from generation to generation,
be glorified by us to all eternity,
and honored among us for ever and all time.
May the Compassionate One
grant us an honorable livelihood.
May the Compassionate One
break the yoke from our neck
and lead us upright to our land.

וּבְנֵה יְרוּשָׁלַיִם עִיר הַקֹּדֶשׁ בִּמְהֵרָה בְיָמֵינוּ.
בָּרוּךְ אַתָּה יהוה, בּוֹנֶה בְרַחֲמָיו יְרוּשָׁלָיִם, אָמֵן.

ברכת הטוב והמיטיב

בָּרוּךְ אַתָּה יהוה אֱלֹהֵינוּ מֶלֶךְ הָעוֹלָם
הָאֵל אָבִינוּ, מַלְכֵּנוּ, אַדִּירֵנוּ
בּוֹרְאֵנוּ, גּוֹאֲלֵנוּ, יוֹצְרֵנוּ, קְדוֹשֵׁנוּ, קְדוֹשׁ יַעֲקֹב
רוֹעֵנוּ, רוֹעֵה יִשְׂרָאֵל, הַמֶּלֶךְ הַטּוֹב וְהַמֵּטִיב לַכֹּל
שֶׁבְּכָל יוֹם וָיוֹם
הוּא הֵיטִיב, הוּא מֵטִיב, הוּא יֵיטִיב לָנוּ
הוּא גְמָלָנוּ, הוּא גוֹמְלֵנוּ, הוּא יִגְמְלֵנוּ לָעַד
לְחֵן וּלְחֶסֶד וּלְרַחֲמִים, וּלְרֶוַח, הַצָּלָה וְהַצְלָחָה
בְּרָכָה וִישׁוּעָה, נֶחָמָה, פַּרְנָסָה וְכַלְכָּלָה
וְרַחֲמִים וְחַיִּים וְשָׁלוֹם וְכָל טוֹב
וּמִכָּל טוּב לְעוֹלָם אַל יְחַסְּרֵנוּ.

בקשות נוספות

הָרַחֲמָן הוּא יִמְלֹךְ עָלֵינוּ לְעוֹלָם וָעֶד.

הָרַחֲמָן הוּא יִתְבָּרַךְ בַּשָּׁמַיִם וּבָאָרֶץ.

הָרַחֲמָן הוּא יִשְׁתַּבַּח לְדוֹר דּוֹרִים
וְיִתְפָּאַר בָּנוּ לָעַד וּלְנֵצַח נְצָחִים
וְיִתְהַדַּר בָּנוּ לָעַד וּלְעוֹלְמֵי עוֹלָמִים.

הָרַחֲמָן הוּא יְפַרְנְסֵנוּ בְּכָבוֹד.

הָרַחֲמָן הוּא יִשְׁבֹּר עֻלֵּנוּ מֵעַל צַוָּארֵנוּ
וְהוּא יוֹלִיכֵנוּ קוֹמְמִיּוּת לְאַרְצֵנוּ.

May the Compassionate One
send us many blessings to this house
and this table at which we have eaten.
May the Compassionate One
send us Elijah the prophet –
may he be remembered for good –
to bring us good tidings of salvation and consolation.

Some say:

May the Compassionate One
bless the State of Israel, first flowering of our redemption.

May the Compassionate One
bless the members of Israel's Defense Forces,
who stand guard over our land.

A guest says:

יְהִי רָצוֹן May it be Your will that the master of this house shall not suffer shame in this world, nor humiliation in the World to Come. May all he owns prosper greatly, and may his and our possessions be successful and close to hand. Let not the Accuser hold sway over his deeds or ours, and may no thought of sin, iniquity or transgression enter him or us from now and for evermore.

הָרַחֲמָן May the Compassionate One bless –

When eating at one's own table, say (include the words in parentheses that apply):
me, (my wife/husband, / my father, my teacher / my mother,
my teacher/ my children,) and all that is mine,

A guest at someone else's table says (include the words in parentheses that apply):
the master of this house, him (and his wife,
the mistress of this house / and his children,) and all that is his,

Children at their parents' table say (include the words in parentheses that apply):
my father, my teacher, (master of this house,) and my mother, my teacher, (mistress of this house,) them, their household, their children, and all that is theirs.

For all other guests, add:
and all the diners here,

הָרַחֲמָן הוּא יִשְׁלַח לָנוּ בְּרָכָה מְרֻבָּה בַּבַּיִת הַזֶּה
וְעַל שֻׁלְחָן זֶה שֶׁאָכַלְנוּ עָלָיו.
הָרַחֲמָן הוּא יִשְׁלַח לָנוּ אֶת אֵלִיָּהוּ הַנָּבִיא זָכוּר לַטּוֹב
וִיבַשֶּׂר לָנוּ בְּשׂוֹרוֹת טוֹבוֹת יְשׁוּעוֹת וְנֶחָמוֹת.

Some say:

הָרַחֲמָן הוּא יְבָרֵךְ אֶת מְדִינַת יִשְׂרָאֵל רֵאשִׁית צְמִיחַת גְּאֻלָּתֵנוּ.
הָרַחֲמָן הוּא יְבָרֵךְ אֶת חַיָּלֵי צְבָא הַהֲגָנָה לְיִשְׂרָאֵל
הָעוֹמְדִים עַל מִשְׁמַר אַרְצֵנוּ.

A guest says:

יְהִי רָצוֹן שֶׁלֹּא יֵבוֹשׁ בַּעַל הַבַּיִת בָּעוֹלָם הַזֶּה, וְלֹא יִכָּלֵם לָעוֹלָם הַבָּא, וְיִצְלַח מְאֹד בְּכָל נְכָסָיו, וְיִהְיוּ נְכָסָיו וּנְכָסֵינוּ מֻצְלָחִים וּקְרוֹבִים לָעִיר, וְאַל יִשְׁלֹט שָׂטָן לֹא בְּמַעֲשֵׂה יָדָיו וְלֹא בְּמַעֲשֵׂה יָדֵינוּ. וְאַל יִזְדַּקֵּק לֹא לְפָנָיו וְלֹא לְפָנֵינוּ שׁוּם דְּבַר הִרְהוּר חֵטְא, עֲבֵירָה וְעָוֹן, מֵעַתָּה וְעַד עוֹלָם.

הָרַחֲמָן הוּא יְבָרֵךְ

When eating at one's own table, say (include the words in parentheses that apply):

אוֹתִי (וְאֶת אִשְׁתִּי / וְאֶת בַּעֲלִי / וְאֶת אָבִי מוֹרִי /
וְאֶת אִמִּי מוֹרָתִי / וְאֶת זַרְעִי) וְאֶת כָּל אֲשֶׁר לִי.

A guest at someone else's table says (include the words in parentheses that apply):

אֶת בַּעַל הַבַּיִת הַזֶּה, אוֹתוֹ (וְאֶת אִשְׁתּוֹ בַּעֲלַת הַבַּיִת הַזֶּה /
וְאֶת זַרְעוֹ) וְאֶת כָּל אֲשֶׁר לוֹ.

Children at their parents' table say (include the words in parentheses that apply):

אֶת אָבִי מוֹרִי (בַּעַל הַבַּיִת הַזֶּה), וְאֶת אִמִּי מוֹרָתִי (בַּעֲלַת הַבַּיִת הַזֶּה), אוֹתָם וְאֶת בֵּיתָם וְאֶת זַרְעָם וְאֶת כָּל אֲשֶׁר לָהֶם

For all other guests, add:

וְאֶת כָּל הַמְּסֻבִּין כָּאן

אוֹתָנוּ – together with us and all that is ours.
Just as our forefathers
Abraham, Isaac and Jacob were blessed in all, from all, with all,
so may He bless all of us together with a complete blessing,
and let us say: Amen.

בַּמָּרוֹם On high, may grace be invoked for them and for us,
as a safeguard of peace.
May we receive a blessing from the Lord
and a just reward from the God of our salvation,
and may we find grace and good favor in the eyes of God and man.

The source of the commandment of *Birkat HaMazon* appears in *Devarim* 8:7–10:

> כי ה׳ א-להיך מביאך אל ארץ טובה, ארץ נחלי מים עינת ותהמת יצאים בבקעה ובהר... ואכלת ושבעת, וברכת את ה׳ א-להיך על הארץ הטבה אשר נתן לך.

> For Hashem your God is bringing you into a good land, a land of brooks of water, rivers of water flowing down from the valley and from the mountains.... And you shall eat and be satisfied, and you shall bless Hashem your God for the good land which He has given you.

According to the plain meaning of the text, this verse is not only a commandment, but also a promise. It includes a promise that when Hashem brings us to the Land of Israel as promised to our forefathers, we will eat its fruit and be satiated and thank Hashem for the land.

It is true that we may not deserve to see the fulfillment of this promise, and even if we deserve to be blessed with dwelling in the Land of Israel, we may not have enough food, and yet we express our gratitude to Hashem for His abundant mercy and grace upon us.

Hashem thus responds to the angels: How can I not show favor to Israel, to whom I said: "And you shall eat and be satisfied," and even when I do not keep this promise and they do not have enough to eat, they show favor to Me beyond the letter of the law and bless for the little that I have bestowed upon them, from the size of an olive to the size of an egg. Therefore, I will also show favor to them and deal with them with mercy, measure for measure, and just as they show favor to Me, I will also show favor to them with mercy and compassion.

At the

אוֹתָנוּ וְאֶת כׇּל אֲשֶׁר לָנוּ, כְּמוֹ שֶׁנִּתְבָּרְכוּ אֲבוֹתֵינוּ
אַבְרָהָם יִצְחָק וְיַעֲקֹב, בַּכֹּל, מִכֹּל, כֹּל
כֵּן יְבָרֵךְ אוֹתָנוּ כֻּלָּנוּ יַחַד בִּבְרָכָה שְׁלֵמָה, וְנֹאמַר אָמֵן.

בַּמָּרוֹם יְלַמְּדוּ עֲלֵיהֶם וְעָלֵינוּ זְכוּת שֶׁתְּהֵא לְמִשְׁמֶרֶת שָׁלוֹם
וְנִשָּׂא בְרָכָה מֵאֵת יהוה וּצְדָקָה מֵאֱלֹהֵי יִשְׁעֵנוּ
וְנִמְצָא חֵן וְשֵׂכֶל טוֹב בְּעֵינֵי אֱלֹהִים וְאָדָם.

BAMAROM – CONNECTING BIRKAT HAMAZON TO THE PRIESTLY BLESSING

דרש רב עוירא... אמרו מלאכי השרת לפני הקדוש ברוך הוא, רבונו של עולם, כתוב בתורתך "אשר לא ישא פנים ולא יקח שחד", והלא אתה נושא פנים לישראל, דכתיב "ישא ה׳ פניו אליך". אמר להם וכי לא אשא פנים לישראל, שכתבתי להם בתורה "ואכלת ושבעת, וברכת את ה׳ א-להיך", והם מדקדקים על עצמם עד כזית ועד כביצה (ברכות כ׳ ע"ב).

Rav Avira stated ... The angels who minister before the Holy One, blessed be He: Master of the Universe, It is written in your Torah, "Who does not show favoritism or accept bribes," but do you not show favoritism to Israel, as it is written [in *Birkat Kohanim*], "May Hashem show favoritism to you"? Hashem replied to the angels: Should I not show favoritism to Israel, for I have written for them in the Torah: "And you will eat and be satisfied, and you will bless the Lord your God," and they are strict about themselves and bless Me even when they eat as little as an olive or an egg! (Berakhot 20b)

Why are we granted the privilege of Hashem showing His favoritism toward us specifically because we are strict about reciting the blessing of *Birkat HaMazon* after having consumed an amount equal to an olive or an egg rather than only upon being fully satiated? Why not merit this blessing for being strict with regard to reciting three *parshiyot* of Shema or for reciting the *Amida* three times a day, both of which are more than the minimum required for each mitzva?

Let's understand the significance of this stringency.

At a circumcision feast add here "May the Compassionate One bless the father" on page 198.

On Shabbat: May the Compassionate One let us inherit the time,
that will be entirely Shabbat and rest for life everlasting.

On Rosh Ḥodesh: May the Compassionate One renew this month for us,
for good and blessing.

On Rosh HaShana: May the Compassionate One renew for us this year,
for good and blessing.

On Yom Tov: May the Compassionate One let us inherit the day,
that is all good.

On Sukkot: May the Compassionate One restore for us,
the fallen Tabernacle of David.

הָרַחֲמָן May the Compassionate One make us worthy
of the Messianic Age and life in the World to Come.
He gives great / *On Shabbat, Festivals, and Rosh Ḥodesh:* He is a tower of / *II Sam. 22*
salvation to His king, showing kindness to His anointed,
to David and his descendants for ever.
He who makes peace in His high places,
may He make peace for us and all Israel, and let us say: Amen.

יְראוּ Fear the LORD, you His holy ones; *Ps. 34*
those who fear Him lack nothing.
Young lions may grow weak and hungry,
but those who seek the LORD lack no good thing.

---

preservation of peace – למשמרת שלום. Then they will all thank and praise Hashem: ישא ה׳ פניו אליך וישם לך שלום – May Hashem lift up His face to you and grant you peace.

ונשא ברכה – And may He bring a blessing from Hashem, as it says: יברכך ה׳ וישמרך – May Hashem bless you and keep you....

ונמצא חן – We will find favor in God's eyes; this is parallel to – ויחנך.

We merit the blessing of peace granted to us through the *kohanim* for taking upon ourselves the stringency of reciting the blessing of *Birkat HaMazon* even if not satiated, having eaten merely an amount equal to an olive or egg.

At a meal after a ברית *add here* הָרַחֲמָן הוּא יְבָרֵךְ אֲבִי הַיֶּלֶד *on page 199.*

בשבת: הָרַחֲמָן הוּא יַנְחִילֵנוּ יוֹם שֶׁכֻּלּוֹ שַׁבָּת וּמְנוּחָה לְחַיֵּי הָעוֹלָמִים.

בראש חודש: הָרַחֲמָן הוּא יְחַדֵּשׁ עָלֵינוּ אֶת הַחֹדֶשׁ הַזֶּה לְטוֹבָה וְלִבְרָכָה.

בראש השנה: הָרַחֲמָן הוּא יְחַדֵּשׁ עָלֵינוּ אֶת הַשָּׁנָה הַזֹּאת לְטוֹבָה וְלִבְרָכָה.

ביום טוב: הָרַחֲמָן הוּא יַנְחִילֵנוּ יוֹם שֶׁכֻּלּוֹ טוֹב.

בסוכות: הָרַחֲמָן הוּא יָקִים לָנוּ אֶת סֻכַּת דָּוִד הַנּוֹפֶלֶת.

הָרַחֲמָן הוּא יְזַכֵּנוּ לִימוֹת הַמָּשִׁיחַ וּלְחַיֵּי הָעוֹלָם הַבָּא
מַגְדִּל/ *On* שבת*,* חגים*, and* ראש חודש מִגְדּוֹל/ יְשׁוּעוֹת מַלְכּוֹ שמואל ב׳ כב
וְעֹשֶׂה־חֶסֶד לִמְשִׁיחוֹ, לְדָוִד וּלְזַרְעוֹ עַד־עוֹלָם:
עֹשֶׂה שָׁלוֹם בִּמְרוֹמָיו
הוּא יַעֲשֶׂה שָׁלוֹם עָלֵינוּ וְעַל כָּל יִשְׂרָאֵל, וְאִמְרוּ אָמֵן.

יְראוּ אֶת־יהוה קְדֹשָׁיו, כִּי־אֵין מַחְסוֹר לִירֵאָיו: תהלים לד
כְּפִירִים רָשׁוּ וְרָעֵבוּ, וְדֹרְשֵׁי יהוה לֹא־יַחְסְרוּ כָל־טוֹב:

At the end of *Birkat HaMazon* we recite the following:

במרום ילמדו עליהם ועלינו זכות שתהא למשמרת שלום.

> In the heights they will learn about them and about us, a merit that will be for the preservation of peace.

We do not find a similar statement in any other prayer, and the words are not easily understood. Rav Asher Weiss (*Birkon Minhat Asher*) offers a fascinating explanation.

Perhaps the paragraph of **במרום** (*Bamarom*) that we recite at the end of *Birkat HaMazon* is linked to *Birkat Kohanim* (blessing of priests), and these two blessings are connected. We ask that in the heights, the angels will attribute to us a merit; when asked how God shows favor to Israel, may they respond that in the name of our forefathers and ourselves we merit the

Thank the Lord for He is good; *Ps. 118*
His loving-kindness is for ever.
You open Your hand, and satisfy every living thing with favor. *Ps. 145*
Blessed is the person who trusts in the Lord, *Jer. 17*
whose trust is in the Lord alone.
Once I was young, and now I am old, *Ps. 37*
yet I have never watched a righteous man forsaken
or his children begging for bread.
The Lord will give His people strength. *Ps. 29*
The Lord will bless His people with peace.

If Birkat HaMazon was made on a cup of wine, t hen the blessing over wine is made and the majority of the cup is drunk, after which the Berakha Me'ein Shalosh, page 172, is said.

At a wedding or Sheva Berakhot, turn to page 182.

---

the verse above can be understood in this fashion as well: I've grown old, and I have experienced a lot in my life, but I never stood idly by when I saw someone in need.

When we express our appreciation to Hashem after consuming our meal, we declare that we will provide for others too, just as Hashem has provided for us. Essentially, we are saying: I never witnessed a *tzaddik* lacking, because I cared for him. We must always focus on other people's physical needs.

In Judaism, the right side of the body is always more significant. Why, then, did Hashem create the heart on the left side of the body? I once heard that it is because it is on the right side of the person facing you; our heart should be focused on that of the other.

הוֹדוּ לַיהוה כִּי־טוֹב תהלים קיח
כִּי לְעוֹלָם חַסְדּוֹ:
פּוֹתֵחַ אֶת־יָדֶךָ תהלים קמה
וּמַשְׂבִּיעַ לְכָל־חַי רָצוֹן:
בָּרוּךְ הַגֶּבֶר אֲשֶׁר יִבְטַח בַּיהוה ירמיה יז
וְהָיָה יהוה מִבְטַחוֹ:
נַעַר הָיִיתִי גַּם־זָקַנְתִּי תהלים לז
וְלֹא־רָאִיתִי צַדִּיק נֶעֱזָב וְזַרְעוֹ מְבַקֶּשׁ־לָחֶם:
יהוה עֹז לְעַמּוֹ יִתֵּן תהלים כט
יהוה יְבָרֵךְ אֶת־עַמּוֹ בַשָּׁלוֹם:

If ברכת המזון *was made on a cup of wine,*
then בּוֹרֵא פְּרִי הַגָּפֶן *is said and the majority of the cup is drunk,*
after which ברכה מעין שלוש*, page 173, is said.*

At a wedding or שבע ברכות*, turn to page 183.*

נער הייתי – NAAR HAYITI

Caring for Others

In *Birkat HaMazon,* we recite: "*Naar hayiti, gam zakanti, velo ra'iti tzaddik ne'ezav.*" Do we ever think about the meaning of this *pasuk*? "I have lived many days and I've never seen a *tzaddik* who was forsaken." Is this statement accurate? Are there no righteous people who suffer?

Rabbi Lord Jonathan Sacks says (*Haggada,* p. 118) that the key phrase here is "*lo ra'iti.*" Think back to *Megillat Esther*. Esther says, "*Eikhakha ukhal vera'iti b'avdan moladeti* – How can I bear to see the destruction of my nation?" (*Esther* 8:6). "*Ra'iti*" means to see something and not react to it. Perhaps

Berakha Me'ein Shalosh

Grace after eating from the "seven species" of produce with which Israel is blessed: food made from the five grains (but not bread or matza); wine or grape juice; grapes, figs, pomegranates, olives, or dates.

בָּרוּךְ Blessed are You, Lord our God, King of the Universe,

After grain products:	*After wine or grape juice:*	*After grapes, figs, olives, pomegranates or dates:*
for the nourishment and sustenance,	for the vine and the fruit of the vine,	for the tree and the fruit of the tree,

After grain products, and wine or grape juice:
for the nourishment and sustenance
and for the vine and the fruit of the vine,

and for the produce of the field; for the desirable, good and spacious land that You willingly gave as heritage to our ancestors, that they might eat of its fruit and be satisfied with its goodness. Have compassion, please, Lord our God, on Israel Your people, on Jerusalem, Your city, on Zion the home of Your glory, on Your altar and Your Temple. May You rebuild Jerusalem, the holy city swiftly in our time, and may You bring us back there, rejoicing in its rebuilding, eating from its fruit, satisfied by its goodness, and blessing You for it in holiness and purity.

On Shabbat: Be pleased to refresh us on this Sabbath Day.

On Rosh Ḥodesh: Remember us for good on this day of the New Moon.

On Rosh HaShana: Remember us for good on this Day of Remembrance.

On Pesaḥ: Grant us joy on this Festival of Matzot.

On Shavuot: Grant us joy on this Festival of Shavuot.

On Sukkot: Grant us joy on this Festival of Sukkot.

On Shemini Atzeret & Simḥat Torah: Grant us joy on this Festival of Shemini Atzeret.

Gemara (Sota 14) declares that Moshe did not plead to be granted the ability to enter Israel because he wanted to eat its succulent fruit, but rather so he would be able to fulfill the mitzvot that can only be performed in *Eretz Yisrael*.

So why

ברכה מעין שלוש

Grace after eating from the "seven species" of produce with which ארץ ישראל *is blessed: food made from the five grains (but not bread or* מצה*); wine or grape juice; grapes, figs, pomegranates, olives, or dates.*

בָּרוּךְ אַתָּה יהוה אֱלֹהֵינוּ מֶלֶךְ הָעוֹלָם, עַל

After grain products:
הַמִּחְיָה וְעַל הַכַּלְכָּלָה

After wine or grape juice:
הַגֶּפֶן וְעַל פְּרִי הַגֶּפֶן

After grapes, figs, olives, pomegranates or dates:
הָעֵץ וְעַל פְּרִי הָעֵץ

After grain products, and wine or grape juice:
הַמִּחְיָה וְעַל הַכַּלְכָּלָה וְעַל הַגֶּפֶן וְעַל פְּרִי הַגֶּפֶן

וְעַל תְּנוּבַת הַשָּׂדֶה וְעַל אֶרֶץ חֶמְדָּה טוֹבָה וּרְחָבָה, שֶׁרָצִיתָ וְהִנְחַלְתָּ לַאֲבוֹתֵינוּ לֶאֱכֹל מִפִּרְיָהּ וְלִשְׂבֹּעַ מִטּוּבָהּ. רַחֶם נָא יהוה אֱלֹהֵינוּ עַל יִשְׂרָאֵל עַמֶּךָ וְעַל יְרוּשָׁלַיִם עִירֶךָ וְעַל צִיּוֹן מִשְׁכַּן כְּבוֹדֶךָ וְעַל מִזְבְּחֶךָ וְעַל הֵיכָלֶךָ. וּבְנֵה יְרוּשָׁלַיִם עִיר הַקֹּדֶשׁ בִּמְהֵרָה בְיָמֵינוּ, וְהַעֲלֵנוּ לְתוֹכָהּ וְשַׂמְּחֵנוּ בְּבִנְיָנָהּ וְנֹאכַל מִפִּרְיָהּ וְנִשְׂבַּע מִטּוּבָהּ, וּנְבָרֶכְךָ עָלֶיהָ בִּקְדֻשָּׁה וּבְטָהֳרָה.

בשבת: וּרְצֵה וְהַחֲלִיצֵנוּ בְּיוֹם הַשַּׁבָּת הַזֶּה
בראש חודש: וְזָכְרֵנוּ לְטוֹבָה בְּיוֹם רֹאשׁ הַחֹדֶשׁ הַזֶּה
בראש השנה: וְזָכְרֵנוּ לְטוֹבָה בְּיוֹם הַזִּכָּרוֹן הַזֶּה
בפסח: וְשַׂמְּחֵנוּ בְּיוֹם חַג הַמַּצּוֹת הַזֶּה
בשבועות: וְשַׂמְּחֵנוּ בְּיוֹם חַג הַשָּׁבוּעוֹת הַזֶּה
בסוכות: וְשַׂמְּחֵנוּ בְּיוֹם חַג הַסֻּכּוֹת הַזֶּה
בשמיני עצרת ושמחת תורה: וְשַׂמְּחֵנוּ בְּיוֹם הַשְּׁמִינִי חַג הָעֲצֶרֶת הַזֶּה

ברכה מעין שלוש – BERAKHA ME'EIN SHALOSH

Fruit of Eretz Yisrael Infused with Kedusha

The Tur (O.C. 208) quotes a *mahloket* with respect to whether one should include in *Al HaMihya* the words "*venokhal mipirya venisba mituva.*" The

For You, LORD, are good and do good to all and we thank You for the land

After grain products:	*After wine or grape juice:*	*After grapes, figs, olives, pomegranates or dates:*
and for the nourishment. Blessed are You, LORD, for the land and for the nourishment.	and for the fruit of the vine.* Blessed are You, LORD, for the land and for the fruit of the vine.*	and for the fruit.** Blessed are You, LORD, for the land and for the fruit.**

After grain products, and wine or grape juice:

and for the nourishment and for the fruit of the vine.*
Blessed are You, LORD, for the land and for the nourishment
and the fruit of the vine.*

* *If the wine is from Israel, then substitute "her vine" for "the vine."*
** *If the fruit is from Israel, then substitute "her fruit" for "the fruit."*

Blessing After Food – Borei Nefashot

After food or drink that does not require Birkat HaMazon or Berakha Me'ein Shalosh – such as meat, fish, dairy products, vegetables, beverages, or fruit other than grapes, figs, pomegranates, olives or dates – say:

בָּרוּךְ Blessed are You, LORD our God, King of the Universe,
who creates the many forms of life and their needs.
For all You have created to sustain the life of all that lives,
blessed be He, Giver of life to the worlds.

---

orla? Do I need to take *teruma* or *maaser* from it? No, it did not grow in Israel. Do I need to be concerned about whether this apple grew during *shemitta*? No, it did not grow in Israel." After realizing that the apple had no inherent *kedusha,* he lost his appetite and put it back. Fruit that grows in Israel is imbued with a certain *kedusha,* and we highlight that fact when we recite the *berakha* of *Al HaMihya.*

כִּי אַתָּה יהוה טוֹב וּמֵטִיב לַכֹּל, וְנוֹדֶה לְּךָ עַל הָאָרֶץ

After grain products:

וְעַל הַמִּחְיָה.
בָּרוּךְ אַתָּה יהוה, עַל
הָאָרֶץ וְעַל הַמִּחְיָה.

After wine or grape juice:

וְעַל פְּרִי הַגָּפֶן.*
בָּרוּךְ אַתָּה יהוה, עַל
הָאָרֶץ וְעַל פְּרִי הַגָּפֶן.*

After grapes, figs, olives, pomegranates or dates:

וְעַל הַפֵּרוֹת.**
בָּרוּךְ אַתָּה יהוה, עַל
הָאָרֶץ וְעַל הַפֵּרוֹת.**

After grain products, and wine or grape juice:

וְעַל הַמִּחְיָה וְעַל פְּרִי הַגָּפֶן.*
בָּרוּךְ אַתָּה יהוה, עַל הָאָרֶץ וְעַל הַמִּחְיָה וְעַל פְּרִי הַגָּפֶן.*

**If the wine is from ארץ ישראל, then substitute* גַּפְנָהּ *for* הַגָּפֶן.
***If the fruit is from ארץ ישראל, then substitute* פֵּרוֹתֶיהָ *for* הַפֵּרוֹת.

בורא נפשות

After food or drink that does not require ברכת המזון *or* מעין שלוש *– such as meat, fish, dairy products, vegetables, beverages, or fruit other than grapes, figs, pomegranates, olives or dates – say:*

בָּרוּךְ אַתָּה יהוה אֱלֹהֵינוּ מֶלֶךְ הָעוֹלָם
בּוֹרֵא נְפָשׁוֹת רַבּוֹת וְחֶסְרוֹנָן
עַל כָּל מַה שֶּׁבָּרָאתָ לְהַחֲיוֹת בָּהֶם נֶפֶשׁ כָּל חָי.
בָּרוּךְ חֵי הָעוֹלָמִים.

So why would we highlight the tasty fruit in our prayers? The Bah explains that the holiness from the dirt of *Eretz Yisrael* flows into its fruit, which as a result contains a certain holiness. When we relate to eating fruit that has grown in Israel, we reflect on its inherent *kedusha*.

Rav Rimon, in his *sefer* on *shemitta*, mentions that when he was once overseas, he picked up an apple in a store and thought to himself, “Is this

חופה, קידושין ושבע ברכות

THE WEDDING CEREMONY AND MEAL

Marriage Service

BLESSINGS OF BETROTHAL

The Rabbi performing the ceremony takes a cup of wine and says:

בָּרוּךְ Blessed are You, LORD our God, King of the Universe, who creates the fruit of the vine.

בָּרוּךְ Blessed are You, LORD our God, King of the Universe,
who has made us holy through His commandments,
and has commanded us concerning forbidden unions,
forbidding us those who are betrothed,
permitting us those who are wedded to us through the rite
of the canopy and sacred covenant of marriage.
Blessed are You, LORD, who sanctifies His people Israel
by the rite of the canopy and sacred covenant of marriage.

The bride and bridegroom both drink from the wine. The bridegroom takes the ring and, holding it ready to be placed on the forefinger of the bride's right hand, says:

הֲרֵי Behold you are consecrated to me by this ring
in accordance with the law of Moses and of Israel.

He then places the ring on the forefinger of the bride's right hand. The Ketuba is read and the bridegroom hands it to the bride. A second cup of wine is taken, and over it, the Sheva Berakhot are recited, beginning with the final blessing of "who creates the fruit of the vine," and proceeding with the remaining six blessings. The same person should preferably recite the first two blessings, "who creates the fruit of the vine" and "who has created all for His glory."

Following the Sheva Berakhot, the bridegroom and the bride both drink from the wine.

The bridegroom breaks a glass in memory of the destruction of the Temple. Some say the following beforehand:

אִם־אֶשְׁכָּחֵךְ If I forget you, O Jerusalem, may my right hand forget *Ps. 137*
its skill. May my tongue cling to the roof of my mouth if I do not remember you, if I do not set Jerusalem above my highest joy.

סדר קידושין ונישואין

ברכות האירוסין

The מסדר קידושין *takes a cup of wine and says:*

בָּרוּךְ אַתָּה יהוה אֱלֹהֵינוּ מֶלֶךְ הָעוֹלָם, בּוֹרֵא פְּרִי הַגָּפֶן.

בָּרוּךְ אַתָּה יהוה אֱלֹהֵינוּ מֶלֶךְ הָעוֹלָם
אֲשֶׁר קִדְּשָׁנוּ בְּמִצְוֹתָיו וְצִוָּנוּ עַל הָעֲרָיוֹת
וְאָסַר לָנוּ אֶת הָאֲרוּסוֹת
וְהִתִּיר לָנוּ אֶת הַנְּשׂוּאוֹת לָנוּ עַל יְדֵי חֻפָּה וְקִדּוּשִׁין.
בָּרוּךְ אַתָּה יהוה, מְקַדֵּשׁ עַמּוֹ יִשְׂרָאֵל עַל יְדֵי חֻפָּה וְקִדּוּשִׁין.

The חתן *and* כלה *both drink from the wine. The* חתן *takes the ring and, holding it ready to be placed on the forefinger of the* כלה*'s right hand, says:*

הֲרֵי אַתְּ מְקֻדֶּשֶׁת לִי בְּטַבַּעַת זוֹ כְּדַת מֹשֶׁה וְיִשְׂרָאֵל.

He then places the ring on the forefinger of the כלה*'s right hand. The* כתובה *is read and the* חתן *hands it to the* כלה*. A second cup of wine is taken, and over it, the* שבע ברכות *are recited, beginning with the final blessing of* בּוֹרֵא פְּרִי הַגָּפֶן*, and proceeding with the remaining six blessings. The same person should preferably recite the first two blessings,* בּוֹרֵא פְּרִי הַגָּפֶן *and* שֶׁהַכֹּל בָּרָא לִכְבוֹדוֹ*.*

Following the שבע ברכות*, the* חתן *and* כלה *both drink from the wine.*

The חתן *breaks a glass in memory of the destruction of the* בית המקדש*. Some say the following beforehand:*

אִם־אֶשְׁכָּחֵךְ יְרוּשָׁלָםִ, תִּשְׁכַּח יְמִינִי: תהלים קלז
תִּדְבַּק לְשׁוֹנִי לְחִכִּי אִם־לֹא אֶזְכְּרֵכִי
אִם־לֹא אַעֲלֶה אֶת־יְרוּשָׁלַםִ עַל רֹאשׁ שִׂמְחָתִי:

Zimmun for a Sheva Berakhot Meal

The leader takes a cup of wine in his hand and says:

Leader Gentlemen, let us say grace.

Others May the name of the Lord be blessed from now and for ever. *Ps. 113*

Leader May the name of the Lord be blessed from now and for ever.

Banish grief and anger.
Let even the mute celebrate in song.
Guide us in the paths of righteousness.
Hear the blessing of the children of Aaron.

Add the appropriate words in parentheses:

With your permission, (my father and teacher / my mother and teacher / the Kohanim present / our teacher the Rabbi / the master of this house / the mistress of this house) my masters and teachers, let us bless our God, in whose dwelling place is joy, from whose food we have eaten.

Others Blessed be our God in whose dwelling place is joy,
from whose food we have eaten, and by whose goodness we live.

Leader Blessed be our God in whose dwelling place is joy,
from whose food we have eaten, and by whose goodness we live.
Blessed be He, and blessed be His name.

Continue with Birkat HaMazon on page 154, at the end of which say the Sheva Berakhot (on the next page) over a cup of wine.

---

together is not totally new. It is built upon a foundation that preceded them. It is based on morals and ethics that were transmitted from previous generations. That is the meaning of the emphasis on building up a ruin.

This relates to a teaching of Rav Shlomo Zalman Auerbach, who notes that we refer to the bride and groom as grape vines intertwining, *invei hagefen b'invei hagefen* (Pesahim 49a). Vines are the only fruit tree that requires support. A vine is supported by a pole. So too, a young couple needs the previous generation to help support it so that it can grow and be fruitful. The couple leans on tradition to successfully build a new home. Our future can only be built on our past.

זימון לסעודת שבע ברכות

The leader takes a cup of wine in his hand and says:

Leader רַבּוֹתַי, נְבָרֵךְ.

Others יְהִי שֵׁם יהוה מְבֹרָךְ מֵעַתָּה וְעַד־עוֹלָם: תהלים קיג

Leader יְהִי שֵׁם יהוה מְבֹרָךְ מֵעַתָּה וְעַד־עוֹלָם:

דְּוַי הָסֵר וְגַם חָרוֹן וְאָז אִלֵּם בְּשִׁיר יָרֹן.
נְחֵנוּ בְּמַעְגְּלֵי צֶדֶק שְׁעֵה בִּרְכַּת בְּנֵי אַהֲרֹן.

Add the appropriate words in parentheses:

בִּרְשׁוּת (אָבִי מוֹרִי / אִמִּי מוֹרָתִי / כֹּהֲנִים / מוֹרֵנוּ הָרַב /
בַּעַל הַבַּיִת הַזֶּה / בַּעֲלַת הַבַּיִת הַזֶּה) מָרָנָן וְרַבָּנָן וְרַבּוֹתַי
נְבָרֵךְ אֱלֹהֵינוּ שֶׁהַשִּׂמְחָה בִּמְעוֹנוֹ שֶׁאָכַלְנוּ מִשֶּׁלּוֹ.

Others בָּרוּךְ אֱלֹהֵינוּ שֶׁהַשִּׂמְחָה בִּמְעוֹנוֹ, שֶׁאָכַלְנוּ מִשֶּׁלּוֹ וּבְטוּבוֹ חָיִינוּ.

Leader בָּרוּךְ אֱלֹהֵינוּ שֶׁהַשִּׂמְחָה בִּמְעוֹנוֹ, שֶׁאָכַלְנוּ מִשֶּׁלּוֹ וּבְטוּבוֹ חָיִינוּ.
בָּרוּךְ הוּא וּבָרוּךְ שְׁמוֹ.

Continue with ברכת המזון *on page 155, at the end of which say the* שבע ברכות *(on the next page) over a cup of wine.*

שבע ברכות – SHEVA BERAKHOT

Building upon a Foundation

The Gemara in Berakhot (6b) states:

> כל המשמח חתן וכלה... רב נחמן בר יצחק אמר כאילו בנה אחת מחורבות ירושלים.
>
> Regarding one who rejoices with a bride and groom, Rav Nahman Bar Yitzhak states: It is as if he has rebuilt a destroyed home in Jerusalem.

Rav Asher Weiss (*Birkon Minhat Asher*) asks: When there is a ruined edifice, one typically knocks it down and then builds a new one. Often this is simpler and safer than seeking to rebuild a dilapidated building. Why is rejoicing with a young couple associated with rebuilding ancient ruins? Perhaps we are to understand that with respect to a marriage, the home the couple builds

THE SEVEN BLESSINGS OF MARRIAGE

בָּרוּךְ Blessed are You, LORD our God, King of the Universe,
who has created all for His glory.

בָּרוּךְ Blessed are You, LORD our God, King of the Universe,
Creator of mankind.

בָּרוּךְ Blessed are You, LORD our God, King of the Universe,
who made humanity in His image, the image of His likeness,
and out of his very self formed a building for eternity.
Blessed are You, LORD,
Creator of mankind.

שׂוֹשׂ Bring great happiness and joy to one who was barren [Zion],
as her children return to her in joy.
Blessed are You, LORD,
who gladdens Zion through her children.

שַׂמֵּחַ Bring great joy to these loving friends,
as You gave joy to Your creations in the Garden of Eden.
Blessed are You, LORD,
who gives joy to the bridegroom and bride.

בָּרוּךְ Blessed are You, LORD our God, King of the Universe,
who created joy and gladness, bridegroom and bride,

---

as one soul is it possible for them to later come together again as one. This creates a natural affinity between them, as they experience a reunification of their souls.

ששון ושמחה – SASSON VESIMHA

Perspective and Appreciation

The Gemara (Kiddushin 2a) teaches us that to complete a marriage, a monetary transaction has to be consummated. This law is derived from Avraham's acquisition of the Me'arat HaMakhpela from Efron. With respect to

שבע ברכות הנישואין

בָּרוּךְ אַתָּה יהוה אֱלֹהֵינוּ מֶלֶךְ הָעוֹלָם
שֶׁהַכֹּל בָּרָא לִכְבוֹדוֹ.

בָּרוּךְ אַתָּה יהוה אֱלֹהֵינוּ מֶלֶךְ הָעוֹלָם
יוֹצֵר הָאָדָם.

בָּרוּךְ אַתָּה יהוה אֱלֹהֵינוּ מֶלֶךְ הָעוֹלָם
אֲשֶׁר יָצַר אֶת הָאָדָם בְּצַלְמוֹ, בְּצֶלֶם דְּמוּת תַּבְנִיתוֹ
וְהִתְקִין לוֹ מִמֶּנּוּ בִּנְיַן עֲדֵי עַד.
בָּרוּךְ אַתָּה יהוה, יוֹצֵר הָאָדָם.

שׂוֹשׂ תָּשִׂישׂ וְתָגֵל הָעֲקָרָה בְּקִבּוּץ בָּנֶיהָ לְתוֹכָהּ בְּשִׂמְחָה.
בָּרוּךְ אַתָּה יהוה, מְשַׂמֵּחַ צִיּוֹן בְּבָנֶיהָ.

שַׂמֵּחַ תְּשַׂמַּח רֵעִים הָאֲהוּבִים כְּשַׂמֵּחֲךָ יְצִירְךָ בְּגַן עֵדֶן מִקֶּדֶם.
בָּרוּךְ אַתָּה יהוה, מְשַׂמֵּחַ חָתָן וְכַלָּה.

בָּרוּךְ אַתָּה יהוה אֱלֹהֵינוּ מֶלֶךְ הָעוֹלָם
אֲשֶׁר בָּרָא שָׂשׂוֹן וְשִׂמְחָה, חָתָן וְכַלָּה

יוצר האדם – YOTZER HAADAM

Creator of Man and Woman

Two of the *sheva berakhot* end with the term *"yotzer haadam* – creator of mankind." The Gemara (Ketubot 8) explains that in the beginning, Hashem designed Adam and Hava to be two beings, but He then created them as one. Later, Hashem split man and woman into two separate beings, yet He has them unite together as one in marriage. What is the message of all these stages? If Hashem wanted us to be together, why create us separately? The Maharsha answers that to have two separate individuals join together as one seems virtually impossible. Only by having the husband and wife start off

happiness and jubilation, cheer and delight,
love, fellowship, peace and friendship.
Soon, LORD our God, may there be heard
in the cities of Judah, and in the streets of Jerusalem,
the sounds of joy and gladness,
the sounds of the bridegroom and bride,
the joyous sounds of bridegrooms
from their wedding canopy
and of young people at their feasts of song.
Blessed are You, LORD,
who makes the bridegroom rejoice with the bride.

בָּרוּךְ Blessed are You, LORD our God, King of the Universe,
who creates the fruit of the vine.

---

do, we should recall the way Adam dealt with Hava. After Hava convinced Adam to eat from the forbidden tree, man was punished, as the Torah dictates: "With the sweat of your brow you shall eat bread." In the very next *pasuk,* Adam named his spouse "Hava." He did not reprimand her or blame his punishment on her wrongdoing; rather, he called her Hava: "*em kol hai* – mother of all life." Adam put everything into perspective. If we recognize and appreciate what we have rather than focusing on what we lack, we will experience happiness with our spouse.

It is interesting to note that we allude to Adam and Hava in the *sheva berakhot* when we say: "*kesamehakha yetzirkha beGan Eden mikedem* – as you gave joy to Your creations in the Garden of Eden." What relevance do Adam and Hava have to the bride and groom? Perhaps this expresses the wish that just as Adam and Hava focused solely on one another, since they were the only couple in the world, so should the new couple's love for each other be exclusive, as if there are no other people in the world.

גִּילָה, רִנָּה, דִּיצָה וְחֶדְוָה
אַהֲבָה וְאַחֲוָה וְשָׁלוֹם וְרֵעוּת.
מְהֵרָה יהוה אֱלֹהֵינוּ יִשָּׁמַע בְּעָרֵי יְהוּדָה וּבְחוּצוֹת יְרוּשָׁלָיִם
קוֹל שָׂשׂוֹן וְקוֹל שִׂמְחָה
קוֹל חָתָן וְקוֹל כַּלָּה
קוֹל מִצְהֲלוֹת חֲתָנִים מֵחֻפָּתָם
וּנְעָרִים מִמִּשְׁתֵּה נְגִינָתָם.
בָּרוּךְ אַתָּה יהוה, מְשַׂמֵּחַ הֶחָתָן עִם הַכַּלָּה.

בָּרוּךְ אַתָּה יהוה אֱלֹהֵינוּ מֶלֶךְ הָעוֹלָם
בּוֹרֵא פְּרִי הַגָּפֶן.

---

the Me'arat HaMakhpela, the *pasuk* states: "*Kesef hasadeh kah mimeni.*" In connection with marriage, the text states: "*Ki yikah ish isha.*" The verb *kah* appears in both verses, and thus we derive a *gezeira shava*: "*Kiha-Kiha misdeh Efron.*" But isn't it a bit peculiar to derive a lesson about a marriage transaction from the acquisition of a burial plot? Couldn't the Gemara have selected a more positive parallel? Perhaps the connection is as follows: If you were to ask Efron who got the better deal, he would have said, "What do you mean? Avraham transferred four hundred shekels to me for a simple cave! I sold an empty plot of land for the highest price per square meter ever – it was the deal of the century!" And if you had asked Avraham, he would have said, "I acquired the entrance to Gan Eden for a few shekels! What a bargain!"

Each party felt that he got the best deal of his life. And that's what marriage is about. Each spouse should look at the other and say, "What a great deal I got!"

It is not always rosy – misunderstandings are bound to occur. When they

סדר ברית מילה
BRIT MILA CEREMONY AND MEAL

Brit Mila Ceremony

When the baby is brought in, all stand and say:

Blessed is he who comes.

The mohel (in some congregations, all) say (in Israel omit):

וַיְדַבֵּר The LORD spoke to Moses, saying: Pinehas the son of Elazar, *Num. 25*
the son of Aaron the priest, turned back My rage from the children of Israel, when he was zealous for Me among them, and I did not annihilate the children of Israel in My own zeal. And so tell him, that I now give him My covenant for peace.

What does the fact that God said "enough" have to do with a *brit mila*?

Third, in *Parashat Tazria* there is a Midrash Tanhuma (5) that cites a discussion between Turnus Rufus and Rabbi Akiva. Turnus Rufus asks Rabbi Akiva: "If Hashem wanted man to have a *brit mila,* why did He not create man already circumcised?" After all, Hashem creates a baby with a heart, brain, lungs, intenstines, fingers, etc., so why couldn't He just finish the job? Rabbi Akiva explained that mitzvot were given to man to purify him. What is the deeper meaning of Rabbi Akiva's words?

The answer to all three of our questions can be found in *Sefer HaHinukh,* mitzva 2:

> ורצה להיות ההשלמה על ידי האדם ולא בראו שלם מבטן, לרמוז אליו כי כאשר תשלים צורת גופו על ידו, כן בידו להשלים צורת נפשו בהכשר פעולותיו.

> And God wanted the completion to be by man, and He did not create him complete from the start, to imply that just as the form of his body is completed by his hand, it is also in his hand to complete the form of his soul through the quality of his actions.

Just like we self-perfect our physical body, so too it is in our control to perfect our spirituality. At a very young age, we already teach the little boy that although Hashem gives us so much, the "finishing touches," the final steps, must be taken by man himself.

That is the meaning of th reference to *Shakai*. God states: I did enough; now it is up to man! So too with Pinhas. Rashi (*Bemidbar* 25:11) claims that

God

סדר ברית מילה

When the baby is brought in, all stand and say:

בָּרוּךְ הַבָּא.

The מוהל *(in some congregations, all) say (in* ארץ ישראל *omit):*

וַיְדַבֵּר יהוה אֶל־מֹשֶׁה לֵּאמֹר: פִּינְחָס בֶּן־אֶלְעָזָר בֶּן־אַהֲרֹן הַכֹּהֵן הֵשִׁיב אֶת־חֲמָתִי מֵעַל בְּנֵי־יִשְׂרָאֵל, בְּקַנְאוֹ אֶת־קִנְאָתִי בְּתוֹכָם, וְלֹא־כִלִּיתִי אֶת־בְּנֵי־יִשְׂרָאֵל בְּקִנְאָתִי: לָכֵן אֱמֹר, הִנְנִי נֹתֵן לוֹ אֶת־בְּרִיתִי שָׁלוֹם: במדבר כה

BRIT MILA

We will raise three questions relating to a *brit mila*:

First, at the beginning of every *brit mila* there is a custom to recite the *pesukim* at the beginning of *Parashat Pinhas* (*Bemidbar* 25:11–12):

> פינחס בן אלעזר בן אהרן הכהן השיב את חמתי מעל בני ישראל בקנאו את קנאתי בתוכם ולא כליתי את בני ישראל בקנאתי. לכן אמר הנני נֹתן לו את בריתי שלום.
>
> Pinhas son of Eleazar son of Aharon the priest diverted My anger from the Israelites by zealously avenging Me among them. I therefore did not destroy the Israelites because of My zeal. Therefore say, "I hereby bestow My covenant of peace upon him."

Why do we recite these verses at a *brit*? Although Kabbalistic sources associate Pinhas with Eliyahu, who appears at each *brit*, and the word *brit* appears in the text, it relates to a covenant not a circumcision. What does the story of Pinhas have to do with a *brit mila*?

Second, the Alshikh posits that the name of God that relates in the context of a *brit* is **שדי** (*Shakai*), as the *pasuk* that introduces the imperative of a *brit* to Avraham is **אני אל שדי, התהלך לפני והיה תמים** – "I am God Almighty. Walk in My ways and be perfect" (*Bereshit* 17:1). The Gemara in Hagiga 12a explains the reference to God as *Shakai:*

> מאי דכתיב "אני א־ל שדי" אני הוא שאמרתי לעולם די.
>
> Why does it state: "I am the Almighty God"? [It reflects the meaning:] the One who said to the world enough!

The following verses, through "Lord, please, grant us success," are only said in Israel.

Mohel: Happy are those You choose and bring near to dwell in Your courts. *Ps. 65*

All: May we be sated with the goodness of Your House, Your holy Temple.

The father takes the baby in his hands and says quietly:

אִם אֶשְׁכָּחֵךְ If I forget you, O Jerusalem, may my right hand forget its skill. May my tongue cling to the roof of my mouth, if I do not remember you, if I do not set Jerusalem above my highest joy. *Ps. 137*

The father says aloud, followed by the congregation:

Listen, Israel: the Lord is our God, the Lord is One. *Deut. 6*

The Mohel, followed by the congregation, recites each of the following three phrases:

The Lord is King, the Lord was King,
the Lord shall be King for ever and all time.
Lord, please, save us. *Ps. 118*
Lord, please, grant us success.

The baby is placed on Eliyahu's seat, and the Mohel says:

This is the throne of Elijah the prophet,
may he be remembered for good.

The Mohel continues:

לִישׁוּעָתְךָ For Your salvation I wait, O Lord. I await Your deliverance, *Gen. 49* *Ps. 119*
Lord, and I observe Your commandments. Elijah, angel of the covenant, behold: yours is before you. Stand at my right hand and be close
to me. I await Your deliverance, Lord. I rejoice in Your word like one *Ps. 119*
who finds much spoil. Those who love Your Torah have great peace,
and there is no stumbling block before them. Happy are those You *Ps. 65*
choose and bring near to dwell in Your courts.

All respond:

May we be sated with the goodness of Your House, Your holy Temple.

The following verses, through אָנָּא ה׳ הַצְלִיחָה נָּא *are only said in Israel.*

המוהל: אַשְׁרֵי תִּבְחַר וּתְקָרֵב, יִשְׁכֹּן חֲצֵרֶיךָ תהלים סה

הקהל: נִשְׂבְּעָה בְּטוּב בֵּיתֶךָ, קְדֹשׁ הֵיכָלֶךָ:

The father takes the baby in his hands and says quietly:

אִם־אֶשְׁכָּחֵךְ יְרוּשָׁלָםִ, תִּשְׁכַּח יְמִינִי: תִּדְבַּק לְשׁוֹנִי לְחִכִּי תהלים קלז
אִם־לֹא אֶזְכְּרֵכִי, אִם־לֹא אַעֲלֶה אֶת־יְרוּשָׁלַםִ עַל רֹאשׁ שִׂמְחָתִי:

The father says aloud, followed by the קהל*:*

שְׁמַע יִשְׂרָאֵל, יהוה אֱלֹהֵינוּ, יהוה אֶחָד: דברים ו

The מוהל*, followed by the* קהל*, repeats each of the following three phrases:*

יהוה מֶלֶךְ, יהוה מָלָךְ, יהוה יִמְלֹךְ לְעוֹלָם וָעֶד.
אָנָּא יהוה הוֹשִׁיעָה נָּא תהלים קיח
אָנָּא יהוה הַצְלִיחָה נָּא:

The baby is placed on the כסא של אליהו*, and the* מוהל *says:*

זֶה הַכִּסֵּא שֶׁל אֵלִיָּהוּ הַנָּבִיא זָכוּר לַטּוֹב.

The מוהל *continues:*

לִישׁוּעָתְךָ קִוִּיתִי יהוה: שִׂבַּרְתִּי לִישׁוּעָתְךָ יהוה, וּמִצְוֹתֶיךָ עָשִׂיתִי: בראשית מט / תהלים קיט
אֵלִיָּהוּ מַלְאַךְ הַבְּרִית, הִנֵּה שֶׁלְּךָ לְפָנֶיךָ, עֲמֹד עַל יְמִינִי וְסָמְכֵנִי.
שִׂבַּרְתִּי לִישׁוּעָתְךָ יהוה: שָׂשׂ אָנֹכִי עַל־אִמְרָתֶךָ, כְּמוֹצֵא שָׁלָל רָב: תהלים קיט
שָׁלוֹם רָב לְאֹהֲבֵי תוֹרָתֶךָ, וְאֵין־לָמוֹ מִכְשׁוֹל: אַשְׁרֵי תִּבְחַר וּתְקָרֵב, תהלים סה
יִשְׁכֹּן חֲצֵרֶיךָ

All respond:

נִשְׂבְּעָה בְּטוּב בֵּיתֶךָ, קְדֹשׁ הֵיכָלֶךָ:

God could have intervened when the Jewish People sinned, but He stepped aside, wanted man to act, as did Pinhas.

Our *berakha* to the young boy, and by extension to ourselves, is to learn the lesson of self-perfection, self-fulfillment. After all of the Godly gifts that we receive, we need to take them and accomplish greatness by ourselves!

The baby is placed on the knees of the Sandak, and the Mohel says:

בָּרוּךְ Blessed are You, LORD our God, King of the Universe,
who has made us holy through His commandments,
and has commanded us concerning circumcision.

Immediately after the circumcision, the father says:

בָּרוּךְ Blessed are You, LORD our God, King of the Universe,
who has made us holy through His commandments,
and has commanded us to bring him [our son]
into the covenant of Abraham, our father.

In Israel the father adds (some outside Israel add it as well):

בָּרוּךְ Blessed are You, LORD our God, King of the Universe,
who has given us life, sustained us, and brought us to this time.

All respond:

אָמֵן Amen. Just as he has entered into the covenant,
so may he enter into Torah, marriage and good deeds.

After the circumcision has been completed, the Mohel
(or another honoree) takes a cup of wine and says:

בָּרוּךְ Blessed are You, LORD our God, King of the Universe,
who creates the fruit of the vine.

בָּרוּךְ Blessed are You, LORD our God, King of the Universe, who made the beloved one [Isaac] holy from the womb, marked the decree of circumcision in his flesh, and gave his descendants the seal and sign of the holy covenant. As a reward for this, the Living God, our Portion, our Rock, did order deliverance from destruction for the beloved of our flesh, for the sake of His covenant that He set in our flesh. Blessed are You, LORD, who establishes the covenant.

אֱלֹהֵינוּ Our God and God of our fathers, preserve this child to his father and mother, and let his name be called in Israel (*baby's name* son of *father's name*). May the father rejoice in the issue of his body, and the mother be glad with the fruit of her womb, as is written, "May your father and mother rejoice, and she who bore you be glad." And it is said, "Then I passed by you and saw you downtrodden in your blood, and I said to you: In your blood, live; and I said to you: In your blood, live."

Prov. 23

Ezek. 16

The baby is placed on the knees of the סנדק*, and the* מוהל *says:*

בָּרוּךְ אַתָּה יהוה אֱלֹהֵינוּ מֶלֶךְ הָעוֹלָם
אֲשֶׁר קִדְּשָׁנוּ בְּמִצְוֹתָיו וְצִוָּנוּ עַל הַמִּילָה.

Immediately after the circumcision, the father says:

בָּרוּךְ אַתָּה יהוה אֱלֹהֵינוּ מֶלֶךְ הָעוֹלָם, אֲשֶׁר קִדְּשָׁנוּ בְּמִצְוֹתָיו
וְצִוָּנוּ לְהַכְנִיסוֹ בִּבְרִיתוֹ שֶׁל אַבְרָהָם אָבִינוּ.

In ארץ ישראל *the father adds (some in* חוץ לארץ *add it as well):*

בָּרוּךְ אַתָּה יהוה אֱלֹהֵינוּ מֶלֶךְ הָעוֹלָם
שֶׁהֶחֱיָנוּ וְקִיְּמָנוּ וְהִגִּיעָנוּ לַזְּמַן הַזֶּה.

All respond:

אָמֵן. כְּשֵׁם שֶׁנִּכְנַס לַבְּרִית, כֵּן יִכָּנֵס לְתוֹרָה וּלְחֻפָּה וּלְמַעֲשִׂים טוֹבִים.

After the circumcision has been completed, the מוהל
(or another honoree) takes a cup of wine and says:

בָּרוּךְ אַתָּה יהוה אֱלֹהֵינוּ מֶלֶךְ הָעוֹלָם, בּוֹרֵא פְּרִי הַגָּפֶן.

בָּרוּךְ אַתָּה יהוה אֱלֹהֵינוּ מֶלֶךְ הָעוֹלָם, אֲשֶׁר קִדֵּשׁ יְדִיד מִבֶּטֶן, וְחֹק בִּשְׁאֵרוֹ שָׂם, וְצֶאֱצָאָיו חָתַם בְּאוֹת בְּרִית קֹדֶשׁ. עַל כֵּן בִּשְׂכַר זֹאת, אֵל חַי חֶלְקֵנוּ צוּרֵנוּ צַוֵּה לְהַצִּיל יְדִידוּת שְׁאֵרֵנוּ מִשַּׁחַת, לְמַעַן בְּרִיתוֹ אֲשֶׁר שָׂם בִּבְשָׂרֵנוּ. בָּרוּךְ אַתָּה יהוה, כּוֹרֵת הַבְּרִית.

אֱלֹהֵינוּ וֵאלֹהֵי אֲבוֹתֵינוּ, קַיֵּם אֶת הַיֶּלֶד הַזֶּה לְאָבִיו וּלְאִמּוֹ, וְיִקָּרֵא שְׁמוֹ בְּיִשְׂרָאֵל (פלוני בֶּן פלוני). יִשְׂמַח הָאָב בְּיוֹצֵא חֲלָצָיו וְתָגֵל
אִמּוֹ בִּפְרִי בִטְנָהּ, כַּכָּתוּב: יִשְׂמַח־אָבִיךָ וְאִמֶּךָ, וְתָגֵל יוֹלַדְתֶּךָ: משלי כג
וְנֶאֱמַר: וָאֶעֱבֹר עָלַיִךְ וָאֶרְאֵךְ מִתְבּוֹסֶסֶת בְּדָמָיִךְ, וָאֹמַר לָךְ יחזקאל טז
בְּדָמַיִךְ חֲיִי, וָאֹמַר לָךְ בְּדָמַיִךְ חֲיִי:

וְנֶאֱמַר And it is said, "He remembered His covenant for ever; the Ps. 105
word He ordained for a thousand generations; the covenant He made with Abraham and gave on oath to Isaac, confirming it as a statute for Jacob, an everlasting covenant for Israel." And it is said, "And Abraham
circumcised his son Isaac at the age of eight days, as God had com- Gen. 21
manded him." Thank the LORD for He is good; His loving-kindness Ps. 118
is for ever.

All respond:

Thank the LORD for He is good; His loving-kindness is for ever.

The Mohel (or honoree) continues:

May this child (*baby's name* son of *father's name*) become great. Just as he has entered into the covenant, so may he enter into Torah, marriage and good deeds.

The Sandak also drinks some of the wine; some drops are given to the baby. The cup is then sent to the mother, who also drinks from it.

תהלים קה וְנֶאֱמַר: זָכַר לְעוֹלָם בְּרִיתוֹ, דָּבָר צִוָּה לְאֶלֶף דּוֹר: אֲשֶׁר כָּרַת אֶת־
אַבְרָהָם, וּשְׁבוּעָתוֹ לְיִשְׂחָק: וַיַּעֲמִידֶהָ לְיַעֲקֹב לְחֹק, לְיִשְׂרָאֵל
בראשית כא בְּרִית עוֹלָם: וְנֶאֱמַר: וַיָּמָל אַבְרָהָם אֶת־יִצְחָק בְּנוֹ בֶּן־שְׁמֹנַת
תהלים קיח יָמִים, כַּאֲשֶׁר צִוָּה אֹתוֹ אֱלֹהִים: הוֹדוּ לַיהוה כִּי־טוֹב, כִּי לְעוֹלָם
חַסְדּוֹ:

All respond:

הוֹדוּ לַיהוה כִּי־טוֹב, כִּי לְעוֹלָם חַסְדּוֹ:

The מוהל *(or honoree) continues:*

(פלוני בֶּן פלוני) זֶה הַקָּטָן גָּדוֹל יִהְיֶה, כְּשֵׁם שֶׁנִּכְנַס לַבְּרִית, כֵּן יִכָּנֵס לְתוֹרָה וּלְחֻפָּה וּלְמַעֲשִׂים טוֹבִים.

The סנדק *also drinks some of the wine; some drops are given to the baby. The cup is then sent to the mother, who also drinks from it.*

Birkat HaMazon at a Brit Mila

Leader Gentlemen, let us say grace.

Others May the name of the Lord be blessed from now and for ever. *Ps. 113*

Leader May the name of the Lord be blessed from now and for ever.

Leader then others We give thanks to Your name among the faithful.
Blessed are you to the Lord.

Leader With permission of the Almighty, awesome and revered,
a refuge in times of trouble,
Almighty, girded with strength –
majestic on high, the Lord.

Others We give thanks to Your name among the faithful.
Blessed are you to the Lord.

Leader With permission of the holy Torah,
pure and clear,
given to us as a heritage
by Moses the servant of the Lord.

Others We give thanks to Your name among the faithful.
Blessed are you to the Lord.

Leader With permission of the priests, the Levites,
I call upon the God of the Hebrews,
declaring His glory to the furthest isles,
and offering blessings to the Lord.

Others We give thanks to Your name among the faithful.
Blessed are you to the Lord.

Leader With the permission of the rabbis, teachers and friends,
I open my lips with song,
saying from my innermost being:
"Blessed is he that comes in the name of the Lord."

Others We give thanks to Your name among the faithful.
Blessed are you to the Lord.

ברכת המזון לברית מילה

Leader רַבּוֹתַי, נְבָרֵךְ.

Others יְהִי שֵׁם יהוה מְבֹרָךְ מֵעַתָּה וְעַד־עוֹלָם: תהלים קיג

Leader יְהִי שֵׁם יהוה מְבֹרָךְ מֵעַתָּה וְעַד־עוֹלָם:

Leader then others נוֹדֶה לְשִׁמְךָ בְּתוֹךְ אֱמוּנַי, בְּרוּכִים אַתֶּם לַיהוה.

Leader בִּרְשׁוּת אֵל אָיֹם וְנוֹרָא
מִשְׂגָּב לְעִתּוֹת בַּצָּרָה
אֵל נֶאְזָר בִּגְבוּרָה
אַדִּיר בַּמָּרוֹם יהוה.

Others נוֹדֶה לְשִׁמְךָ בְּתוֹךְ אֱמוּנַי, בְּרוּכִים אַתֶּם לַיהוה.

Leader בִּרְשׁוּת הַתּוֹרָה הַקְּדוֹשָׁה
טְהוֹרָה הִיא וְגַם פְּרוּשָׁה
צִוָּה לָנוּ מוֹרָשָׁה
מֹשֶׁה עֶבֶד יהוה.

Others נוֹדֶה לְשִׁמְךָ בְּתוֹךְ אֱמוּנַי, בְּרוּכִים אַתֶּם לַיהוה.

Leader בִּרְשׁוּת הַכֹּהֲנִים וְהַלְוִיִּם
אֶקְרָא לֵאלֹהֵי הָעִבְרִיִּים
אֲהוֹדֶנּוּ בְּכָל אִיִּים
אֲבָרְכָה אֶת יהוה.

Others נוֹדֶה לְשִׁמְךָ בְּתוֹךְ אֱמוּנַי, בְּרוּכִים אַתֶּם לַיהוה.

Leader בִּרְשׁוּת מָרָנָן וְרַבָּנָן וְרַבּוֹתַי
אֶפְתְּחָה בְּשִׁיר פִּי וּשְׂפָתַי
וְתֹאמַרְנָה עַצְמוֹתַי
בָּרוּךְ הַבָּא בְּשֵׁם יהוה.

Others נוֹדֶה לְשִׁמְךָ בְּתוֹךְ אֱמוּנַי, בְּרוּכִים אַתֶּם לַיהוה.

Leader With your permission, my masters and teachers,
let us bless (*in a minyan:* our God,) the One
from whose food we have eaten.

Others Blessed be (*in a minyan:* our God,) the One
from whose food we have eaten,
and by whose goodness we live.

Leader Blessed be (*in a minyan:* our God,) the One
from whose food we have eaten,
and by whose goodness we live.
Blessed be He, and blessed be His name.

Continue with Birkat HaMazon on page 154 until "in the eyes of God and man" on page 166. Then continue:

Someone other than the father says:

הָרַחֲמָן May the Compassionate One
bless the father and mother of this child.
May they be worthy to raise him,
educate him, and train him in wisdom.
From this eighth day onward may his blood be accepted,
and may the LORD his God be with him always.

Someone other than the Sandak says:

הָרַחֲמָן May the Compassionate One bless him [the Sandak]
who assisted in the covenant of circumcision
and rejoiced to do this pious deed.
May God doubly reward him for his deed,
exalting him ever higher.

הָרַחֲמָן May the Compassionate One
bless the tender child, circumcised on his eighth day.
May his heart and hands be firm with God,
and may he be worthy to witness the Divine Presence
three times a year.

Leader בִּרְשׁוּת מָרָנָן וְרַבָּנָן וְרַבּוֹתַי
נְבָרֵךְ (במנין: אֱלֹהֵינוּ) שֶׁאָכַלְנוּ מִשֶּׁלּוֹ.

Others בָּרוּךְ (במנין: אֱלֹהֵינוּ) שֶׁאָכַלְנוּ מִשֶּׁלּוֹ
וּבְטוּבוֹ חָיִינוּ.

Leader בָּרוּךְ (במנין: אֱלֹהֵינוּ) שֶׁאָכַלְנוּ מִשֶּׁלּוֹ
וּבְטוּבוֹ חָיִינוּ.
בָּרוּךְ הוּא וּבָרוּךְ שְׁמוֹ.

Continue with ברכת המזון *on page 155 until* בְּעֵינֵי אֱלֹהִים וְאָדָם *on page 167. Then continue:*

Someone other than the father says:

הָרַחֲמָן הוּא יְבָרֵךְ אֲבִי הַיֶּלֶד וְאִמּוֹ
וְיִזְכּוּ לְגַדְּלוֹ וּלְחַנְּכוֹ וּלְחַכְּמוֹ
מִיּוֹם הַשְּׁמִינִי וָהָלְאָה יֵרָצֶה דָמוֹ
וִיהִי יהוה אֱלֹהָיו עִמּוֹ.

Someone other than the סנדק *says:*

הָרַחֲמָן הוּא יְבָרֵךְ בַּעַל בְּרִית הַמִּילָה
אֲשֶׁר שָׂשׂ לַעֲשׂוֹת צֶדֶק בְּגִילָה
וִישַׁלֵּם פָּעֳלוֹ וּמַשְׂכֻּרְתּוֹ כְּפוּלָה
וְיִתְּנֵהוּ לְמַעְלָה לְמָעְלָה.

הָרַחֲמָן הוּא יְבָרֵךְ רַךְ הַנִּמּוֹל לִשְׁמוֹנָה
וְיִהְיוּ יָדָיו וְלִבּוֹ לָאֵל אֱמוּנָה
וְיִזְכֶּה לִרְאוֹת פְּנֵי הַשְּׁכִינָה
שָׁלֹשׁ פְּעָמִים בַּשָּׁנָה.

Someone other than the Mohel says:

הָרַחֲמָן May the Compassionate One
bless him who performed the circumcision,
and fulfilled every part of the precept.
The service of the faint-hearted would not be acceptable
if he failed to perform the three essentials of the precept.

הָרַחֲמָן May the Compassionate One
send us His anointed, blameless in life,
through the merit of this child
groomed by the blood of circumcision,
to proclaim good news and consolations
to the unique people scattered
and dispersed among the nations.

הָרַחֲמָן May the Compassionate One
send us the righteous priest, who was taken into hiding,
until a throne, bright as the sun, radiant as a diamond,
is prepared for him;
the prophet who covered his face with his mantle
and wrapped himself in it [when God declared]:
My covenant is with him for life and peace.

Continue with "May the Compassionate One make us worthy of the Messianic Age" on page 168.

On Shabbat, Rosh Ḥodesh or Yom Tov, continue with the appropriate "May the Compassionate One" on page 168.

Someone other than the מוהל *says:*

הָרַחֲמָן הוּא יְבָרֵךְ הַמָּל בְּשַׂר הָעָרְלָה
וּפָרַע וּמָצַץ דְּמֵי הַמִּילָה
אִישׁ הַיָּרֵא וְרַךְ הַלֵּבָב עֲבוֹדָתוֹ פְּסוּלָה
אִם שְׁלָשׁ אֵלֶּה לֹא יַעֲשֶׂה לָהּ.

הָרַחֲמָן הוּא יִשְׁלַח לָנוּ מְשִׁיחוֹ הוֹלֵךְ תָּמִים
בִּזְכוּת חֲתַן לַמּוּלוֹת דָּמִים
לְבַשֵּׂר בְּשׂוֹרוֹת טוֹבוֹת וְנִחוּמִים
לְעַם אֶחָד מְפֻזָּר וּמְפֹרָד בֵּין הָעַמִּים.

הָרַחֲמָן הוּא יִשְׁלַח לָנוּ כֹּהֵן צֶדֶק אֲשֶׁר לֻקַּח לְעֵילוֹם
עַד הוּכַן כִּסְאוֹ כַּשֶּׁמֶשׁ וְיַהֲלוֹם
וַיָּלֶט פָּנָיו בְּאַדַּרְתּוֹ וַיִּגְלֹם
בְּרִיתִי הָיְתָה אִתּוֹ הַחַיִּים וְהַשָּׁלוֹם.

Continue with הָרַחֲמָן הוּא יְזַכֵּנוּ לִימוֹת הַמָּשִׁיחַ
on page 169.

On שבת, ראש חודש *or* יום טוב,
continue with the appropriate הָרַחֲמָן *on page 169.*

סדר פדיון הבן
REDEMPTION OF THE FIRSTBORN

Redemption of the Firstborn

A firstborn male child must be redeemed on the 31st day of his birth – unless the father is a Kohen or Levi, or the mother is a daughter of a Kohen or a Levi. If the 31st day falls on Shabbat or Yom Tov, the ceremony is postponed to the following weekday.

The father, presenting his child to the Kohen, declares:

זֶה This is my firstborn son, the first issue of his mother's womb.
The Holy One, blessed be He, has commanded us to redeem him,
as is said,

> "Those who are to be redeemed, you must redeem from the age of one month, at the fixed price of five shekels of silver by the sacred standard, which is twenty gerahs to the shekel." *Num. 18*

And it is also stated,

> "Consecrate to Me every firstborn; the first of every womb among the people of Israel, whether of man or beast, belongs to Me." *Ex. 13*

The Kohen checks with the mother that this is her firstborn, and then asks if she has miscarried before this child. If her answer is no, he asks the father:

מַאי Which do you prefer:
to give me your firstborn son, the first birth of his mother,
or to redeem him for five selas
as you are bound to do according to the Torah?

The father replies:

חָפֵץ I wish to redeem my son.
I present you with the cost of his redemption
which I am bound to give according to the Torah.

Holding the redemption money, the father says:

בָּרוּךְ Blessed are You, LORD our God, King of the Universe,
who has made us holy through His commandments,
and has commanded us concerning the redemption of a son.

סדר פדיון הבן

A firstborn male child must be redeemed on the 31st day of his birth – unless the father is a כוהן *or* לוי*, or the mother is a daughter of a* כוהן *or a* לוי*. If the 31st day falls on* שבת *or* יום טוב*, the ceremony is postponed to the following weekday.*

The father, presenting his child to the כוהן*, declares:*

זֶה בְּנִי בְכוֹרִי הוּא פֶּטֶר רֶחֶם לְאִמּוֹ
וְהַקָּדוֹשׁ בָּרוּךְ הוּא צִוָּה לִפְדּוֹתוֹ
שֶׁנֶּאֱמַר
וּפְדוּיָו מִבֶּן־חֹדֶשׁ תִּפְדֶּה, בְּעֶרְכְּךָ כֶּסֶף חֲמֵשֶׁת שְׁקָלִים בְּשֶׁקֶל הַקֹּדֶשׁ, עֶשְׂרִים גֵּרָה הוּא׃ במדבר יח
וְנֶאֱמַר
קַדֶּשׁ־לִי כָל־בְּכוֹר פֶּטֶר כָּל־רֶחֶם בִּבְנֵי יִשְׂרָאֵל בָּאָדָם וּבַבְּהֵמָה, לִי הוּא׃ שמות יג

The כוהן *checks with the mother that this is her firstborn, and then asks if she has miscarried before this child. If her answer is no, he asks the father:*

מַאי בָּעֵית טְפֵי
לִתֵּן לִי בִּנְךָ בְּכוֹרְךָ שֶׁהוּא פֶּטֶר רֶחֶם לְאִמּוֹ
אוֹ בָּעֵית לִפְדּוֹתוֹ בְּעַד חָמֵשׁ סְלָעִים, כְּדִמְחֻיַּבְתְּ מִדְּאוֹרַיְתָא.

The father replies:

חָפֵץ אֲנִי לִפְדּוֹת אֶת בְּנִי
וְהֵילָךְ דְּמֵי פִדְיוֹנוֹ כְּדִמְחֻיַּבְנָא מִדְּאוֹרַיְתָא.

Holding the redemption money, the father says:

בָּרוּךְ אַתָּה יהוה אֱלֹהֵינוּ מֶלֶךְ הָעוֹלָם
אֲשֶׁר קִדְּשָׁנוּ בְּמִצְוֹתָיו וְצִוָּנוּ עַל פִּדְיוֹן הַבֵּן.

בָּרוּךְ Blessed are You, Lord our God, King of the Universe,
who has given us life, sustained us, and brought us to this time.

The redemption money is given to the Kohen, who then returns the child to his father.
The Kohen takes a cup of wine and says:

בָּרוּךְ Blessed are You, Lord our God, King of the Universe,
who creates the fruit of the vine.

Placing his right hand on the head of the child, the Kohen blesses him as follows:

יְשִׂמְךָ May God make you like Ephraim and Manasseh. May the Lord bless you and protect you. May the Lord make His face shine on you and be gracious to you. May the Lord turn His face toward you and grant you peace. The Lord is your Guardian; the Lord is your protection at your right hand. The Lord will guard you against all harm. He will guard your life. For length of days, years of life, and peace He will increase for you.

Gen. 48
Num. 6
Ps. 121
Prov. 3

בָּרוּךְ אַתָּה יהוה אֱלֹהֵינוּ מֶלֶךְ הָעוֹלָם
שֶׁהֶחֱיָנוּ וְקִיְּמָנוּ וְהִגִּיעָנוּ לַזְּמַן הַזֶּה.

The redemption money is given to the כוהן*, who then returns the child to his father.*
The כוהן *takes a cup of wine and says:*

בָּרוּךְ אַתָּה יהוה אֱלֹהֵינוּ מֶלֶךְ הָעוֹלָם, בּוֹרֵא פְּרִי הַגָּפֶן.

Placing his right hand on the head of the child, the כהן *blesses him as follows:*

יְשִׂמְךָ אֱלֹהִים כְּאֶפְרַיִם וְכִמְנַשֶּׁה: יְבָרֶכְךָ יהוה וְיִשְׁמְרֶךָ: יָאֵר — בראשית מח / במדבר ו
יהוה פָּנָיו אֵלֶיךָ וִיחֻנֶּךָּ: יִשָּׂא יהוה פָּנָיו אֵלֶיךָ וְיָשֵׂם לְךָ שָׁלוֹם:
יהוה שֹׁמְרֶךָ, יהוה צִלְּךָ עַל־יַד יְמִינֶךָ: יהוה יִשְׁמָרְךָ מִכָּל־רָע, — תהלים קכא
יִשְׁמֹר אֶת־נַפְשֶׁךָ: כִּי אֹרֶךְ יָמִים וּשְׁנוֹת חַיִּים וְשָׁלוֹם יוֹסִיפוּ לָךְ: — משלי ג

KOREN JERUSALEM